Designing High-Speed Interconnect Circuits

Advanced Signal Integrity for Engineers

Dennis Miller

Publisher: Rich Bowles
Assistant Editor: Lynn Putnam
Managing Editor: David B. Spencer
Text Design & Composition: Wasser Studios, Inc.
Graphic Art: Wasser Studios, Inc. (illustrations), Ted Cyrek (cover)

Printed in the United States of America

        10 9 8 7 6 5 4 3 2

First printing, July 2004
Second printing December 2006

Contents

Appendix A Signal Integrity 261

Appendix B Matlab 101 267

Appendix C Further Reading 279

Preface

This book is intended for working engineers in the field of digital design and signal integrity, with emphasis on interconnect design. The whole point of this book is to enable you to join the movement to create digital interconnections that operate at microwave frequencies.

Books on the various topics commonly required for the design of digital circuit boards that run at microwave frequencies are scarce. As a designer, you are faced with inadequate literature to help you with unfamiliar design problems.

Companies that make a profit designing or selling digital devices cannot afford to wait for a new generation of engineers to graduate from schools, or for a new generation of professors to generate curricula that address this type of design. Some day, all that information will be readily available. Until then, this book is for the engineer who needs to design now and is not averse to studying new concepts along with a bit of mathematics.

Acknowledgements

Rarely is a book with this much information created by one person. Fortunately, I had help from numerous experts within Intel Corporation and from many more throughout the industry.

This book contains references to great discoveries and useful methods that were invented by real people. They were discovered and perfected by people other than me. As this book is not written to be an academic research report, it is not filled with footnotes and credits. Instead, I give the inventors and discoverers their well-deserved credit in Appendix C.

For their time, support, and expertise, I would like to thank Christine Griffen and Nick Peterson, managers who could see past their day-to-day schedules and allocated the large chunk of time for me to write a book; Ahmad Arabi, Alok Tripathi, and Xiaoning Ye, who do their best to keep my technical descriptions honest; and Jerry Bolen, who kept us in lab equipment, measurements, and test probes.

About the Terminology

Those of you involved in PC design will find that many of the terms are familiar, but that I've expanded the definitions. Some terms and concepts may be new, but they are still based on familiar physics. Most importantly, you should recognize that you have already demonstrated enough brain power to deal with this new material. The material has to be clearly explained, of course. You might need to refresh some of your math, but the time will come when these subjects are as clear and obvious as are the principles you are now using in designing circuitry. Of course, those who don't know what they are doing now may have alternate experiences. But that's not you, obviously!

To help you out, the book has a glossary. When you encounter a new term in the body of this book, check the glossary. If the term is italicized when it first appears, you'll find a full definition in there.

Overview of the Chapters

Although I intend the chapters to be read in the order that they are presented, you don't have to take them in order. You could skip directly to Chapters 3, 4, or 5, and the material would probably make sense. If you read Chapter 2 first, the later chapters will make more sense. The order presented yields the highest score on the sense-o-meter. This annotated table of contents should help you decide what you want to do.

Chapter 2 covers the physical objects that make up circuitry, mostly transmission lines. Relevant physical concepts are introduced and technical terms are defined or given expanded definitions. For example, the concept *impedance* must be defined and understood much more broadly than was required for lower-speed circuitry. You should find this chapter a fairly easy read.

Chapter 3 is partly a refresher on mathematics, partly new material. It refreshes your knowledge of how complex numbers and matrices are used in design. Then I introduce key concepts such as scattering or *S* parameters, peeling, and Mason's Rule.

To make use of *S* parameters, the concepts of frequency and time domains must be understood. That subject requires an explanation of how you make use of Fourier transforms. No need to fear a lot of pencil pushing, because software that does the work is easily available, yet you should have a good understanding of how and why these things work.

Chapter 4 introduces the subject of peeling. Remember the movie *Jurassic Park*? At the beginning, they pinged the ground acoustically, and their computer displayed the bones of the dinosaur in the ground beneath them. That technique was peeling: extracting information from a reflected signal. I am not going to tell you how to find buried dinosaurs, but when this section is done, you will see how it might be accomplished. Peeling is a fascinating subject whose surface I can only scratch here, explaining how you can ping a transmission line and interpret its characteristics from the reflection.

I also discuss the great subject of Mason's Rule. Again, this fundamental area of mathematics is immensely useful for high-speed circuit design. The chapter explains how Mason's Rule applies to interconnect circuitry; the method is used in conjunction with *S* parameters. When you are done with this chapter, you should believe that it is possible to model an entire interconnect circuit and derive its characteristics without having to simulate the link.

Chapter 5 is the home of the heaviest mathematics in the book. This chapter brings you to a point where you can say confidently that you understand Maxwell's equations. Many of the characteristics of interconnect circuitry at microwave frequencies can be determined only through analysis with field solvers. You need to understand what field solvers are about in order to understand the words and concepts used with field solvers. To that end, I explain Maxwell's equations, fundamental to all field solvers, then work through an example showing how a fully functional field solver—the FDTD method—can be created. When you see how this is done, you immediately should see some of the advantages and limitations of this particular type of field solver. That thought is expanded by briefly describing several other common types of field solvers and what is good and bad about each.

The transmission of data through circuit boards is electrically described by a piece of mathematics called *the telegrapher's equation*. This equation is the fundamental model of how signals travel and reflect on a transmission line. This chapter shows how to derive the telegrapher's equation from the wave equation, and how to derive the wave equation from Maxwell's equations. When done, you too will be able to do this

Chapter 6 is unique. The entire chapter is dedicated to defining a single word—*differential*. The word is used in many ways: differential signaling, differential impedance, differential drivers, and so on. Experience has shown that many engineers initially presume that they know perfectly well what this simple word means, and then they become very confused by subtle aspects of its meaning. Differential signaling is very important; it is a primary element enabling high-speed, microwave frequency data rates. I define the word in the interconnect context and explain why it is important enough to require an entire chapter. This is a short chapter and should be a fairly easy read, but don't skip over it. The concept is central, yet sometimes leads to big confusion.

Chapter 7 brings us to issues and problems you will encounter when you begin applying this information. One of the cornerstones of interconnect analysis has been the tool called SPICE. This powerful tool is still useful at microwave frequencies, but you should recognize that there are circuit features that no SPICE-based tool directly understands. These include things like bends in transmission lines, return paths, and vias. SPICE can deal with them if they are modeled as separate elements, but only then. These types of issues are described here with suggestions for how to deal with them. The thrust of the chapter is to demonstrate what types of things can be directly handled by SPICE tools, what types cannot, and what to do about it.

The chapter also introduces a range of concepts that become important at microwave frequencies. Entire books are devoted to subjects such as slot lines and patch antennas, so we will not be able to cover all of them in depth in this one book. Yet, it is extremely important for you to recognize what they are and what they do. When you design a board and a structure you intended to be a power fill, starts operating as a dielectric resonator or as a patch antenna, you will be glad you recognized these terms and what they are about.

Chapter 8 covers the practical issues of board layout. Consider, for example, designing an audio amplifier for use in an intercom. It probably wouldn't make sense to start by making a study of the frequency response of the typical human ear. No, you would probably go with some rule of thumb such as AM radio quality. Rules of thumb are time savers, and familiarity with them contributes greatly to your engineering capabilities. They enable you to skip full analysis in cases where nothing new will be contributed by that full analysis.

This chapter proposes some rules of thumb for board layout to bootstrap you to productivity. As with all rules of thumb, they are not always applicable nor are they absolute. You are always free to do the analysis and modify the rule to your particular needs. But when you need to get a circuit board out and time does not allow full analysis, these recommendations are reasonably benign. Sometimes the rule is not even quantified but only points you in a direction that is likely to be fruitful.

Chapter 9 describes wide-band test equipment and how it is used. It includes definitions and descriptions of the most important and fundamental test equipment used in designing for microwave frequencies. It describes what these devices do and things you need to know about them. It describes the basics of how signals are measured in circuits that operate at microwave frequencies.

The days of making measurements by placing a hand-held probe on a node are quickly waning. Beyond a few hundred megahertz, this method of making measurements is totally impractical. Yet *microwave probes* are not always the right answer either. Have you ever made a signal measurement that required use of a *vibration isolation table*? That day is upon us, too.

Appendices

Appendix A is a definition of the term *signal integrity*. This book is targeted at engineers who have experience in signal integrity work, but there will be the occasional person who doesn't fit that description. If you are that person and are not sure what signal integrity work is all about, start by reading Appendix A and then come back to the body of the book.

Appendix B is a very brief tutorial for Matlab[†], a tool that facilitates mathematical calculations. Many engineers are very familiar with SPICE simulators but not at all familiar with Matlab. Many of the calculations described in this book can easily be implemented with this tool. This tutorial gives you enough information about how to run Matlab to make you, as the saying goes, dangerous. From it, you can learn how to perform calculations, access the help system, and make plots of your results. You should gain enough information to get a feel for what this tool might be able to do for you.

Appendix C accomplishes two goals. First, it provides you with a list of additional material you can read to expand your understanding of material presented here. Second, it partially fills my obligation to let you know who the people are that really deserve the credit for concepts presented here.

—Dennis Miller
Hillsboro, Oregon

Chapter 1

A Short History of Digital Interconnection

Throughout their history, computers have had one characteristic of progress: newer generations of hardware provided greater capabilities in smaller boxes. One major contributor to these greater capabilities has been the increased speed of interconnect circuitry on circuit boards. Early generations of personal and hobbyist computers operated with bus cycle speeds in the range of one megahertz. They could complete about a million transactions per second. That speed worked well because the central processing units (CPUs) of these machines also operated at such speeds. Approximate parity between CPU speed and bus speed continued to be the norm while processors evolved through various generations so that, when the PCI bus was introduced at 32 megahertz, microprocessors were also running at that speed.

Then came the introduction of Intel486™ microprocessor. In subsequent editions of this microprocessor, developers found that system performance could be enhanced by running the internal CPU at a frequency that was a multiple of the bus frequency. This enhancement was significant for several reasons. Processing was faster, but the bus and related hardware could remain as they had been. That is to say, the investment that people had made in purchasing or in designing various peripheral devices was not wasted. For example, the video chip that had been designed for the 32-megahertz bus and its 32-megahertz processor still worked with the new faster CPUs.

Subsequent generations of personal computers saw an ever-growing disparity between bus speeds and CPU speeds. Perhaps it was easier to squeeze more performance out of silicon circuitry than out of the circuit boards and bus architectures that used these devices. Perhaps it was more economically feasible to invest engineering in CPU design than in board design. Whatever the reason, the situation eventually got to where CPU operation was proceeding at 10 and 20 times the speed of the busses on the circuit boards. Performance was being strangled by the inability to get data in and out of the CPU. If CPU speed were doubled, would the user be able to see proportionately enhanced performance? With the buses saturated by data, additional CPU speed was not going to improve system performance all that much. It was like trying to push more water through a hose that was already too small.

Various solutions were tried, and slight gains were made. For example, some buses were doubled in width. Doubling the width trades throughput for board area and number of package pins. Board area and pin counts have costs, too. As packages shifted to greater numbers of pins, it became more and more difficult to route signals out from the inner rows of pins. To accommodate the larger number of traces, boards needed more routing layers. The number of routing layers became a function of the density needs of one or two devices on that board. And the problem persisted: input-output (I/O) throughput was still not growing at a rate adequate to support CPU improvements.

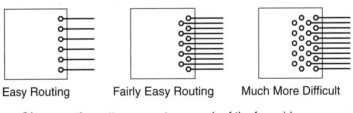

Easy Routing   Fairly Easy Routing   Much More Difficult

Of course, the pattern repeats on each of the four sides.

Figure 1.1   Routing Versus Number of Pins

Design labs began experimenting with various possible solutions. It was found that the packages and board materials commonly used in the personal computer (PC) industry were capable of supporting data rates above one gigahertz if differential signaling were used, a concept that will be fully explored. It was found that microwave frequencies could be supported over useful distances on the very inexpensive materials used for circuit boards in the PC industry. Perhaps the biggest shock came when it was realized that it was practical to transmit data so fast that a four-wire link could transport an equivalent amount of data to a double-speed, double-wide PCI bus, that it could transport this amount of data on a set of only four wires; whereas, the PCI bus required over a hundred wires. This was the breakthrough that the industry had needed. New standards for I/O methodologies were quickly developed, and that brings the story up to the present.

Interconnect circuitry is now entering an era of microwave frequencies, yet most engineers currently designing computers and their circuit boards are not familiar with methods appropriate for work at these frequencies. Neither has the microwave community yet dealt with many of the issues that are faced in such a design effort. For example, a recently published microwave textbook speaks of a particular lossy transmission line and then makes the statement that this example is only for the sake of demonstrating the issues, for nobody would consider designing a practical transmission line in so lossy a medium. The example the textbook gave was of a material with less than half the loss of the materials regularly used in printed circuits for computers.

Digital Transforms to Microwave Design

In school, digital designers concentrated on things like Karnaugh maps; microwave designers studied things like field theory and wave equations. The mathematics of digital circuitry design is not the same as the mathematics of field theory and of wave equations. To design circuit boards for signals at microwave frequencies, computer board designers must either learn or refresh some mathematics that they may not have used since their days in school. This book presents a subset of various mathematics that are necessary to understand in order to do this type of design work. For example, when the subject of Scattering Parameters is covered, you will have to be familiar with the structure and some of the fundamental operations of matrices and vectors. Similarly, when Maxwell's equations are discussed, you will have to recognize some of the terminology of partial differential equations. In each case, the subjects and material required for understanding will be presented in clear statements of the fundamentals. You will not need to perform such operations as inverting matrices, finding eigen values, or solving generalized partial differential equations. Where these capabilities are needed, it is common practice to use some of the readily available software that performs these tasks.

On the other hand, you must be able to read—emphasis on *read*—equations of various types, including matrix equations and differential equations. The need to understand the meaning of equations that are presented cannot be avoided. In that area, assistance is provided in the form of an entire chapter dedicated to refreshing the mathematics. Although tools can do many of the complex tasks, the maxim of "garbage in, garbage out" still holds. You must understand the task to be performed, what information is needed to perform that task, and what various results mean.

Mathematical Approximations

One possible world view is that everything can be modeled by non-linear partial differential equations. A response to that view is that a model that cannot be solved is of limited use. A solution that applies to a single special case is also of limited use. I once had a textbook that developed a clear, concise method for solving a particular example field problem. It was an analytic solution. It provided an exact result. It was easy to understand. And yet, I was never able to make the method work on any problem of my own. Recently I read another book with the same development of the same analytic solution for the same problem. However, the second book closes the problem with a statement that this example comprises the "majority" of cases where this method can be applied. The reality is that though it might be true that most of world can be modeled by partial differential equations, it is also true that there are very few cases where anyone has found a method to generate an analytic solution for many of those equations. Even where such solutions exist, it is often completely impractical to deal with anything other than a very crude approximation to the total problem.

When you plug your coffee pot into the wall, you probably don't care that what is called 120-volt AC is 120-volt nominal RMS voltage, not peak voltage. You probably don't care that the waveform is only nominally a sine wave, probably significantly distorted. You don't care that fields radiate around the power cord, that the insulators aren't perfect, that loss occurs in the outlet. You just want a cup of coffee. Similarly, though they are just an approximation of some partial differential equations, concepts such as *impedance* are good enough for many engineering applications.

Throughout the engineering world, practical approximations are used. Though exact analytic solutions are not available for most problems, methods of approximation are available for many. An approximation that can be made arbitrarily accurate with limited effort is good enough for engineering use. Much of the information developed here in this book consists of such approximations. The electrical characteristics of the materials, used to interconnect active devices such as circuit boards, are strongly dependent on the physical geometry of these materials and nearby objects. Analytic solutions simply don't exist for the electrical characteristics of the great majority of useful configurations of traces on circuit boards. This difficulty does not cause everybody to throw their hands up and go home. Rather, the solution requires alternative methods: often iterative methods, often approximations.

As a working engineer, you are expected to be familiar with the approximation methods that pertain to the work you do. But here we are introducing microwave data rates and new types of approximations will be needed. In some cases, new tools will be needed. In others, it is a little surprising that some very old tools can still be used. It is important to recognize, and you will be informed, that the old tools work in some circumstances and in others they don't. Recognizing which is which represents a major aspect of upgrading your skills.

Chapter 2

Transmission Lines

In this chapter, you will explore the physical features that compose a transmission line. You will examine how the geometries of chunks of metal influence the flow of electrical signals, terminology used to describe this flow, and the mathematical models that explain it. When these chunks of metal become large compared to signal wavelengths, interesting things happen. Of course, these things happen at lower frequencies, too, but often they can be ignored. When signals were running in the low hundreds of megahertz, wavelengths were meters long, and circuit board sizes were small compared to wavelengths. Now with signals in the mid-gigahertz range, board sizes are large compared to wavelengths. Even individual traces are often long compared to wavelengths. In some instances, even board thicknesses are large compared to wavelengths. Effects that were too small to be of concern when frequencies were lower now can become dominant factors.

The full, exact evaluation of a complicated arrangement of metals and dielectrics at microwave frequencies is often not possible. Good approximations are often possible, but they take excessive amounts of time. Running a model of a few inches of transmission line in SPICE takes a millisecond or so. Running a full-wave analysis of a square inch of multi-layer circuit board takes hours to days. The engineering question is, how good is good enough?

Electrical Characteristics

To make practical use of microwave frequencies on production-level boards, design engineers need useful approximations and simplifications that allow them to quickly identify critical issues while ignoring those issues that will not have a significant impact on the resulting product. To get there, you need to understand the physics of what goes on at microwave frequencies. You need to understand Maxwell's equations.

You may have heard the expression that all electronics can be derived from Maxwell's equations. From some perspectives, this is true. We will examine these equations, but we won't derive all electronics from them. Our quest is not perfection; it is practical engineering.

Early in the previous century, several events occurred that sent mathematicians into a panic. One, called the ultraviolet catastrophe, was when physicists applying the mathematics of Newtonian physics could *prove* that the universe could not exist. Pause for a moment to consider the word "prove." Used as a technical term, prove has a specific meaning. The word means that in some logic system, a path can be found from one set of statements to other statements, which path doesn't violate any of the rules of the logic system. That is, if A and B are accepted, steps 1, 2 and 3 produce the conclusion that C follows. C is proven. Contrary to the popular wisdom preached by television commercials, proof does not imply truth. If you accept that four-legged animals are cows, I can prove that a dog is a cow.

Back to the physicists. They could prove that the universe couldn't exist. Both Newtonian physics and the existence of the universe were thought to be experimentally verified. Though not everyone agrees with this assertion, the presumption will be accepted here. The mathematicians seem to have accepted it. Their problem was that they couldn't find the flaw in the argument. What if the physicists were right? What if mathematics doesn't work? The only answer seemed to be to start over and carefully examine every presumption used in generating all of mathematics. To this end, two young mathematicians began an attempt to do just that.

Russell and Whitehead tried to derive all mathematics from first principles. Their work was never finished. It took several hundred pages of derivations to get to the provable statement that 1 plus 1 equals 2. Meanwhile, a German philosopher had come up with the question: so what? Even if you prove all mathematics from first principles, aren't you still presuming that proof somehow implies truth? As strange as it may seem, this question yields useful results.

Using set theory, Kurt Gödel was able to demonstrate that, in any logic system capable of self-reference, it is possible to simultaneously prove some statements true and false. Logic systems that are not capable of self-reference are virtually useless. But Gödel's result yielded much more than this. He showed that there are truths expressible in a logic system, but with no paths to them. There are truths with many paths to them, and, most importantly, truths with only partial paths to them. He showed that the perfectly logical man, the Mr. Spock of *Star Trek* fame, is not the best scientist. Rather it is the educated artist who is most productive. It is the one who can say, "What if?" It is the one who can reach out to grab one of those partial strands, but also has the education to follow it to the truth at its end.

While all electronics can be derived from Maxwell's equations, that effort is also more than likely not the best use of design engineering resources. This book identifies practical simplifications that yield usable results, plus it delineates theoretical justifications and trade-offs that design engineers and signal integrity engineers can use in making design decisions.

Describing a signal path interconnecting two active devices requires numerous electrical parameters: characteristic impedance, insertion loss, return loss, crosstalk, EMI, and others. Many of these terms are familiar to any designer of computer circuit boards; others are probably not. All these terms must be understood in the context of differential signals at microwave frequencies. To gain that understanding, read on.

Characteristic Impedance: Zo

Impedance is the ratio of voltage to current, and it is often usefully treated as a constant. Of course, it is only approximately constant while conditions are held within some range. In the case of digital data in PC boards, the frequency range could be from zero through several gigahertz. That is simply too great to expect impedance or any other element of electrical performance to be characterizable by a single constant. One way to retain the usefulness of the concept of impedance is to tie impedance to frequency. The microwave characterization of components commonly presumes that constants are tabulated as functions of frequency. For example, rather than a component being characterized as having some value of capacitance, it will be characterized as having a set of capacitance values at a corresponding set of frequencies. Impedance is then no longer a single value; it is a table of values versus frequencies.

Figure 2.1 shows what a plot of impedance versus frequency might look like for some specific device. Impedance that looks somewhat constant at low frequencies may change significantly as frequency increases.

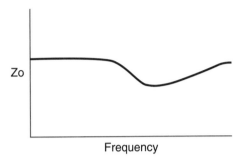

Figure 2.1   An Example of Frequency-Dependent Impedance

When an impulse—a short voltage transient—is applied to a transmission line, it causes a particular ratio of current and voltage. This ratio is called the characteristic impedance, or *Zo*, of the line. If a steady-state sinusoidal signal is applied to the line, the ratio of current and voltage at an arbitrary point of application will not generally equal that of the characteristic impedance, unless the far end of the line is terminated such that it prevents reflections. Characteristic impedance is not the same as ordinary impedance. If a particular steady-state current is run through an ordinary component, a particular steady-state voltage can be predicted based only on knowledge of the impedance. This is not always true for the characteristic impedance of a transmission line.

The AC voltage resulting from some applied current is a constant with ordinary impedance, but usually it varies with position for characteristic impedance. And to make things more interesting, it varies in a manner that depends, among other things, on aspects of the geometry of the transmission line. This characteristic doesn't mean that the concept of impedance is less useful, only that the concept needs to be expanded.

Geometry and Impedance: Zo

The value of the characteristic impedance, Zo, is established by the geometry of the line and the electrical characteristics of the surrounding space. It is approximately true to say that Zo remains constant as geometry scales; as long as two lines and their dielectrics have congruent cross-sectional geometries, they will have the same Zo. In fact, it is strictly true if the materials are lossless and dielectric constants are the same. It's important to note that this is only approximately true in the real world because all lines have loss, that loss is a function of scale, and it does form a minor part of the Zo. However, in many practical geometries, the inaccuracy of the lossless presumption is less than the variability of the manufacturing process. Figure 2.2 shows cross-sections of transmission lines of various sizes. These cross-sections are identical in proportion, so effectively they have identical characteristic impedance.

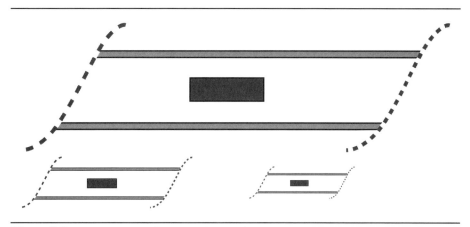

Figure 2.2   Various Scales, Equal Impedances

As the geometric scale is varied, impedance remains constant because it is a ratio of characteristics that depend on geometric proportions. Characteristic impedance varies as a function of inductance divided by capacitance. As long as any change in capacitance is accompanied by an equal change in inductance, the ratio remains constant and so does characteristic impedance. On the other hand, changing the dielectric constant changes *capacitance* without changing *inductance*, therefore impedance changes.

The cross-sectional geometric profile and materials establish the characteristic impedance. But what about the length of the line? If the length doubles, the total capacitance doubles, and so does the total inductance. Zo, the ratio of the two, remains the same. With transmission lines, capacitance and various similar parameters usually are specified on a per-unit basis. That is, a statement of the capacitance or inductance really means capacitance per inch and inductance per inch or per meter.

The software tools—field solvers—that are used to calculate the characteristic impedance resulting from a specific choice of geometry typically produce a capacitance matrix and an inductance matrix. The elements of these matrices, though it isn't always stated, are always in terms of some unit of length. Typically, the unit is meters.

Some interesting interactions among the parameters are involved in establishing the characteristic impedance. With Zo and capacitance (C) known, inductance (L) can be calculated. Because Zo equals the square root of inductance over capacitance, knowing any two allows the third to be calculated. Other similar relationships among parameters exist, such that with any two of the four known—inductance, capacitance, impedance, or effective dielectric constant—the rest can be calculated.

Purists are happy to tell you that the following equations are true only for perfect conductors, metals that have no resistance, or lossless conductors. It is true, but the differences in magnitude generated by including loss are very small for situations shown here and are not particularly relevant to this discussion.

$$Zo = \sqrt{L/C}$$
$$L = Zo^2 C$$
$$C = L/Zo^2$$

Another set of relationships tie in the velocity (v) of signals on the transmission line. Velocity is expressed in the same units of length as capacitance and inductance.

$$v = 1/\sqrt{LC}$$
$$L = 1/Cv^2$$
$$C = 1/Lv^2$$

Finally, in a uniform dielectric material, the velocity of the signal equals the velocity of light (C) in the material. The velocity of light in a medium (v) is a function of the relative dielectric constant (er), so that constant can be also tied into this system.

$$v = c / \sqrt{\varepsilon \mu}$$

In most systems of interest, if any two of the above four parameters (C, L, v, er) are known, the remaining two can be determined through calculation. Given these equations, you can see that the system contains a lot more interdependencies than you might first expect. However, you also face a lot more complications than you might first expect. The above equations have been developed as though the transmission line exists in total isolation. That assumption is not realistic. More realistic models account for the presence of other things in the vicinity of the transmission line.

Moving on to Fields

Consider the situation from the perspective of capacitance. Capacitance is the ratio of a change in charge on an object to the change in voltage. Voltage comes from the electrical force of a charge. And fundamental physics says that force, multiplied by the distance over which it is applied, equals work.

Things are about to get real dry for a few pages. Hang in there. This concept is important to understand. You need to know how and why a group of identical conductors can have more than one characteristic impedance. Which of these impedances applies depends on how voltages are assigned to the conductors. This relativity is important because only in understanding it can you understand what differential impedance is.

In assembling a group of charges, the repulsion between the charges causes a force, depicted by an arrow in Figure 2.3, to be overcome in moving each unit of charge from some original position to its position in the assembled group.

Figure 2.3   Force in Assembling Charges

This force is likely to vary with position in space, so it is often described as a mathematical field—the electrical field, E. Because work may be done in moving a charge from one position in this field to another, there is a "potential" for work between any two locations in that field. That potential is quantified in units called *volts*. If a charge is so small as to not disturb the field, the work done in moving that charge from some initial position *a* to a final position *b* is the sum of all the incremental products of force and charge along the path, as indicated in Figure 2.4. Voltage is the line integral of that charge multiplied by the force, the E field, at each point along the path.

Figure 2.4   Moving a Charge

The charge is a constant, but the field may vary over position. So, in integrating the product, the charge can be brought outside the integral. The remaining integral, the line integral of the E field from point *a* to point *b*, is called the *voltage* between points *a* and *b*. A fundamental characteristic of the static E field is that the voltage between any two points in the field is independent of the path of the integral, independent of the path a charge takes in going from one point to the other. Figure 2.5 shows three different paths through which you could push the charge at *a*. The total work done is the same for each.

Figure 2.5   Multiple Paths, Equal Voltage

For a particular quantity and arrangement of charges, the work required in moving from point *a* to point *b* has a particular value. What happens if the positions of all the individual charges remains fixed but somehow the magnitude of each charge is changed? The result has to be that the voltage between *a* and *b* changes in proportion. The electronics industry makes great use of this. Metals are used to contain, and therefore to establish, the positions of charges. In this case, a constant relates charge and voltage between two metal structures. That ratio is called the capacitance of the structure. As depicted by Figure 2.6, points *a* and *b* are the terminals of the capacitor constructed of those two metal bodies.

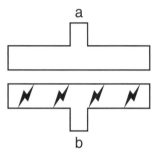

Figure 2.6   Charge on a Capacitor

In the case of a transmission line, one plate of a capacitor is the conductor of the transmission line itself; the other is the ground-reference that is associated with the transmission line. But what if there is a second nearby transmission line, as illustrated in Figure 2.7?

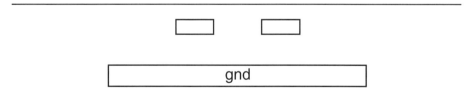

Figure 2.7   Cross-Section of Two Transmission Lines

Consider the case where that second transmission line is held by attachment at ground potential. The charges now distribute themselves over this added area. Changing the shape of the charges changes the shape of the fields and so changes the capacitance.

Consider adding a fixed amount of charge to the ground side of the two-wire system shown on the left side of Figure 2.8. The added area provided by this second body of metal attached to the ground conductor means that the fixed quantity of charge can spread out over more area and becomes less dense at any particular point. The decrease in density means that it would be easier to move a small test charge from any point on the remaining conductor to a point on this ground assemblage. That means the capacitance has increased.

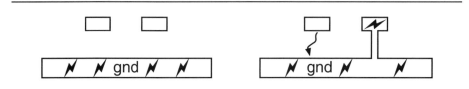

Figure 2.8   Redistributing Charges

Other possibilities exist. This is a key point. What would happen if the second transmission line were held at the same potential with respect to ground as the first transmission line? They are not connected together, but some outside agent keeps them at the same potential. Now no current flows from one transmission line to the other. Consider two cases. If the second conductor is held at ground potential while voltage on the first conductor is varied, current flows through the capacitance from the first to the second conductor, and through the capacitance from the first conductor to ground. If the second conductor is held at the same potential as the first, then as voltage on the first is varied, current flows as before, through the capacitance to ground but not through the capacitance to the second conductor. In this case, the capacitance to the second conductor is not seen; it might as well not exist.

Back to Characteristic Impedance

As we've seen, an equation relates characteristic impedance and capacitance. We've also seen that in a system of more than two conductors, a relationship exists between how voltages are applied and which capacitances are seen by the resulting current. Combining these two results compels you to conclude that, in a system of more than two conductors, there is a relationship between how voltages are applied and characteristic impedance. When voltages can be applied more than one way, the system can have more than one characteristic impedance.

With two transmission lines, three ways that voltage might be applied are of practical importance. In the first case, the voltage applied to the one line has no relationship with the other. In the second case, the voltage applied to each is always equal. In the third case, the voltage on one transmission line is always equal and opposite to the voltage on the other. Two of these cases are regularly used in the transmission of information; the third is important for other reasons.

The first case, where no relationship exists between the voltage variations on one line and those on any nearby lines, corresponds to the transmission mode traditionally used in computer buses. This mode often goes by the name *single-ended transmission*. All engineers with experience in designing digital circuitry are familiar with this mode. Many are less familiar with the other modes.

The second case places the same voltage variations on the two lines of a pair. This mode is called *common mode*. Given two or more transmission lines in a set, when the same voltage variations are placed on all simultaneously, the term common mode applies. This mode is not very useful for the transmission of information, but is very important in the analysis of various types of interference that can occur in the transmission of information.

The last case applies only to lines taken in pairs. The case where the voltage variation on one line of the pair is always forced to be complementary, equal and opposite to that of the other of the pair, is called *differential mode*. Differential mode of transmission becomes extremely important. For various reasons, this mode enables the circuit board connections between digital components to operate at microwave frequencies in practical applications.

Even and Odd Impedance

An alternative set of terms that is often found in the literature of differential circuitry is *even* and *odd mode* impedance. Strictly, these two terms apply only in the case of a pair of traces. An assemblage of more than two traces cannot be validly characterized in terms as simple as even and odd mode impedances. Yet, since differential pairs are often designed to be somewhat isolated from other nearby traces on a board, it is practical to treat such pairs as though they existed in true isolation and use the mathematics of even and odd mode impedances.

It may be helpful to go through this in another way. Though I claim characteristic impedance depends on how signals are applied, you may not be convinced yet. Consider two identical side-by-side traces. Each has capacitance to ground and each has capacitance to the other. Two voltage sources are used to drive these two lines. Call these voltage sources A and B. They also could be called Fred and Rita, but then descriptions further down this discussion might get a little strange. On the other hand, I apologize now to anyone who might have named their children A and B. Voltages A and B are applied to the same ends of the two side-by-side traces.

In the first instance, voltage A is always held equal to voltage B, so no current flows through the capacitance between the two lines. The capacitance is still there, but no current flows through it because no voltage difference exists cross that capacitance. Current does flow through the capacitance to ground. In the second instance, voltage A is always held complementary to voltage B. If B goes up, A goes down; if B goes down, A goes up. In this case, current flows in the capacitance between the two lines. Looking at either individual line, the current that flows as a result of applying a particular voltage depends on what the voltage at the other is doing. The current out of supply A depends not only on the voltage applied at A, but also on the voltage applied at B. This dependency can mean only one thing. The impedance, the ratio between voltage and current seen at either port, depends on what is being done with the voltage at the other port.

Differential Impedance

Transmission line impedance is important in the design of high-speed interconnects because, as will be detailed later, impedance mismatches result in reflections. Reflections increase signal loss. Reflections can also reduce the available bandwidth and the maximum data rate of the interconnect.

Unlike single-ended signaling, differential signaling involves more than one impedance; namely, *odd impedance*, *even impedance*, and *single-ended impedance*. That which is mathematically called odd-mode impedance relates to differential impedance in that differential impedance in an uncoupled or very loosely coupled pair is defined as twice the odd-mode impedance. Even-mode impedance is also called *common-mode impedance*. Single-ended impedance is the vector sum of the two orthogonal impedances: even and odd. The mathematics used to compute these parameters reflects these relationships.

The starting point is an inductance matrix (L) and a capacitance matrix (c). These matrices usually are obtained through use of a field solver, a program that calculates electrical characteristics given geometric and physical characteristics. The field solver needs to know the shapes of the metal and dielectric parts, the related conductivity, the loss tangent of the dielectric, and the dielectric constant. It is fairly common to simplify this list by specifying a perfect electrical conductor (*PEC*) and a lossless dielectric.

A differential pair can usually be simulated in a two-dimensional (2D) field solver. This simplified field solver presumes structures are uniform in one dimension of space. That is, the conductors are treated as extrusions. The desired output of the field solver is the inductance and capacitance matrices. Additional outputs are set aside for the moment.

Given these two matrices, the three characteristic impedances for a differential pair are calculated as shown here.

$$L = \begin{bmatrix} l_{11} & l_{12} \\ l_{21} & l_{22} \end{bmatrix} \quad C = \begin{bmatrix} c_{11} & c_{12} \\ c_{21} & c_{22} \end{bmatrix}$$

$$Z_o = \sqrt{\frac{l_{11} - l_{12}}{c_{11} - c_{12}}} \quad Z_e = \sqrt{\frac{l_{11} + l_{12}}{c_{11} + c_{12}}}$$

$$Z_o Z_e = \sqrt{\frac{(l_{11} - l_{12})(l_{11} + l_{12})}{(c_{11} - c_{12})(c_{11} + c_{12})}} = \sqrt{\frac{l_{11}^2 - l_{12}^2}{c_{11}^2 - c_{12}^2}} \cong Z_{se}^2$$

$$v_o = \frac{1}{\sqrt{(l_{11} - l_{12})(c_{11} - c_{12})}} \quad v_e = \frac{1}{\sqrt{(l_{11} + l_{12})(c_{11} + c_{12})}}$$

The preceding formulae apply to all structures, including *microstrip*, *stripline*, and *offset stripline*. In most differential applications, only the differential impedance is of significant interest and the other two are discarded. It is significant that each impedance has an associated phase velocity, and the even (v_e) and odd (v_o) mode phase velocity are not always equal. This velocity difference becomes significant when *mode conversions* are examined.

Length-Related Issues

The characteristic impedances so far considered are all independent of length. That is, characteristic impedance does not say anything about the length of a transmission line. A 50-ohm line can have any length and still be a 50-ohm line. Yet if you attempt to measure the impedance at an end of this line, the value measured can be strongly dependent on the length of the line.

Consider a voltage driven across a pair of resistors in series. They have resistance values r1 and r2, as illustrated in Figure 2.9. The voltage-divider equation states that the relative voltage at the junction between the two has some specific value. That value (Vo) is described by the voltage divider equation and is independent of time.

$$Vo = ViR2/(R1 + R2)$$

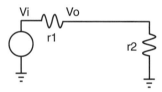

Figure 2.9   A Simple Voltage Divider

What would happen if the circuit had a transmission line between r1 and r2, as illustrated in Figure 2.10? We are talking about a real long transmission line, long enough that it takes notable time for a signal to get from one end to the other. Suppose this transmission line has characteristic impedance Zo. Now when Vi is initially applied, the value of Vo at the junction of r1 and the transmission line is set by the values of r1 and Zo. The voltage at Vo is still described by the voltage divider equation, but the impedance of the ground leg is Zo, not r2—initially. At the beginning, the value of r2 doesn't come into the picture at all. Later, after voltages on the transmission line have had time to come to a steady state, Vo depends on r2 and not on Zo at all. If you try to measure impedance of the transmission line-r2 system, the value obtained depends on the instant in time that the measurement is made.

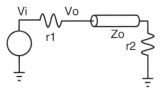

Figure 2.10   A Voltage Divider with Transmission Line

These effects are best envisioned in terms of forward and reverse waves on the transmission line. When a voltage is first applied to a transmission line, a forward wave proceeds down the transmission line, as you can see at time T0 in Figure 2.11. At some point it encounters the other end of the line or a change in impedance, and the wave may be absorbed or partially or fully reflected. The voltage measured at any point along the line at any time is the sum of the forward and reflected waves at that point and time.

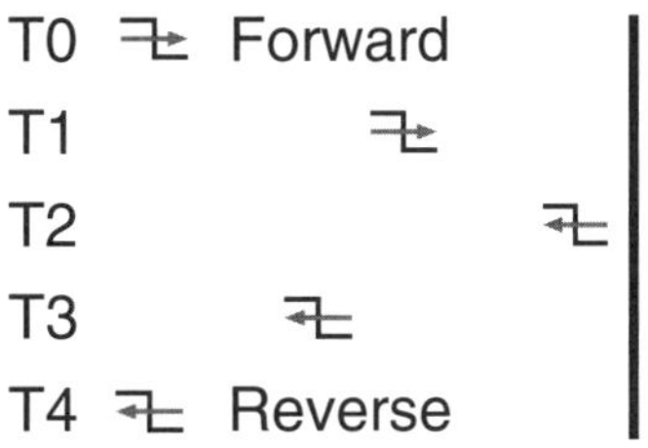

T0 ⎍ Forward

T1   ⎍

T2   ⎍

T3   ⎍

T4 ⎍ Reverse

Figure 2.11   Waves Front Versus Time

Consider the case where the far end of the transmission line is shorted. A short circuit does not support voltage so, at the shorted end of the line, voltage must always be zero. In terms of forward and reflected waves, the short circuit produces a reflected voltage wave that, at the short, is equal in magnitude and opposite in sign to the forward wave; their sum is zero. Similarly, an open circuit produces a voltage reflection that is equal in both magnitude and sign to the incident wave. In the range between open and short circuits is a value where positive reflections transition to negative reflections. At this value of termination, the magnitude of reflection falls to zero, and the transmission line is said to be *fully terminated*. This value of termination impedance precisely equals the characteristic impedance of the line.

Of course, the fully terminated line is the most boring, though desirable, structure you can build on a circuit board. It is only when lines are not fully terminated that things get exciting. Consider the case of the shorted transmission line driven by a sinusoid of a particular frequency, as illustrated in Figure 2.12. At the short, the phases of the incident and reflected voltage waves must always line up to precisely cancel each other. Envision the incident wave arriving at the short at the instant its voltage is half-way up its rising phase. Then, the reflected wave must be half-way down its negative phase. Now, following the incident wave back toward the generator, you should see that a quarter wavelength from the short the sum of the incident and reflected wave traverses its maximum swing. A half-wave back from the short, the waves always sum to zero.

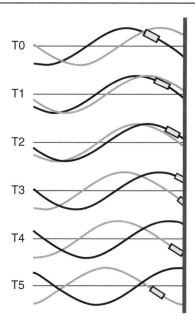

Figure 2.12   Sinusoidal Waves Reflecting

The open-circuited transmission line acts in a similar way. A quarter-wave back from an open circuit, this transmission line looks like a short circuit; the voltages always sum to zero. At half-wave intervals further back, this pattern repeats.

Just as a quick estimation, signal travels though traces internal to FR4 circuit boards at a speed of about six inches per nanosecond. For data rates of 2.5 gigabits per second, many of the signal-edge features are due to harmonics between about 2.5 and 5 gigahertz. At 5 gigahertz, a quarter wavelength is about 0.3 inch long. As any open stub nears this length, it looks more and more like a total short for nearby harmonics. When data rates get up to 10 gigabits, that stub length gets proportionally smaller. An open stub of 0.125 inch will clearly impact 10-gigabit signals.

Voltage and Current Envelopes

When you measure a sinusoidal voltage at a point on a shorted or opened transmission line, the voltage is a function of the distance from the open or short. Figure 2.13 depicts the voltage envelope observed on an open-circuit transmission line as the measurement point moves away from the open circuit.

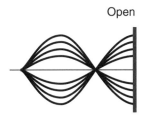

Open

Figure 2.13   The Voltage Envelope of an Open Transmission Line

The right end of the line is open. This signal envelope is caused by the summing of the incident and reflected waves at each point. The picture shows that the forward and reverse voltage waves always sum to zero at a quarter wavelength from the open circuit, so that point looks like a short-circuit. It is also evident that moving toward the driver, at a half wavelength from the open, the line again looks like an open circuit, voltage is maximum, and so on at half wavelengths up the line.

Next, consider the same view of the current on an open-circuited transmission line. We examined voltage; now we shall examine current in Figure 2.14.

Open

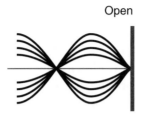

Figure 2.14   The Current Envelope of an Open Transmission Line

At the open end of the line, current must be zero; there is no place else for it to go. To make it zero there, the reflected current wave must be the negative of the incident wave at that point. So now, the wave envelope is as in Figure 2.14. These figures show the case for an open line. The case for a shorted line is similar to these if the vertical line, here depicting the open-circuit end of the trace, is moved a quarter wavelength to the left. In that case, the current is always maximum at the short and the voltage is always minimum. Note that an alternate way of viewing it is that, in the shorted case, the images for voltage and for current can simply be exchanged for each other, and the label "Open" can be exchanged for "Short."

Things get interesting if these two, the current wave and the voltage wave, are superimposed on each other. Again, the open-circuited case is viewed, but the short-circuited case should be obvious. Only the maximum voltage and current traces are displayed in Figure 2.15, but both current and voltage are shown together.

Open

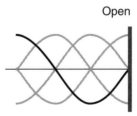

Figure 2.15   Combined Current and Voltage Envelopes

Again, at the right, open-circuited end, voltage goes through its maximum value while current is minimum. But impedance is the voltage-to-current ratio. And that is the point of this whole development. If a sine wave is placed on the line, and if the impedance is measured by the standard method of dividing the voltage by the current, the measured impedance is found to be a function of the distance from the termination. The measured impedance at any particular distance is constant, but the value of that constant varies with distance from the termination. Only when the line is terminated in its own characteristic impedance does the measured impedance become a fixed value independent of distance from the termination.

For some reason, people seem to have difficulty with the concept of impedance that varies with position. Hopefully, this clears up some of the confusion. Is it possible to calculate what the impedance at a particular point and frequency is? Of course. The voltages can be calculated. The currents can be calculated. In fact, if the envelope of the voltage is viewed as a sine function of distance, the current must be a cosine function of the same distance argument. The impedance, voltage divided by current, must be a tangent function of wavelength and distance from the termination. In the simple, lossless case, this becomes these equations:

$$Zin(d) = Zo \frac{Z_L + jZo \tan(\beta d)}{Zo + jZ_L \tan(\beta d)}$$

$$\beta \equiv \frac{\omega}{v_p}$$

In the more complicated case, where you have loss in the transmission line, the equation is cast in the more general form below, where the hyperbolic tangent is used to accommodate the possibility of a complex argument.

$$Zin(d) = Zo \frac{Z_L + Zo \tanh(\gamma d)}{Zo + Z_L \tanh(\gamma d)}$$

$$\gamma \equiv \alpha + j\beta$$

The symbol d is distance from the termination, but nothing has been said about where this gamma, alpha, and beta, came from. Don't worry, those symbols and their meaning will be detailed in Chapter 4. After you read Chapter 4, come back and look at these again. They will make sense. Here and now, the point is that these equations describe the impedance at a spot in the line, in terms of distance from the termination and characteristic impedance.

Smith Chart

You probably won't work directly with these equations. If the measured impedance at a point on a transmission line is needed, it is usually easier to employ a graphical chart. Since the impedance variations are periodic, it is convenient to plot the complex impedance versus distance on a circular graph, a polar plot. The most common such chart is the *Smith chart*, shown in Figure 2.16, invented in 1939 by P.H. Smith.

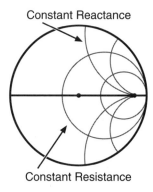

Constant Reactance

Constant Resistance

Figure 2.16   Circles on the Smith Chart

The reflection coefficient for sinusoids, the ratio of reflected to incident voltage, is designated by the upper-case gamma.

$$\Gamma = \frac{Z - Zo}{Z + Zo}$$

Z, of course, is the measured impedance as is being discussed here; Zo is the characteristic impedance. As a complex number, gamma can be plotted on the complex plane. That plane can be mapped into a circular format. The normalized gamma plane in circular format is called the Smith chart. The Smith chart can also be used with other complex entities such as the impedance of lumped elements, as it is simply a normalized graph of complex numbers.

In a rectangular format, you would expect to see horizontal lines that correspond to constant reactance, and vertical lines corresponding to constant resistance. You would plot a particular complex impedance by traversing the real axis till the point equaling the real part of the impedance was found. Then, following the vertical line, traverse to the point where the imaginary part was found. The same is true for plotting on the

Smith chart, except that the mapping changes the vertical lines from straight to circular, as illustrated by Figure 2.17. One follows the horizontal center line till the real part of the number is found, then follows the intersecting circle till the imaginary part is found.

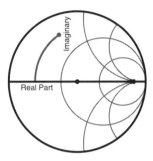

Figure 2.17   Plotting a Complex Value on a Smith Chart

Of course, with lumped elements such as capacitors or inductors, the imaginary part is specific to a frequency. Recall, for example, that the imaginary part of the impedance of an inductor has a magnitude of two *pi* times the frequency (Ω) times the inductance. On the simplest level, the real part, the resistive part, will be independent of frequency. So the impedance of this inductor will traverse one of the constant resistance circles as frequency varies, as indicated in Figure 2.18.

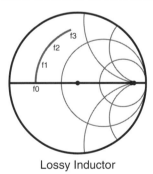

Lossy Inductor

Figure 2.18   Plotting a Frequency-Dependent Value on a Smith Chart

In plotting on the Smith chart, impedances are normalized; that is, they are divided by 50, if that is the chosen normalization value. When the inductor is plotted, the impedance at low frequencies is low, so the inductor plot starts near the left edge of the chart. As frequency increases, the plot traverses the circular path up and around to the right edge of the chart. In real circuits, there would always be some parasitic capacitance, so for a real component the plot would not simply approach the center horizontal axis, the real axis, at the right side of the chart, but would pass through it and continue into the negative, or lower, half of the chart. In this region, the component looks like a capacitor. The frequency where the trace passed through the real axis is the resonance frequency.

This discussion has proceeded entirely in terms of impedances. It is equally valid to use the Smith chart in terms of admittances and to adjust the interpretations accordingly. In such uses, it is advisable to explicitly describe the charts as impedance or admittance Smith charts.

Going back to where the Smith chart discussion began, transmission lines can be used with this chart, too. Consider a particular example where a transmission line is terminated by some particular impedance, as illustrated in Figure 2.19.

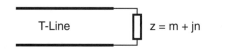

Figure 2.19 Transmission Line with Complex Termination

Start by calculating the reflection coefficient at the load and normalizing this value; that is, by dividing the real and imaginary parts by 50. Then locate the corresponding point on the chart, as illustrated in Figure 2.20.

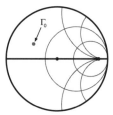

Figure 2.20 Plotting a Reflection Coefficient

If that location includes an imaginary part, the termination must have been calculated at a particular frequency. To examine a transmission line with the Smith chart, a particular frequency must be chosen. The termination is evaluated at that frequency, and the transmission line is characterized in terms of that frequency. The length of the line is specified in terms of wavelengths at this frequency. The wavelength is the velocity in the line divided by the frequency, so divide the physical length of the transmission line by the wavelength. Transmission down the line corresponds to traversing a circle centered at the center of the chart. This circle is not one of those already included on the bare Smith chart; it can be drawn with a compass. Along the outside of commercially available Smith charts are several setting circles. Some are in wavelengths, others in degrees. Here it might be easier to explain in degrees. Convert the length of the transmission line from wavelengths to degrees by multiplying the wavelengths by 360 degrees. Now draw a line from the center of the chart to the outside edge, passing through the termination impedance that was previously plotted. Note what angle on the periphery this line passes through. Now traverse the circle that was drawn with a compass, depicted in Figure 2.21 by the number of degrees corresponding to the length of the transmission line, in a clockwise direction—or use a protractor. The point at the end of this corresponds to the value of the reflection coefficient of this transmission line at its input end. This value can now be read back as the normalized impedance at the input of the line at this frequency.

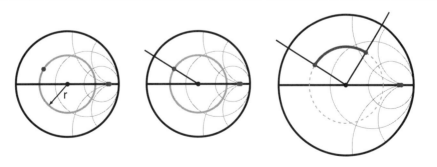

Figure 2.21   Transmission Line Impedance Calculations on the Smith Chart

Some of the equations that relate to this use of the Smith chart can now be shown:

At the load :

$$\Gamma_0 = \frac{z-1}{z+1}$$

At the input :

$$\Gamma(d) = \Gamma_0 e^{-j2\beta d}$$

ie : *rotated*.

$$z(d) = \frac{1+\Gamma(d)}{1-\Gamma(d)}$$

In these equations, *d* is distance and beta is the propagation constant. Chapter 5 will go into greater detail, so don't worry if these equations make no sense to you at this point.

In the Smith chart, both axes get warped into circles. Constant resistance circles all center on the horizontal center line, and are tangent to the right side of the circle that bounds the chart. Constant reactance circles are all tangent to the horizontal center line, and they pass through the point where that line passes through the right side of the bounding circle. The resistance is normalized, so the center of the impedance chart is one. The left end of the center line is a short circuit; the right side is an open circuit. The upper half of the impedance plane is inductive; the lower half is capacitive. Loops in the frequency response indicate resonances. The Smith chart can be used to plot impedances, admittances, and transmission lines.

The information presented here is not enough to make you an expert on Smith charts. It is intended to familiarize you with the fundamental terms, concepts, and uses of this tool. It is intended to pique the interest and to encourage further study. Hopefully you realize that powerful tools can come in forms other than software. In signal integrity applications, this tool is seldom used, but there are a few places where it can be valuable.

Reflection Coefficient

In circuitry consisting of discrete elements, resistors, capacitors, and so on, voltages are often calculated by use of the voltage-divider equation. When distributed elements such as transmission lines or volumes of space are involved, the voltage-divider and similar circuit approaches are usually inadequate. The underlying concept, a wave arriving at a boundary and part of it bouncing back, is very simple. The ramifications in complex systems can be intense. Understanding this phenomenon and how to deal with it is the core of learning to cope with microwave frequencies.

At this point, I'm going to introduce some terminology. Microwave studies involve a lot of Greek letters—alphas, betas, gammas, and so on. The discussion of what is physically happening is simplified by assigning standard meanings to such symbols and using them as abbreviations.

The proportion of a transient signal reflected at a boundary, relative to incident signal, is a constant called the *reflection coefficient*, designated in the transient case as the lower-case Greek letter rho (ρ). The ratio of forward-to-reverse amplitudes of a steady-state signal at any arbitrary point in a transmission line is designated by the upper-case Greek letter gamma (Γ). That is, lower-case rho corresponds to transient; upper-case gamma corresponds to steady-state. A matrix element called S11, explained in Chapter 3, corresponds to gamma at the source of the transmission line. Gamma at the termination end of the line equals rho at that point. In the design of interconnect circuitry, what usually happens at the two ends is the dominant point of interest. The symbols and equations for the two ends of a transmission line are shown here:

$$\Gamma(0) = \rho$$
$$\Gamma(l) = S_{11}$$

A schematic representation of the same thing is shown in Figure 2.22. Once again, remember that S11 and the upper-case gamma refer to the steady-state conditions, not the transient. Rho, at the end of the line, is valid for both the transient and steady-state case.

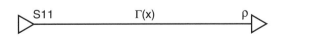

Figure 2.22 A Schematic View of Reflection Coefficients

Unfortunately, this gamma and rho are often given the same name, *reflection coefficient*, but they aren't really the same thing. They are merely similar. Rho is the reflection coefficient for a signal edge. It is the time-domain reflection coefficient. Rho is the transient case, the case that is seen in time-domain reflectometry. When a transient is launched down the transmission line and that signal encounters some entity that reflects a portion of the signal, the ratio of signal arriving to signal reflected is designated by the constant, rho. This situation is almost but not quite the same as gamma at x. When a steady-state sinusoid is on a transmission line, and that sinusoid encounters some entity that reflects a portion of the signal, the ratio of signal arriving to signal reflected is designated by the constant, gamma. The difference is this: rho measures the reflection of a transient event. The arriving signal edge is not impacted by anything that is going to happen another half inch or whatever further down the line. This reflection coefficient is based on the impedance of the line immediately prior to the reflection point and the impedance of the line, or load, immediately after the reflection point. The fact that the signal may or may not encounter more reflections further down the line has no bearing on the reflection coefficient at this point.

Gamma, however, is the reflection coefficient for a sinusoid in a steady-state condition. The downstream impedance may well not be the characteristic impedance of the downstream transmission line. The downstream impedance will be the measured impedance, the actual ratio of voltage and current, at that point, x. It will only be the characteristic impedance of the downstream transmission line if the far end of the downstream transmission line is terminated in its characteristic impedance. In all other cases, gamma, measuring a steady-state condition, will be impacted by all the reflections that take place downstream from the measurement point.

In the case of rho, the calculation is as simple as comparing the two characteristic impedances. In the case of gamma, the calculation can be much more complicated. Starting at the farthest downstream termination, the reflection coefficient at the end of the line is calculated. This is rho at the far end of the line. Then this impedance is translated by a transmission line transformation, perhaps with aid of a Smith chart, into the impedance it represents at this particular frequency at the upstream point where the next previous reflection took place. This transformed impedance is used to calculate the reflection coefficient there. This new reflection is again transformed by the length of the next upstream segment of transmission line to a new impedance. The process is repeated until the point, x, is achieved. There, the value of gamma at x can be calculated.

If you have a transmission line of known impedance profile and known termination, this is how you would calculate the gamma-at-x quantity. Tools such as the Smith chart exist to assist in making this calculation. If the transmission line is being simulated in a tool such as a SPICE simulator, it can be much simpler than this. The impact of all down-stream reflection is already present in the voltage and current at the point of interest. The impedance presented at the downstream side of the reflection point can be easily calculated by simply dividing the voltage by the current. Keep in mind that these are both complex numbers and must be mathematically manipulated as such. SPICE defaults to outputting magnitudes rather than complex numbers. When you need complex numbers, you have to explicitly tell SPICE to print the real and imaginary parts.

It is easy to confuse rho and gamma because the formulas are identical. At the termination end-point, the same equation can be used for either. The formula is simply the difference between the impedance downstream and the impedance upstream, divided by the sum of the two. Stated that way, the formula is the same for both. The difference is that the downstream impedance for the steady state is not equal to that for the transient case, except at the terminated end of the line. In the case of rho, the reflection coefficient for signals in one direction is simply the negative of that for signals in the other direction. The magnitudes are the same. In the case of gamma, the magnitude in one direction will probably not equal the magnitude in the other.

Energy that is reflected at one end of a transmission line is energy that is not available for use in the other end. As such, it is one source of loss in a transmission line.

$$\Gamma(0) = (Z_L - Zo)/(Z_L + Zo)$$

In this equation, Z_L is the impedance of the termination at the end of the transmission line. You can see an interesting thing in that equation. If you had a junction between two transmission lines with impedances Z1 and Z2, the magnitude of rho is the same for waves from either direction. But notice, the sign is different.

When the mathematics are worked out and the magnitude of the forward voltage passing a boundary of specified reflection coefficient is calculated, you find this:

$$v_2/v_1 = \sqrt{(Z_2/Z_1)(1-\rho^2)}$$

Where:

$v1$ is the forward traveling voltage wave before the boundary

$v2$ is the forward traveling voltage wave after the boundary

Z1 is the line impedance before the boundary

Z2 is the line impedance after the boundary

rho is the reflection coefficient at the boundary, for forward waves

The previous equation is found by calculating the forward and reflected energy on the incident side of the boundary, and applying conservation to determine the energy downstream from the boundary. Recognize that if the reflection coefficient is calculated for a signal arriving at a boundary from the left, it does not equal the reflection coefficient that would be calculated for a signal arriving at the same boundary from the right. The reflection coefficient for current is always the negative of that for voltage.

Insertion Loss

The signal loss measured between one port and another is *insertion loss*. It is made up of resistive, often called *copper*, losses, dielectric losses, reflections, and radiation. In the case of a transmission line at microwave frequencies, the insertion loss does not remain precisely constant as cross-sectional geometry scales. Resistive loss is a function of trace cross-sectional area. As cross-sectional geometry is reduced, the insertion loss increases. This increase can impact design engineering because designs are often required to use all available margin; even the quantity of data that can be pushed through a given volume of circuit board needs to be maximized. If trace width is reduced, maximum allowable trace length at high frequencies will likely also be reduced. This result is because copper loss, the resistive loss of the conductor, increases with frequency.

At data rates of only a few hundreds of megahertz, transmission line losses were typically ignored. Compared to the reflected signals, the actual losses of the transmission line were trivial. At microwave frequencies, that situation sometimes reverses. By the time a signal line gets 7 or 8 inches long, the transmission line losses usually dominate all other effects. Those losses consist mostly of copper losses, resistive losses, and of dielectric losses. It is common for receivers to see a fourth or less of the signal amplitude that was launched a few inches away. This loss becomes a dominant reality in signal integrity work. The reason the resistive loss of copper increases so dramatically as frequency increases is the phenomenon called *skin effect*. This greatly reduces the cross-sectional area available for current flow, as frequency increases.

The dilemma you will often face is that maximizing the distance available for a given data rate on an interconnect requires maximizing trace cross-section. But for a given characteristic impedance, the relation between geometry and impedance makes this equivalent to requiring thicker boards. Manufacturing or other considerations often set limits on acceptable board thickness.

A second major contributor to insertion loss is a parameter called the *loss-tangent* of the dielectric material. One theory, not accepted here, suggests that there is a simple painless fix for loss. This theory is treated as an "ace in the hole." The theory says that if the allocated budgets can't be achieved, changing to *low-loss materials* fixes all budgeting problems. Literature is available at numerous Websites describing materials with *dielectric losses* at half to less than a tenth that of FR4. But while using these new materials sounds like the solution to all loss and signal budgeting problems, their impact is limited to dielectric loss.

Dielectric loss is only one of the loss mechanisms in an interconnect link. Alternate dielectric materials do nothing for copper losses, connector losses, or for via losses. They don't correct for the loss incurred due to impedance mismatches between boards that are plugged together, or even for impedance mismatches incurred by changing routing layers on a single board. Impedance mismatches cause reflections, and it has already been shown that reflections reduce the transmitted signal.

An important term, loss tangent, needs explanation. In the study of how dielectric constants enhance field strength, a theory comes forward in which, as frequency increases, a lag grows between applied stimulus and the resulting field. This lag is measured as a phase difference and can be expressed by modeling the relative dielectric constant (er) as having a real and an imaginary part, shown in Figure 2.23. When the mathematics of energy encounters an imaginary part in the dielectric constant, that part is a dissipater of energy, a loss mechanism. The angle defined by the real and imaginary part of the dielectric constant is identified in the literature by the term *loss tangent*. This value, usually very small, goes to zero as loss goes to zero.

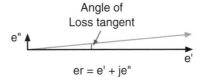

Figure 2.23   The Loss Tangent

When evaluating the total loss budget of an interconnect using a material with no dielectric loss, emphasize *none*, is likely to improve the total loss budget by perhaps 10 to 30 percent. While you can certainly find instances where this level of improvement will save a design, this result demonstrates that using low dielectric loss materials is not a panacea, but rather only one of the possible tools that you can use to manipulate loss budgets.

A better solution in a multi-board link, for example, may be to choose tightly controlled impedance. The determination of which solution is more cost effective must be based on the particular implementation that you are addressing, and the constraints, even non-electrical, your design requirements impose.

So, to reiterate, insertion loss is the loss a signal sees in traversing a transmission line from one end to the other. It is usually a strong function of frequency and expressed by a table of values versus frequency. More will be said of it in Chapter 3.

First, consider this. The loss tangent is described as a part of the dielectric constant. It is the imaginary part of the dielectric constant. Electric field strength could be calculated if you had the dielectric constant, the voltage, and the capacitance. But dielectric loss is proportional to field strength so this loss has to be proportional to capacitance. One way that transmission lines are often described is in terms of a capacitance matrix, an inductance matrix, a resistance, and a conductance matrix—RLGC. But as you see, the G matrix can be derived from the C matrix through use of the loss tangent, as long as the surrounding medium is homogeneous.

$$[G] = \varpi \tan \delta [C]$$

For short transmission lines, insertion loss tends to be dominated by energy reflected at impedance mismatches. For long transmission lines, insertion loss tends to be dominated by dissipative and radiated effects. Radiated loss is minimized by using carefully balanced differential transmission. At low-to-mid frequencies, dissipative loss tends to be dominated by copper loss. This loss is minimized by using large traces. At high frequencies, dissipative loss tends to be dominated by dielectric loss, which is loss proportional to the dielectric loss tangent. You minimize dielectric loss by selecting materials with a small dielectric loss. Proportions vary, but all loss mechanisms are always present.

Return Loss

The ratio of reflected signal to forward signal at a port is *return loss*. A mathematical description of return loss is in the section detailing S parameters in Chapter 3. It will resurface again in Chapter 4, in which Mason's Rule is covered. This characteristic, the return loss of an interconnect link, impacts the signal source in several ways. The return loss of a circuit alters the voltage waveforms that you measure at a driver or a receiver. It can increase the jitter measured at a driver or receiver. Return loss alters the measured impedance of the transmission line. An important significance of return loss is that this parameter can cause resonances that severely distort the electrical characteristics of the interconnect, limiting usable bandwidth and data rate. That is, if a low-loss section is bounded by two very reflective interfaces, a standing wave builds between those interfaces. That wave can enhance losses, radiation, and crosstalk. In short, ignoring return loss is a bad idea and needs to be avoided.

In differential signaling, the norm is to terminate both ends of the pair in their nominal characteristic differential impedance. It is possible to terminate a differential pair in two different ways, as seen in Figure 2.24. The odd-mode-impedance component could be placed between each individual line and ground. Alternatively, a single component of twice that value could be placed across the pair, with no connection to ground. Either one terminates the differential signal equally well. Either one can prevent all reflections of the differential signal. Yet one of the two can present serious problems.

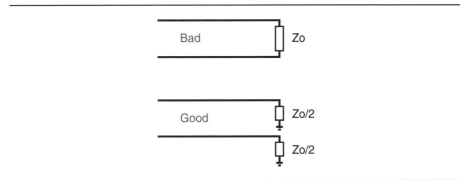

Figure 2.24   Terminating Differential Lines

The termination method that leaves both lines open to ground looks like an open circuit to any common-mode signal that is present on the pair. If a large common-mode return loss occurs at any other point in the link, a common-mode standing wave can build up on the pair and cause serious problems through crosstalk, radiation, or mode conversions.

Even a device that is intended to present a specific differential impedance at an interface will have some manufacturing tolerance. That tolerance will impact return loss. In a perfectly terminated line, return loss is zero. Later, when additional details have been presented on how interconnects are designed, you will see that return loss is a key parameter. This importance becomes evident in Chapter 4 in the study of Mason's Rule.

Both insertion loss and return loss are often expressed in *decibels*. A decibel can be defined as 20 times the log—base 10—of a voltage ratio. A decibel always expresses a ratio, not an absolute value. Notice that the term dBm, which implies a reference of one miliwatt, isn't used here. As an exponential, a decibel value that is positive corresponds to a ratio that is greater than one. Negative decibels correspond to ratios less than one. It is common to hear or see phrases such as "a loss of 20 dB." Mathematically, this phrase usually means a value of negative twenty decibels. But how should a phrase such as "20-dB insertion loss" be interpreted? If the device is known to be passive, you can safely assume the statement really intended to mean negative twenty. But if the device is not known to be passive, the same statement could mean an actual significant amount of gain. I strongly recommended that whenever decibel notation is used, in speech or in text, the proper sign be included.

Crosstalk

Most engineers with experience in designing printed circuit boards will recognize at least two varieties of *crosstalk*. The interference between signals on two different interconnects is called crosstalk, and if the case is a receive signal being impacted by the action of a nearby transmitter, the crosstalk is called near-end crosstalk (NEXT). If the receive signal is being impacted by signal arriving at a nearby receiver, it is called far-end crosstalk (FEXT), shown in Figure 2.25. The source of the interfering signal is often called the aggressor, and the signal impacted by the crosstalk is often called the victim. When microwave frequency signals are transmitted across a circuit board, crosstalk becomes a very important issue. A lot of the reason for this is that the large amount of signal loss at these frequencies increases the impact of crosstalk.

Consider two links adjacent to each other. Each transmits at a level of one volt, and the receive signal on each is one-tenth volt. They run in opposite directions so that the transmitter of one is next to the receiver of the other. Say there is five percent crosstalk. That five percent of the transmit amplitude, corresponds to half of the amplitude of the receive signal. That is what the problem is. The impact of crosstalk always has to be referenced to the signal amplitude at the receiver. The heavy loss incurred at microwave frequencies has the effect of magnifying the impact of crosstalk.

The characteristics of NEXT, sometimes also called reverse crosstalk, and FEXT, sometimes called forward crosstalk, are quite different. Near-end crosstalk is called reverse crosstalk because the victim signal is traveling in a direction opposite that of the aggressor. With FEXT they both travel in the same direction—forward. In the case of FEXT, the fact that each part of the traveling aggressor wave remains adjacent to the same part of the traveling victim wave, results in the amplitude of the crosstalk being proportional to the coupled-path length.

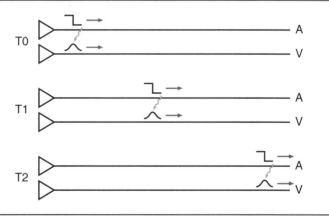

Figure 2.25   FEXT

In the case of NEXT, Figure 2.26, the fact that the two travel in opposite directions has the effect that the amplitude of the crosstalk can be somewhat independent of line length. In the case of NEXT, the pulse-width of the crosstalk signal is proportional to the length of the coupled section, though pulse amplitude tends not to vary with length. Thus, the two types of crosstalk have significantly different characteristics. Traces that are interior to a circuit board have crosstalk characteristics that are different than those of traces on the outside surfaces of the board, too.

Depending on how you are inclined to count, there are two or four different types of crosstalk familiar to most circuit board designers—near end, far end, each on microstrip, and each on stripline.

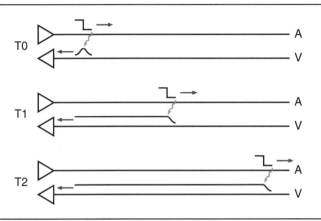

Figure 2.26   NEXT

Differential signaling is different than single-ended signaling, and crosstalk is one of the bigger differences. It is fairly easy to have crosstalk for differential signals an order of magnitude lower than that of single-ended traces with similar trace separations.

In differential signaling you have six fundamental types of crosstalk: three types of NEXT and three of FEXT. A differential signal in one signal pair can show up as a differential signal in an adjacent differential pair. A differential signal in a pair can show up as a common-mode signal in an adjacent pair. A common-mode signal can show up as a common-mode signal in an adjacent pair. Each of these has distinct characteristics. The cases of common-mode showing up as differential and of differential showing up as common-mode are identical. So, six rather than eight types of crosstalk exist between differential pairs. And of course, you still have the fact that stripline crosstalk is not like microstrip crosstalk.

To maximize the throughput density of the circuit board, understand how the various crosstalk types relate to geometric aspects of the layout. In Chapter 6, substantially greater details illustrate how crosstalk interacts with differential signals and the methods of working with common mode issues.

Various geometries can be imposed on the traces of a differential pair and can cause significant conversions of differential energy in the pair to common-mode energy. Common-mode energy generates crosstalk far more severely than does differential energy. This greater crosstalk reduces the usable receiver sensitivity and so reduces the available insertion loss budget. Reducing the available loss budget reduces the maximum usable length of an interconnect. The point is that geometric considerations impact a design on multiple levels. An important goal of subsequent chapters will be to clarify how you recognize and deal with these interactions.

EMI

Law tightly regulates electromagnetic interference with other devices. When circuit boards make use of microwave signals, they can generate a serious EMI issue. When circuit boards employed signals only in the bottom few hundreds of megahertz, most structures on the board, and the board itself, were small compared to the wavelengths involved. At microwave frequencies, the board and most structures on it are large compared to the wavelengths involved. The result is that various objects—the traces, the heat sinks, the ground, and power planes—can become resonant structures and enhance emissions. They can become good antennae. Similarly, apertures in a chassis that were effective blocks to EMI at lower frequency can become efficient *slot antennas* for microwave frequencies.

Such geometric considerations as the distances between the *reference planes,* power and ground on the circuit board that a signal passes through influence the amount of energy that can be coupled into the *planar waveguide* formed by the reference planes. Energy coupled in that waveguide can leak out the edges. The presence of a bend in a differential pair can cause conversion of differential energy to common mode. Common mode energy radiates much better than does differential mode energy because of the field-cancellation effect of the complementary signals. Distance to a second bend can form an antenna to radiate that energy.

■ Conclusion

This chapter introduced you to electrical characteristics that are crucial to understanding how microwave signals work on printed circuit boards. Several key terms and concepts were described, discussed, and graphically depicted. But to "talk the talk and walk the walk", more is needed than just the words. Subsequent chapters introduce a fundamental set of mathematical concepts to enable calculations. At low frequencies, most important electrical parameters can be directly measured. At microwave frequencies, that is often no longer true. Yes, we make measurements and acquire data, but that data must be further processed to extract most of the required information. You need to be able to do the mathematics. To enable you to get good data, measurement methods will be presented, modeling methods will be described, and recommendations will be made.

The need to calculate rather than directly measure circuit parameters doesn't mean that you are going to spend the rest of your life pushing a pencil and doing pages and pages of mathematics. We have computers for that. But as always, if you don't understand how and why the procedures work, you won't be likely to use them correctly either. Now I am going to shift from mostly hand-waving to the fun stuff: mathematics.

Chapter **3**

Mathematical Background For Microwaves

You can't see electrons, current, or voltages in ordinary conductors. Only through mathematics can we see electronics in action. Our interest is not electronics as a whole, but in just one very specialized area of electronics. This area, high data-rate transmission, can be seen through the application of a particular set of mathematics. That set probably doesn't exactly coincide with the set that you have been using. While the mathematics used to describe microwaves is not totally new, it might be a bit rusty from disuse. So here is a refresher on some of the applicable mathematics.

At microwave frequencies, you cannot directly measure many parameters needed for your designs. Rather, you make measurements and then mathematically extract the needed information. How is that done? This chapter tells you. It covers concepts and procedures needed to read and use the material presented in this book.

First, we refresh the most basic complex number operations, and then we cover fundamental matrix manipulations. This material is used in the description of scattering, or S, parameters.

Why, you may ask, do we need to study this? For several reasons. Your real-time oscilloscope is not likely to be capable of a bandwidth of more than a few gigahertz. A really good time-domain reflectometer (TDR) may have an effective bandwidth of six or seven gigahertz. Network analyzers capable of 50-gigahertz bandwidth are readily available. And, not only can they measure this range, they can achieve accuracies orders of magnitudes better than either the oscilloscope or the TDR.

Your wideband tools, network analyzers and field solvers, typically output scattering parameters. Scattering parameters are important for interpreting measurements, and the mathematics to deal with them will enable you to extract information from such measurements.

The range and the variety of information that can be extracted is amazing! The details of six different kinds of crosstalk are available from a single measurement set. Single-ended, differential, and common-mode characteristics, along with losses and conversions, are all there. If you want the single-ended impedance, it is there. If you want the differential impedance, it is there. If you prefer to work in the time domain, you convert frequency domain measurements to the time domain. Yes, you can generate the TDR curves from the scattering parameters. You want the impulse response? You want the step or the pulse response? Yes, they are there. And if you like, we'll throw in the slicer-dicer for free!

I want to emphasize that this chapter is not a substitute for the appropriate mathematics, physics, and electronics courses. It is a refresher and perhaps somewhat of an introduction to terms that the microwave guys use. If you already understand S parameters and how they apply to differential signals, skip to the next chapter. If S parameters are new to you, you will find them both fascinating and useful.

Analytical Procedures

Analytical procedures are algebraic or calculus methods that produce a precise numerical result in a single pass. The term is used here to distinguish such methods from others in which a numerical result is obtained by subdividing a problem into numerous simpler problems, or methods that approximate a numerical result by recycling the procedure over and over to produce an ever-decreasing error in an approximation.

Analytic formulae can come about in various ways. An exact solution to a physical problem may have been found through application of algebra or calculus. That solution may be available as a formula used to calculate a particular parameter. Alternatively, an exact solution may have been found but it might be too complex for ordinary day-to-day use, and someone may have generated a simple formula that reasonably well matches the exact one. My personal favorite is the method in which a problem whose solution takes too much computational time to be practical in day-to-day use is solved for a range, or a few discrete samples of input parameters and a simple curve-fit are used to interpolate results for all intermediate sets of parameters. Once the analytic formula is present, each of these is blindingly fast.

The advantage of analytic methods is excellent speed; a common disadvantage is inappropriate use. Consider the problem of determining the inductance of a wire. You need to know the inductance of a length of wire. You look in your books and find an equation. Calculus has been applied to the physics of the problem, and an exact and simple solution has been found for the inductance of a wire. There is a formula. The formula is correct, accurate, and all that you could desire of a simple formula. Everyone agrees that it is right. If you take this formula and calculate the inductance of your wire, the answer will always be wrong.

Perhaps wrong is too strong a word. The formula is indeed exact, but a real answer will always be inexact. Sometimes it will be so inexact that it can only be called wrong! The reason is that the formula is for the inductance of a section of an infinitely long wire and there can be no infinitely long wire in the real world. Yes, someone has modified the formula to account for wire length, but you still cannot necessarily guarantee a right answer. Even if we presume the wire is straight, not curled, the inductance provided by the formula can be very wrong. Even if we specify the wire is round, not rectangular, and we are looking for the low frequency inductance, the answer can still be wrong.

If somehow a formula for a finite length of straight wire were found and that formula was applied to a specific length of straight wire, would the answer necessarily be right? Such a formula, one that is fairly accurate, has been found. Can an engineer always rely on it? By now you know the answer is going to be a resounding no! So, why not?

Take that wire. Clamp it sideways in a vise. Measure the inductance from one jaw of the vise to the other. It won't equal the inductance predicted by the formula. The analytic formula presumes current is going the long way down the wire. This example is not unrealistic. If a signal on a circuit board is routed from one layer to an adjacent layer through a via, the current is more likely to be diagonal than coaxial with the via. With a little thought, it is evident that a current truly coaxial with a short wire will be the exception rather than the rule.

The point of all this is that, though analytic solutions are very fast at providing an answer, they almost always require careful consideration to be sure that the formula is being used properly, under the conditions for which it was intended, and within the range of input values for which it was intended. Yes, by all means use analytic methods, but use them carefully and correctly.

Refresher: Complex Numbers and Matrices

This section covers the most basic aspects of complex numbers and then does the same for matrix operations. It is a launching point for the discussion of scattering parameters, a subject that involves matrices of complex numbers. Scattering parameters are indispensable in working with microwaves because they are generated by the only practical method known for measuring and characterizing microwave components over a very wide bandwidth. Since this chapter is a refresher, you can simply skim or even entirely skip this short section, but don't skip the section on scattering parameters.

Complex Numbers

Complex numbers are numbers that are represented by two parts: the *real* part and the *imaginary* part. These are just names that come from the tradition of complex numbers. In an existential sense, there is nothing more or less real about the real part than there is about the imaginary part. They could just as well be divided into part u and part v.

A complex number is usually represented by printing two values. The first, on the left side of the pair, is the real part. The second, on the right side of the pair, is the imaginary part. The imaginary part is usually clarified by prefixing the letter i or the letter j to the number. This serves to distinguish a complex number from a number pair that might designate a position in two-dimensional space. A second clarification is added by always explicitly stating the sign of the imaginary part before the i or j. Numerically, whichever is used, i or j, it equals the square root of negative one.

Addition and subtraction of two complex numbers, detailed below, is very simple. It consists of adding or subtracting the real parts of each to generate the real part of the result, and the imaginary parts of each to generate the imaginary part of the result.

$$u = a + jb$$
$$v = c + jd$$
$$u + v = (a + c) + j(b + d)$$
$$u - v = (a - c) + j(b - d)$$

Multiplication is handled in the same way that multiplication of polynomials is handled. One cross-product generates j multiplied by j. This product is defined to equal negative one, a real quantity.

$$uv = ac + jad + jbc + j^2bd$$
$$= (ac - bd) + j(ad + bc)$$

Division of complex numbers is slightly trickier, as it involves the complex conjugate. The complex conjugate is the number generated by changing the sign of the imaginary part of a complex number. The procedure for division is to multiply both the numerator and denominator by the complex conjugate of the denominator, equivalent to multiplying the fraction by one. This operation has the impact of changing the denominator to a strictly real number. Once done, the real and imaginary parts of the resulting numerator are each divided by this real number.

$$u/v = (a + jb)/(c + jd)$$
$$= ((a + jb)(c - jd))/((c + jd)(c - jd))$$
$$= ((a + jb)(c - jd))/(c^2 + d^2)$$
$$= (ac + bd)/(c^2 + d^2) + j(bc - ad)/(c^2 + d^2)$$

You might encounter an alternate representation of complex numbers. This alternative presents the number in the form of magnitude and angle. This form is very useful for graphing functions of complex numbers but a poor choice for some types of mathematics. Multiplication is easy—just multiply the magnitudes and add the angles. For division, divide the magnitudes and subtract the angles. There is no practical way to add or subtract in this form.

$$u = a + jb$$
$$mag(u) = \sqrt{a^2 + b^2} = f$$
$$ang(u) = \tan^{-1}(b/a) = g$$
$$u = f\angle g$$

As a final note, some software, such as Matlab, uses the j as a postfix rather than a prefix.

That set of operations—add, subtract, multiply, and divide—is all you need to make the complex-number material in this book readable. Next comes a similar refresher on matrices and vectors.

Matrices

One way of viewing a matrix is as a shorthand way of representing a set of simultaneous equations. Of particular interest is any set of linear equations that all have the same form and variables but different coefficients. In this case, the coefficients can be arranged in an array that is called a matrix, and the input variables and output solutions are arranged in lists called *vectors*. In this format, the relationship between a bunch of output values that will here be called b_i, and a bunch of input variables that will here be called a_i, is represented by the simple form:

$$b = Ma$$

In this representation, b represents the list of output values or a vector, M represents the coefficients of the linear equations that relate the outputs to the inputs, and a represents the list of input values, another vector. Often a matrix is represented in the literature with brackets around it [M] to make it clear that it is a matrix and not an ordinary number. The standard mathematical operations all apply in some form to matrices, but they can get a bit complicated. A vector or matrix can be multiplied or divided by a number. And a matrix can be multiplied by a matrix, but that is a different sort of operation. The tough one is division. There is no simple division of a matrix by a matrix, and that is where all the interesting procedures become involved. Typically, for division, you find and then multiply by the inverse of the divisor matrix. Finding the inverse of a matrix is not always possible and, even when it is possible, it is seldom easy.

This refresher covers some basic matrix operations, but will not cover inversions, the finding and uses of eigenvalues, nor other of the more complicated operations. A starting point is the nomenclature of matrix elements. A matrix is an array of numbers, arranged in rows and columns. These individual numbers are the elements of the matrix. Each element has a specific row and column where it resides and so can be designated by its position. As a whole, a matrix is usually designated by a single capital letter. In this case the same letter, in lower case and subscripted by the row and column, can designate an individual specific element in the matrix. This notation is not exclusive. Sometimes, the same capital letter is used both for the matrix and for an element of the matrix. To avoid ambiguity, the element always has the row and column as a subscript.

$$[A] = \begin{matrix} a_{11} & a_{12} & a_{13} \\ a_{21} & a_{22} & a_{23} \\ a_{31} & a_{32} & a_{33} \end{matrix}$$

One hard, fast rule always used in representing a matrix element is that the first, left-hand, subscript value is always the row, and the second, right-hand, value is always the column. Usually these numbers are represented by subscripts, but sometimes even that is ignored. But the row-column order is always in that order. None other is accepted.

Elements

A generalized element of matrix [M] is m_{ij}. The particular element of [M] that resides in, for example, the third column and second row is m_{23}. Columns are numbered from the left. Column values become larger proceeding to the right. Rows are numbered from the top down. The left-most column is numbered one. The top row is numbered one.

Multiply

Two types of multiplication occur in matrices, the first by a number and the other by another matrix. It is common to see matrices multiplied by vectors but that is not a third instance because a vector is just a one-column matrix. Multiplying a matrix by a constant is simply multiplying each element individually by the constant.

If [K] = [M]a, where a is a number, then for all i and j, $k_{ij} = am_{ij}$.

Multiplication of a matrix by a matrix is more complicated. Each row-element of the product is formed of the sum of the products of the elements of the corresponding row of the multiplicand matrix, with the corresponding elements of the corresponding column of the multiplier matrix. Though true, that mess of words is not likely to communicate the procedure required in this form of multiplication.

The easiest case to describe is that in which a matrix is multiplied by a column vector. The product is another column vector. Each row-element of the product vector is the sum of each element in the same row of the matrix, multiplied in pairs; each column element of the matrix, with row element with the same index number, of the multiplier vector. Is it still not clear enough?

Then try taking the multiplier vector and laying it horizontally across the top of the multiplicand matrix. The top element of the original vector is now on the left. Each vector element is above a corresponding column of the matrix. The first, or top, element of the product vector is formed by multiplying the top element of each matrix column with the corresponding element of the vector and then summing all these products. The second element of the product vector is formed by summing the products of each vector element with the corresponding matrix column element in the second row of the matrix. The third product element is formed in a similar manner of the third matrix row, and so on.

The multiplication of a matrix by another matrix is just more of the same. The first column of the product is formed by multiplication with the first column vector of the multiplier matrix. The second column of the product is the product formed using the second column of the multiplier, and so on. The product will be a matrix with the same number of columns as the multiplier matrix has rows, and the same number of rows as the multiplicand matrix. Clearly, the multiplier must have the same number of rows as the multiplicand has columns.

In practice, the notation is always such that the multiplier is shown on the right and the multiplicand on the left. This is another hard and fast rule because in matrix multiplication the product [A][B] need not be equal to the product [B][A]. For that matter, if one or both matrices are not square, only one order, if any, will have a defined product. A square matrix is a matrix with the same number of rows as columns. S, the scattering matrix, is a square matrix.

Usage

Matrix notation is used in many electronic applications where several results relate linearly to several inputs. Examples include such things as an impedance matrix [Z], an admittance matrix [Y], a capacitance matrix, an inductance matrix, and, of special interest here, scattering parameters [S]. Each of these is similar in that an individual output element equals the sum of a group of coefficients multiplied by a group of input elements. The coefficient-group is the matrix.

$$b_1 = k_{11}a_1 + k_{12}a_2 + \ldots + k_{1n}a_n = \sum k_{1j}a_j$$
$$b_2 = k_{21}a_1 + k_{22}a_2 + \ldots + k_{2n}a_n = \sum k_{2j}a_j$$

etc.

$$b = [K]a$$

Filling out the Matrix

Given such a system, whether Z or S or C or Y—whatever—the individual elements of the matrix can be found through a simple procedure of either measurement or mathematics. If all the elements but one in the input vector are set to zero, the matrix elements of the column corresponding to the non-zero input element are simply found by measuring or calculating the output and dividing.

$$b_1 = k_{11}a_1 + k_{12}*0 + \ldots + k_{1n}*0$$
$$b_2 = k_{21}a_1 + k_{22}*0 + \ldots + k_{2n}*0$$

etc.

$$k_{11} = b_1 / a_1$$
$$k_{21} = b_2 / a_1$$

etc.

An example is the impedance matrix, defined by the equation $v=[Z]i$. The vector, i, is made up of the currents into the ports of the device. Of course, such a matrix is always square. When all ports but one are open circuited, voltage can be generated at all ports by applying current at that one port. The ratio of the voltage at each port to that current is the value of the matrix element in the column corresponding to the port where current is applied. In a similar manner, the elements of an admittance matrix can all be measured by shorting to ground all ports but one, applying a voltage to that one, and measuring current at each port. Unfortunately, at microwave frequencies, neither of these methods works.

At microwave frequencies, a truly open circuit is very difficult to create because some capacitance always exists across the supposedly open circuit. A truly shorted port is difficult because a short circuit always has some inductance. It is impractical to characterize a microwave component by measuring either the impedance or the admittance matrix. Yet, you need to be able to characterize microwave components.

In an ideal world, some parameter could be unambiguously set to zero, even in microwave circuits. This parameter would be readily stimulated and readily measured, and it would be adequate to fully characterize a device. While in this ideal world, you might also wish that this parameter would yield a matrix that could be converted into an impedance matrix or an admittance matrix by some simple procedure. And the parameter would be such that it could be accurately measured over an extremely wide dynamic range—something like a range of nearly a billion to one. The parameter would be measurable over an exceedingly wide frequency range—perhaps 20 or even 50 gigahertz. Again, you have probably guessed by now that said perfect world is the one we live in. The parameters of interest are incident and reflected waves. The coefficients that relate them are called scattering parameters, and the matrix made up of scattering parameters is called [S].

Introducing S parameters

It works like this. A test generator is provided with a precisely 50-ohm output impedance and a precisely 50-ohm measuring port. These two ports connect to the device under test through cables that also are precisely 50 ohms. The test generator measures the scattering parameters relative to a 50-ohm system. From there the data can be converted to any other desired reference impedance. The parameter that can be set to zero at any port is the wave entering the device. The response that can be measured is the wave exiting the device. Any transmission line terminated by precisely its characteristic impedance has no reflection. So, by terminating the line in 50 ohms, it is possible to guarantee that no wave enters a port from a 50-ohm line.

Another characteristic of microwave systems is that the precise values of parameters usually are frequency dependent. In practice, sine waves are applied over a range of frequencies to make measurements. The measured values at each frequency are tabulated, and, what is spoken of as an S matrix, is actually a set of matrices, one for each frequency in the range. And again, it is not expected that you would work the various conversions or deal with the hundreds of matrices by hand. Rather, these are dealt with by plugging the appropriate matrix expressions into an appropriate software tool such as Matlab or Octave.

The resulting data is said to be in the *frequency domain*; that is, a value is presented for each frequency step used in the range. Digital designers typically do not work in the frequency domain but rather in the time domain, a voltage or current value at each moment in time. Once again, this is an ideal world in which it is not difficult to convert time domain information into the frequency domain and frequency domain to time domain. Details will come shortly. Life is good.

Standard Terminology

A two-port example is presented below to help define and clarify some of the standard terminology.

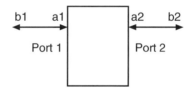

Figure 3.1   A Two-Port Object

A two-port device can be as simple as a piece of wire. At one end something goes in, and, at the other, something comes out.

Figure 3.2   A Simple Wire

The signal coming out, that is, the outward-bound portion of the total wave, is referred to as b; the signal going in, the inward-bound portion or the total wave, is a. There is an element of the a vector at each port and an element of the b vector at each port. The values of the b vector relate to the values of the a vector through the scattering matrix, S. Each of these vectors has one element for each port of the device. The real, total, as-official-as-it-gets definition of the scattering matrix is $b=Sa$. All else that can be said is just polishing this.

The value of $a2$ can be set to zero by placing a 50-ohm termination on port 2. In that case, the value of S11 is simply the amount of signal reflected at port 1 relative to a unit of applied signal at port 1. It is the reflection coefficient at port 1. Similarly, S22 is the reflection coefficient at port 2. Measuring the signal level at port 2 while port 2 is terminated, also gives you the value of $b2$. When a unit of signal is applied at port 1, and measured at port 2, the measured value is the loss or gain from port 1 to port 2. The corresponding matrix element is S21. Thus S21 is the gain or loss through the device.

$$\begin{bmatrix} b_1 \\ b_2 \end{bmatrix} = \begin{bmatrix} s_{11} & s_{12} \\ s_{21} & s_{22} \end{bmatrix} \begin{bmatrix} a_1 \\ a_2 \end{bmatrix}$$

Generalizing this, an n-port device is characterized by an n-by-n matrix. The S matrix is measured by applying signal to each port, one at a time, while all other ports are terminated at 50 ohms. The diagonal elements of the S matrix correspond to the reflection coefficients at each port. Sii is the reflection coefficient at port i. The off-diagonal elements correspond to the gain or loss between two ports. Sij is the gain or loss from port j to port i. Finally, standard terminology throughout the microwave literature is that a general element, Sij, is called an *insertion loss* if i doesn't equal j, and is called a *return loss* if i does equal j. Yes, crosstalk is characterized as an insertion loss.

A particular S matrix is typically only valid at a single frequency. In making the measurements, the equipment usually measures the parameters at hundreds of frequencies, yielding hundreds of S matrices to characterize this single device at those hundreds of frequencies. All those hundreds are presumed included in the concept. Each matrix equation is true for each of the hundreds of frequencies, and must be applied at each of them.

The device that is used to characterize microwave equipment is the network analyzer, which is a sine-wave generator and receiver capable of measuring amplitude and phase. The amplitude of the sine-wave output is not critical because the measurements are of voltage ratios rather than absolute values. This equipment delivers a sine wave from a precisely calibrated, typically 50-ohm port, and measures the amplitude and phase at that port. It also provides a second receive port, again precisely the same termination impedance, where it can again measure amplitude and phase. A third measurement, voltage and phase at a point before the transmitter's terminator, can be used to calculate the current out of the transmit port. With these three measured values, it is possible to determine with great precision the S11 and S21 values of the device under test. The equipment usually has the ability to reverse its direction and make the same measurement sourcing from the second port and receiving at the first. This reversal enables measurement between the two ports of all four elements—S11, S21, S12, and S22—with only one hookup.

Many devices of interest have more than two ports. Network analyzer builders would love to sell multi-port machines. A two-port analyzer can measure almost any device of any number of ports, but undoubtedly for some situations convenience is more important than capability. And as long as the device is passive and linear, the qualification of almost is not needed.

Measuring n-Ports

The generalized element in an *n*-port matrix is S*ij*. To measure the value of S*ij* with a two-port network analyzer, connect port 1 of the analyzer to port *i* of the device under test (DUT) and connect port 2 to port *j* of the DUT. Make the measurements and retrieve what the machine designates S11, S12, S21, and S22. Rename these measured values such that, for any element with a subscript 1, the one gets changed to the numerical value of port *i*; for any element with subscript 2, the two gets changed to the numerical value of the port designated *j*. The network analyzer is reconnected in the various configurations to enable measurement of all the elements in the S matrix.

It is true that a four-port network analyzer would be able to measure all the elements for a four-port device, but a simple differential pair is a four-port device. So, measuring crosstalk between two differential pairs would require, at a minimum, an eight-port measurement. The point is: practical cases exist of dimension greater than is likely practical for any multiport analyzer. Each laboratory will get what is needed for their particular circumstance, but if the system is linear, nothing can be measured with an *n*-port analyzer that cannot also be measured with a two-port analyzer.

Use of S Parameters

Of themselves, S parameter data tables have a lot of numbers and make great plots but don't directly answer many important questions. How much crosstalk is present? What is the differential impedance? How much skew, differential loss, and so on, are involved? All the answers are there, but you must use mathematical manipulations to get at them. Next you will see those manipulations and why they work.

Consider an object consisting of two nets, parallel to each other and close together enough to have significant coupling. We want to determine the differential characteristics of this object. First, this network has 4 ports. Port numbers are assigned such that ports 1 and 3 are the near ends, 2 and 4 are the far ends, 1 connects to 2, and 3 connects to 4. The order in which the ports are numbered is totally arbitrary, yet once chosen, all the element numbers in the calculations are specific to that particular ordering.

The matrix form, abbreviated, is shown here.

$$b = [S]a$$

This is shorthand for the matrix equation below. In most applications, the shorthand is preferred. Filling out all the entries takes a lot of time and often adds little clarity. Here the full matrices are being filled out because the individual parts of the equations are being examined.

$$
\begin{bmatrix} b_1 \\ b_2 \\ b_3 \\ b_4 \end{bmatrix} =
\begin{bmatrix} s_{11} & s_{12} & s_{13} & s_{14} \\ s_{21} & s_{22} & s_{23} & s_{24} \\ s_{31} & s_{32} & s_{33} & s_{34} \\ s_{41} & s_{42} & s_{43} & s_{44} \end{bmatrix}
\begin{bmatrix} a_1 \\ a_2 \\ a_3 \\ a_4 \end{bmatrix}
$$

We will examine the case of differential drive so the voltage at port 3 is, by definition of differential, the negative of the voltage at port 1. In general, apply the drive conditions to be investigated at the a vector, and S will yield the resulting outputs in the b vector.

$$
\begin{bmatrix} b_1 \\ b_2 \\ b_3 \\ b_4 \end{bmatrix} =
\begin{bmatrix} s_{11} & s_{12} & s_{13} & s_{14} \\ s_{21} & s_{22} & s_{23} & s_{24} \\ s_{31} & s_{32} & s_{33} & s_{34} \\ s_{41} & s_{42} & s_{43} & s_{44} \end{bmatrix}
\begin{bmatrix} a_1 \\ a_2 \\ -a_1 \\ a_4 \end{bmatrix}
$$

In use, we terminate the receive ports, 2 and 4. That eliminates reflections from ports 2 and 4 so the corresponding elements in the a vector are zero.

$$
\begin{bmatrix} b_1 \\ b_2 \\ b_3 \\ b_4 \end{bmatrix} =
\begin{bmatrix} s_{11} & s_{12} & s_{13} & s_{14} \\ s_{21} & s_{22} & s_{23} & s_{24} \\ s_{31} & s_{32} & s_{33} & s_{34} \\ s_{41} & s_{42} & s_{43} & s_{44} \end{bmatrix}
\begin{bmatrix} a_1 \\ 0 \\ -a_1 \\ 0 \end{bmatrix}
$$

Multiply it out to find the individual formula for each of the b elements.

$$b_1 = a_1(s_{11} - s_{13})$$
$$b_2 = a_1(s_{21} - s_{23})$$
$$b_3 = a_1(s_{31} - s_{33})$$
$$b_4 = a_1(s_{41} - s_{43})$$

But the differential signal at the transmit port is the value at port 1 minus that at port 3, and the input signal swing at each input port corresponding to a unit of differential is one-half unit of single-ended swing—a half positive and a half negative add to one—so we name the differential reflection parameter DS_{11} and find that:

$$DS_{11} = 0.5 * (s_{11} + s_{33} - s_{13} - s_{31})$$

As expected, this shows that you can have a perfect match with no reflections for the differential component, but a mismatch for single-ended signals. That observation is important; so be certain that you understand it. A perfect match is when DS_{11} equals zero. By similar calculations, the differential insertion loss—the loss from differential port 1,3 to port 2,4—is found by applying the same stimulus but calculating the differential at ports 2 and 4.

$$DS_{21} = 0.5 * (s_{21} + s_{43} - s_{23} - s_{41})$$

It is important, even critical, to note in all this that the particular matrix elements used in calculations depend on the way the ports of the DUT were assigned. If, for example, one implementation assigns the number five where another assigns one, all the elements subscripted as *one* in an equation for the one device will have to be *five* for the other device. For this reason, it is more important to understand how the equations are formed than to try to memorize the equations or to just flip to the page and blindly apply a formula that is found there.

As a last example, consider the same differential drive being applied and the common-mode output being measured. This is referred to as the common-mode conversion in the device under test. The common mode output is the same thing as the combined average of the two output ports, 2 and 4. Their common mode is the sum of their outputs divided by the number of outputs: two. But because the nets have been driven differentially, that factor of 0.5 is also present.

We name the differential-to-common-mode conversion factor DCS_{21}, shown in the next equation.

$$DCS_{21} = 0.25 * (s_{21} - s_{43} - s_{23} + s_{41})$$

A convention being used here is to prefix the differential version of scattering parameter with the letter D, for differential, to distinguish it from ordinary single-ended scattering parameters. Similarly, C designates common mode. When the input mode is the same as the output mode, I use only a single prefix letter. When the input mode differs from the output mode, I add two prefixes. The left-most prefix indicates the input mode, the second letter indicates the output mode. Finally, when I am using these forms, I usually don't subscript the row and column designators. These conventions will be particularly important in the case of crosstalk where the aggressor can be a differential component on a pair, or it might be a common-mode component on a pair. Similarly, the interference at the victim pair may be a differential or a common-mode component.

Examples:

DS11   differential input and differential output at port 1

DCS11   differential input reflected as common mode at port 1

CDS21   common mode input at port 1 seen as differential at port 2.

Crosstalk

Crosstalk in differential circuitry is particularly interesting. The signal mode on the aggressor pair can be the same or the alternate mode of that on the victim pair. Two input modes and two output modes yield four types of crosstalk. But two cases—differential in with common mode out, and common mode in with differential out—have the same coefficient values. So there are three distinctly different kinds of near-end crosstalk and three of far-end. In considering crosstalk between two differential pairs, the minimum system is an eight-port device.

Again, begin with the fundamental equation: $b = Sa$. Apply the signal, the stimulus of correct sign and magnitude, to the input port elements of the a vector. Terminate all undriven ports by setting their corresponding elements in a to zero. Calculate all the elements of the b vector. Then choose the output ports of interest and the signal mode of interest and calculate that voltage from the elements of b. If the calculation is finding output on the same ports that are driven, it is a return loss that is calculated. If the output ports are the other end of the lines driven, it is an insertion loss or a mode conversion that is being calculated. If the output ports are neither of these, it is a crosstalk that is being calculated.

Manipulations that have been described here are readily performed, even in a spreadsheet. Again, remember that the numbers are all complex and so all these calculations must be handled as complex mathematics. When the calculations are complete, you will want to graph the results. The usual way of displaying the results is in the form of magnitude versus frequency. The magnitude of a complex number is the square root of the sum of the square of the real and the square of the imaginary part. Though most calculations are performed with the raw numbers, it is common to convert the magnitudes to a decibel scale for display. Voltage magnitudes are converted to decibels by multiplying the base-10 logarithm of the magnitude by 20.

In examining the various types of crosstalk that associate with differential signals, the advantages of differential signaling begin to become obvious. The first step in the investigation of crosstalk is to assign port numbers. Always start with a sketch with the port numbering clearly marked. Any discrepancy between the way the equations are set up and the way the ports are numbered produces wrong results. Also, it is usually a very good idea to keep all procedures so clearly documented that a second party can readily check the work and verify it.

Figure 3.3 illustrates crosstalks modes in differential pairs.

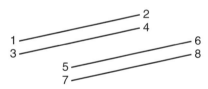

Figure 3.3   Two Differential Pairs

The matrix equation is set up to clearly show all the relationships. You can trust me that writing out all the elements by hand, as has been done here, is not fun.

$$
\begin{bmatrix} b_1 \\ b_2 \\ b_3 \\ b_4 \\ b_5 \\ b_6 \\ b_7 \\ b_8 \end{bmatrix} = \begin{bmatrix} s_{11} & s_{12} & s_{13} & s_{14} & s_{15} & s_{16} & s_{17} & s_{18} \\ s_{21} & s_{22} & s_{23} & s_{24} & s_{25} & s_{26} & s_{27} & s_{28} \\ s_{31} & s_{32} & s_{33} & s_{34} & s_{35} & s_{36} & s_{37} & s_{38} \\ s_{41} & s_{42} & s_{43} & s_{44} & s_{45} & s_{46} & s_{47} & s_{48} \\ s_{51} & s_{52} & s_{53} & s_{54} & s_{55} & s_{56} & s_{57} & s_{58} \\ s_{61} & s_{62} & s_{63} & s_{64} & s_{65} & s_{66} & s_{67} & s_{68} \\ s_{71} & s_{72} & s_{73} & s_{74} & s_{75} & s_{76} & s_{77} & s_{78} \\ s_{81} & s_{82} & s_{83} & s_{84} & s_{85} & s_{86} & s_{87} & s_{88} \end{bmatrix} * \begin{bmatrix} a_1 \\ a_2 \\ a_3 \\ a_4 \\ a_5 \\ a_6 \\ a_7 \\ a_8 \end{bmatrix}
$$

Again the driven port is designated as the port 1,3. Any end of any differential pair could equally well be designated as the driven port for a particular instance. Here, only one instance is shown, where 1 and 3 are driven. In examining crosstalk, it is necessary to drive these differentially only because the crosstalk coefficients for the case of differential drive showing up as common-mode receive are the same as the case for common-mode drive showing up as differential at the receiver.

Applying a unit of differential signal at ports one and three is equivalent to setting $a1$ to 0.5, $a3$ to minus 0.5, and all other elements of the a vector to zero. Carrying out the matrix multiplication, the elements of b are found:

$$
\begin{bmatrix} b_1 \\ b_2 \\ b_3 \\ b_4 \\ b_5 \\ b_6 \\ b_7 \\ b_8 \end{bmatrix} = 0.5 * \begin{bmatrix} s_{11} - s_{13} \\ s_{21} - s_{23} \\ s_{31} - s_{33} \\ s_{41} - s_{43} \\ s_{51} - s_{53} \\ s_{61} - s_{63} \\ s_{71} - s_{73} \\ s_{81} - s_{83} \end{bmatrix}
$$

Choosing the output port of interest and calculating the value of the common-mode or the differential component are simple matters. For example, the near-end, differential-to-differential crosstalk, DDNEXT, at port 5, 7 becomes the value of $b5$ minus the value of $b7$. Similarly, the differential to common-mode crosstalk at this port, DCNEXT, is the sum of $b5$ and $b7$ divided by two.

The procedure is the same and independent of the number of ports in the device under test. The input ports are identified and driven with appropriate levels. All other ports are driven with a value of zero. The matrix multiplication is carried out to evaluate the b vector. Finally, the elements of the b vector are evaluated in terms of the desired output port and output mode.

It is particular interesting to view the plot of a typical differential system's various crosstalk modes, as in Figure 3.4.

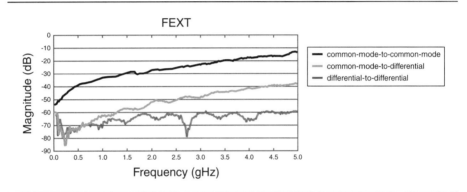

Figure 3.4   Three Varieties of FEXT

If nothing else, it becomes clear that the crosstalk of the differential component is substantially lower than that of the common mode component. This result is typical and is one of the major advantages that differential signaling holds for high-speed data signals. This graph also should be convincing evidence that familiarity with crosstalk in single-ended systems is not enough to give one a feel for what crosstalk is like in a differential system. Until you have accumulated experience with differential circuitry, it is safest to presume that there are six modes, three near end and three far, all of which are totally new, and all the old rules of board layout need to be reevaluated.

Impedance

So far it has been shown that reflections, through-loss, mode conversions, and six types of crosstalk can all be calculated from a scattering matrix that characterizes a particular device. Next you will see that various impedances can also be calculated. Unlike the above material, step-by-step derivations will not be provided for this section. These derivations are readily available in the literature, whereas the application of scattering parameters to differential systems is often not included in the literature.

Diagonal elements of the scattering matrix correspond to the single-ended reflection coefficients at each of the ports of the device. Knowing the source impedance, in this case 50 ohms, with the reflection coefficient S*ii* is enough information to calculate the effective impedance at the port. I need to stress that this is not the characteristic impedance of the trace unless the trace is uniform and is itself terminated in its characteristic impedance. In this book, the impedance that is found is called the *measured impedance*, to distinguish it from the characteristic impedance. The single-ended measured impedance at the port is simply:

$$Z_i = 50 * \frac{1 + s_{ii}}{1 - s_{ii}}$$

This thing we are calling measured impedance differs from characteristic impedance in that, by definition, characteristic impedance is the impedance seen by a transient signal. The measured impedance is the impedance seen by a sine wave at steady state.

This equation yields the single-ended measured impedance, but that number is actually of very little significance for differential signaling. The differential and common mode impedances are the values that are important for differential signaling. The differential impedance is what needs to be matched to maximize signal transfer. The differential and common mode impedances are what need matching to minimize reflections. If significant coupling exists between the two traces of the pair, matching the single-ended impedance of each line in a pair is guaranteed to be an incorrect termination for the differential component of signal on the pair.

Back to the statement just made about the value Zi, shown above. You may ask, if this value isn't the characteristic impedance, then what is it? The answer is that this value is the impedance that would be measured for a steady-state sine wave at this port. Recall that a forward wave and a backward wave usually exist on every line. A line with only a forward wave or only a backward wave has a constant ratio of voltage to current throughout the line, and the ratio has been given the name Zo. But most lines have both a forward and a backward wave. So, the ratio varies with position along the line, and the impedance measured at a point along the line is a function of distance from the termination. This impedance is what is produced by the above equation and it, too, is of little interest except in narrow-band situations. It is completely possible to calculate the characteristic impedance from a table of S parameters. That procedure is tricky and gets covered in the section on peeling.

In similar manner the value of DS*ii*, the differential return loss at port *i*, could be calculated, and the measured differential impedance at the port could be produced. Transmission lines of interest are seldom totally uniform, and characteristic impedance changes along the line. In this case, the lines of most interest cannot be characterized by a single number called the characteristic impedance. Rather, they are characterized by a scattering matrix and leave it at that, or they are characterized by an impedance profile, a list of impedance verses position on the line. One of the fascinating aspects of all this is that the two representations actually have the same information content. The scattering matrix can be used to generate the impedance profile within conditions, and the impedance profile can be used to generate the scattering matrix. Details on how this works are in the next section.

Format and Reference Conversions

The same information content can be displayed in various formats. Common representations include scattering [S], impedance [Z], and admittance [Y]. Of particular interest here is conversion between [S] and [Z]. [Z] is the impedance matrix of the device. To generate [Z], an auxiliary matrix, [Zo] is generated. [Zo] is a matrix with all off-diagonal elements set to zero and every diagonal element set to the same value, Zo. Here Zo is the reference impedance of [S], typically 50 ohms. A second auxiliary is defined as [1], a matrix of all zeros except the diagonal that is all ones. With this information, the impedance matrix is found:

$$[z] = [z_o]([1]+[s])([1]-[s])^{-1}$$

The conversion in the other direction is equally simple. Using the same auxiliary matrix definitions as above, the scattering matrix is:

$$[s] = ([z]+[z_o])^{-1}([z]-[z_o])$$

The interesting thing about these two equations is that they provide a simple mechanism to convert scattering parameters from one reference impedance to another. That is, though test equipment is typically referenced to 50 ohms, it can be used to determine scattering parameters for any other reference impedance by use of the above two equations. The procedure is to use the first equation with the impedance of the test equipment to calculate the impedance matrix. Then use the impedance matrix with the desired reference impedance in the [Zo] matrix to calculate the new [S] matrix.

You can create a scattering matrix that has each port referenced to a different impedance, but why would you want to? The procedure is easy to implement, but caution is needed in use of such a form. In all the preceding material of this book, the definition of the scattering matrix has been that [S] is the matrix that produces the vector b when multiplied by the vector a. That definition is valid. So far everything is correct. Then the manipulations of this equation have proceeded as though the elements of the a and b vectors were voltages or forward and reverse voltage waves. That progression is not always valid. What is precisely true is that the ratios of a and b elements equal the ratios of forward and reverse voltage waves, as long as the reference impedance at each port is the same. In systems of interest here, the reference impedance at all ports will be equal, but that is not an absolute necessity for all systems.

The precise definition is that the vector components, in terms of voltages, are the forward and reverse wave voltages, each divided by the square root of the reference impedance for the particular port where the voltage is measured. If all the reference impedances are equal, they cancel out when ratios are taken. But, if all the reference impedances are not equal, these terms need to be carried through all the calculations made with scattering parameters.

The procedure for converting scattering parameters from a single reference impedance to multiple different reference impedances is:

$$[F] = diag(1/2\sqrt{Z_i})$$
$$[G] = diag(Z_i)$$
$$[S] = [F][[Z]-[G]][[Z]+[G]]^{-1}[F]^{-1}$$
$$[Z] = [F]^{-1}[[I]+[S]][[I]-[S]]^{-1}[F][G]$$

Here, the function diag( ) signifies that the matrix is a diagonal matrix whose elements are those specified in the argument of the function. The individual Zi value is the impedance desired at port-i. The procedure, going from a scattering matrix with all ports referenced to a single impedance, to one that has individual reference impedances at each port, is first to convert the [S] matrix to a [Z] matrix, and then use the formula presented here to calculate the multi-referenced scattering matrix. The reverse procedure involves using the last formula presented here to calculate the [Z] matrix, and then convert that to [S].

These procedures are presented for the sake of completeness, and their presence here is not to be construed as a recommendation that this approach be used. As always, I do not expect you to perform any of these manipulations by hand. Use an appropriate software tool to facilitate the mathematics.

Chaining

A typical interconnect circuit is likely to have several devices: a package, some trace, a connector, more trace, and another package, all concatenated together. The question arises, how do you determine the scattering matrix of a pair of devices each individually characterized by scattering matrices? It would be nice if it were as simple as finding the product of the two scattering matrices, but this won't work. The reason this won't work is that the scattering matrix expresses the output at every port in terms of the input at every port, and what is needed is the total voltage at the output ports in terms of the total voltage at the input ports.

Calculating such a matrix is just an exercise in algebra, and examples are given in many textbooks. It is unfortunate that such examples often lead you down a garden path. They show a procedure that works well in the example but is useless in any realistic application. They will set up and solve the two-port example, and the solution will be found by application of Gaussian elimination. After a few pages of calculation, you'll find this approach still works for a four-port device. Trying this method on an eight-port or 12-port device is an exercise in futility. One method that works for these cases is application of Cramer's Rule. An even simpler method is discussed below.

The matrix that results, that expresses total voltage at output ports in terms of total voltage at input ports, is called the chain matrix and is designated T. Concatenating devices characterized by T matrices is simply a matter of calculating the product of those matrices. The result is the T matrix of the combination. That resulting matrix can then be again algebraically manipulated to convert it back to the S format.

ABCD

The ABCD matrix describes the voltage and current at an output pin, in terms of the voltage and current at an input pin.

$$\begin{bmatrix} v2 \\ -i2 \end{bmatrix} = \begin{bmatrix} A & B \\ C & D \end{bmatrix} \begin{bmatrix} v1 \\ i1 \end{bmatrix}$$

The T matrix is the most general case but is often difficult to use. A simpler system that applies to discrete two-port devices and can be used occasionally in distributed systems is the ABCD matrix. Because this form applies only to two-port systems, it is not useful when things such as crosstalk need analysis. The conversion from S to ABCD is:

$$ABCD \equiv \begin{bmatrix} AB \\ CD \end{bmatrix}$$

$A = ((1 + S11)(1 - S22) + S12S12)/2S21$

$B = Z_0((1 + S11)(1 + S22) - S12S12)/2S21$

$C = ((1 - S11)(1 - S22) - S12S12)/2S21Z_0$

$D = ((1 - S11)(1 + S22) + S12S12)/2S21$

The scattering parameters for each device are converted to an ABCD matrix for each device. The product of those component matrices is calculated, resulting in the ABCD matrix for the combined assemblage. Then that matrix is converted back to the scattering matrix of the combined assemblage. The conversion from ABCD to S is:

$S11 = (A + B/Z_0 - CZ_0 - D)/\Delta$

$S12 = 2(AD - BC)/\Delta$

$S21 = 2/\Delta$

$S22 = (-A + B/Z_0 - CZ_0 + D)/\Delta$

where:

$\Delta \equiv A + B/Z_0 + CZ_0 + D$

The very form of the ABCD matrix makes it clear that this method can only be used in two-port instances.

Frequency Domain and Time Domain

Data that is presented in terms of values versus time values is said to be time-domain data or in the time domain. Data that is presented in terms of values verses frequency values is said to be frequency-domain data or in the frequency domain. The image that you might see displayed on an oscilloscope is in the time domain. The image you might see on a spectrum analyzer is in the frequency domain.

The time domain is important because it is easy to measure, display, and understand. The frequency domain is important because it is the domain of much of electronic analysis, the domain of many specifications such as FCC regulations, and it is the domain in which many of the best measurements in all electronics are possible.

Neither domain has a monopoly on utility; neither is appropriate for all uses. Fortunately, it is possible to convert data in either domain to the other domain. Perhaps that is better stated differently: it is mathematically possible to convert, but a good conversion requires conditions. The first condition needed to facilitate conversion between the two is that data points are evenly spaced in their domain. This requirement is usually obvious in the time domain but not as obvious in the frequency domain. Display in the frequency domain is often on a logarithmic scale. Sometimes data is acquired on a logarithmic scale. That data is not suitable for conversion—it needs modification. Similarly, data in the frequency domain must be in the form of complex numbers rather than magnitudes. And it must be in the form of real and imaginary parts, not magnitude and phase. Data in the frequency domain must also extend to adequately high and low frequencies and must have enough data points between. These requirements may seem obvious and yet they need to be stated. Many network analyzers acquire data that is great for display purposes but is inadequate for conversion. Particularly, they default to too few data points. Though a few hundred data points are adequate for drawing a nice picture on a display, they are too few for useful calculations. Considering the degree of effort typically involved in setting up a particular measurement, why settle for the minimal number of data points? Twenty years ago it was important to conserve memory space. Today it makes a lot more sense to acquire massive amounts of data and conserve engineering time rather than computer memory.

Consider an example in the time domain. A pulse is formed consisting of 10 steps at zero, 90 more at one, and the remainder of 1,000 all at zero. The fast Fourier transform (FFT) is taken of this data set and the magnitude of the result is plotted. Figure 3.5 shows what you see. It appears symmetrical about a center frequency and has a nice bathtub shape.

An interesting aspect of the frequency domain graph is that it is mirrored through the center, right to left. This characteristic results when this transform is applied to any real function. When this graph is compared to the magnitude of a data set from a scattering parameter measurement, it becomes evident that the network analyzer provides only the left half of this data set. To perform the conversion from frequency domain to time domain, it is necessary to reconstitute the right hand of the data set. To do so, reflect the real part of each data point across the right end of the S data set boundary, and reflect the negative of each imaginary part. The resulting data set is then capable of generating time-domain data through use of the inverse fast Fourier transform (IFFT). But is it?

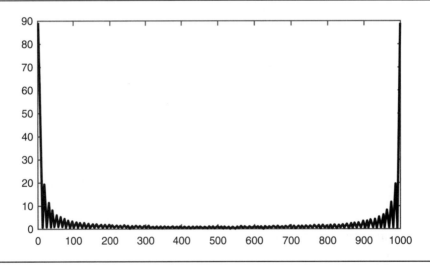

Figure 3.5   The FFT of a Square Pulse

Examine the graph more closely. Use the same time-domain wave but only sample it at 40 points. Implement the FFT on it and graph the magnitude of the result: the symmetry is not quite perfect. The center of the reflection is offset one data point to the right. In fact, the entire reflected half is the mirrored conjugate of the left half, except for the first data point of the left half. Why is that first point different? The answer comes from recalling how the Fourier series is calculated. That first element, called $a0$, is calculated in a manner different than all the remaining terms. This offset and reflection, seen in Figure 3.6, are what you will have to emulate with your S parameters to make them suited to conversion with the IFFT.

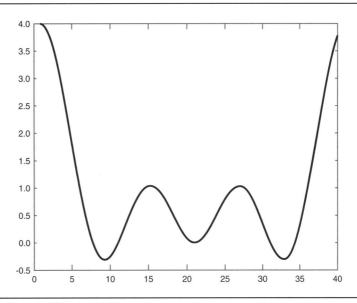

Figure 3.6   A 40-Point FFT

While thinking about the Fourier transform, recall that it produces a harmonic series. A harmonic series has elements that fall on integer multiples of some fixed frequency. Data that meets this requirement is called a harmonic sequence. Nothing in the definition of S parameters includes this requirement. Odds are that your measured S parameters don't meet this requirement. To use the IFFT, you have to produce a harmonic sequence from the data you have. You probably have to apply some sort of curve fit and interpolation scheme to obtain data in the harmonic sequence that the IFFT requires. Fortunately there is software, both commercial and free, that is designed to enable such conversions without much work on your part. The effort required to do these manipulations on the frequency domain data is well worth the effort.

Through this method, for example, the S11 data can be transformed into equivalent time-domain-reflectometer (TDR) data. Of course that too needs a little thought. Applying the IFFT to S11 data results in an impulse response. Integrating the impulse response generates the step response. Finally, getting a graph that totally mimics TDR data may require addition of an offset, an integration constant. Also, by the way, the pulse response can be generated from the step response. To do so, form the sum of the step response and a negated copy of the step response that has been time-shifted by one unit interval, that is, by the width of the desired pulse. You get the pulse response.

These procedures allow the extraction not only of TDR data, but also crosstalk wave forms and amplitudes, from a set of S parameters. It was stated previously that the most accurate measurements at microwave frequencies are made with network analyzers. These mathematical procedures enable the engineer who is accustomed to working in the time domain to work with the resulting data in familiar terms.

Sometimes you have access only to time domain data. An example is the lab that has a TDR machine but not a network analyzer. It is easy to say that the data can be transformed to the time domain by applying an FFT to the data, but is that really all? Yes, it is easy to say that, and yes we were all taught that in school, but in practice it simply isn't true! It was shown above that actual application of the IFFT to measured data requires "faking" half the data set. Again, the data set acquired from the TDR machine is likely to be inadequate for actual application of the FFT. The reason is the unspoken presumptions in this process.

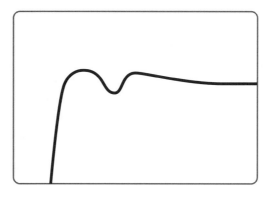

Trace seen on TDR

Figure 3.7   The TDR View

Looking at the TDR machine, you see a trace and presume that the wave extends to forever at the right. That is the presumption, but the data doesn't actually say that. For mathematical manipulations, the presumptions need to be replaced by explicit statements.

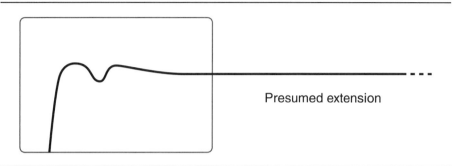

Presumed extension

Figure 3.8   The TDR Presumption

The acquired data probably ends at about the right-hand side of the display. When this data is fed to the FFT, the FFT doesn't know about the above presumption. The FFT sees a data set that extends to the right of the screen and presumably repeats this pattern forever. The spectrum of that case is not the spectrum of the wave with the presumed extension. The calculated frequency response will be quite different than that of the circuit being analyzed. The FFT is going to see that abrupt end of the data and treat it as though the data made a sudden transition to zero. That sudden transition is going to transform into a lot of high-frequency harmonics that are not supposed to be there.

So now what? Well, of course, more faking of data. All engineers know that it is wrong to fake data. Give it another name. Perhaps call it "completing the data set." Then it is okay to fake the data. If the data set can be adequately completed, a correct or acceptable spectrum will be generated.

One procedure, certainly not the only one, is to pad the right hand with a constant value for a while, then slowly taper it off to zero to avoid adding high-frequency components. Then pad on additional data at zero to push any added components into the very low frequencies. This modified data set is then run through the FFT and will produce a valid frequency spectrum everywhere but at the low frequency, where the added data create a low-frequency component.

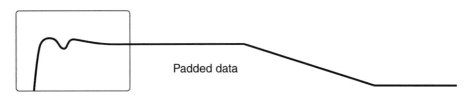

Padded data

Figure 3.9   The TDR Fix

Peeling

Peeling is an alternate way of handling TDR data. With peeling you can generate very good SPICE models directly from measurements. The method is easy and fast. Though it is not appropriate everywhere, in the many places where it applies, it is an excellent option. It gets covered in detail in the next chapter.

Chapter 4

Peeling and Mason's Rule

Peeling is one of the truly awesome procedures. It is used by oil companies looking for oil deep in the ground. It has shown up in movies, with famous actors searching for bones of Jurassic-era dinosaurs. And now it is right here in your hands. Peeling is a procedure that generates a physical profile of some embedded object by *deconvolving* reflections in the time domain. What that means in English, what that means for you, is that you can quickly generate high-quality SPICE models directly from the electrical measurements of connectors and similar devices.

How Peeling Works

Envision a voltage source with known output resistance (*Rs*) that connects to a second resistor (*Rl*) to ground. It is easy to calculate the value of the second resistor by measuring the open circuit voltage (Vo) and the connected voltage (Vc) using the voltage-divider equation:

$$Vc = Vo \frac{Rl}{Rs + Rl}$$

The schematic version of the system is displayed in Figure 4.1. This circuit is one of the most fundamental in electronics, and the sad truth is that if you connect the two resistors with a transmission line, the voltage divider equation only works when a lot of qualifiers surround its application.

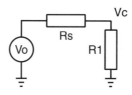

Figure 4.1 A Voltage Divider

If the load is a transmission line and the source voltage is a transient, the transient impedance of the line can be measured by the same procedure. However, if the *source* impedance is a transmission line, this procedure no longer works very well. When something drives or is driven by a transmission line, you calculate with the reflection coefficient for transients, ρ, rather than the voltage-divider equation, as follows:

$$\rho = \frac{Z1 - Z2}{Z1 + Z2}$$

This equation holds for all cases, whether Z1 and Z2 are discrete elements, the characteristic impedances of transmission lines, or any mixture of the two. Through use of this equation, we can extract the impedance profile of a device by analysis of the reflected signal seen at the input to that device.

Starting with some known source impedance and given a lossless non-uniform transmission line, it is possible to extract the impedance values of each segment of the line. The procedure is called the *peeling algorithm*. Figure 4.2 depicts a coaxial transmission line with variation in characteristic impedances through the length of the line.

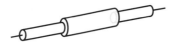

Figure 4.2 A Co-ax of Varying Impedance

When a transient is applied to such a line, each discontinuity in impedance produces a reflection. Some energy goes forward, some reflects back. Following the path of the forward energy, the forward wave encounters the next discontinuity and, again, some reflects and some goes forward. Now, following the reflected energy, it encounters that original discontinuity and, again, some reflects and some proceeds.

A typical device has numerous small and sometimes big variations in impedance, each causing another point of reflection. The result can become very complicated. A reflection diagram, sometimes called a lattice diagram, can be used to help envision the situation, as illustrated in Figure 4.3.

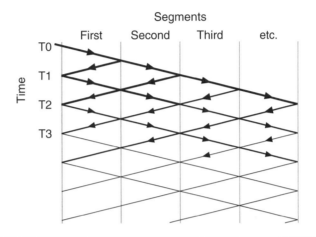

Figure 4.3   Signal Reflections

Here's the way peeling works. You start at the first segment, and from the known voltage and source impedance, calculate the reflection coefficient at the beginning time (*t0*) of the first segment. Knowing this coefficient, you can calculate the impedance of that first segment and, more importantly, the forward and reverse energy in that first segment. Knowing these waves, you can calculate the reflection coefficient at the right side of this second segment. That information allows you to calculate the forward and reverse energy in the next segment, and so on. This series of calculations is called the peeling algorithm. Though it sounds easy, it can be a little tricky to implement.

Implementing Peeling

For an applied transient starting at the left, the information needed to calculate the reflection coefficient at the right side of any segment is the forward and reverse energy in this segment. The procedure starts with only the voltage at the driving port, the step response. The calculation presumes that the device under test (DUT) was in a non-excited steady state to begin with, and so it has no initial reflected wave in any segment of the device. If this is true, the first change of voltage from the initial voltage must include two pieces of information: first, the magnitude of the change is the sum of the initial applied wave and the reflected wave; second, the time it took for this to return equals twice the electrical length of the first segment. Using this information, you calculate reflection coefficient at the right side of the first segment. To continue the solution, calculate the forward and reverse wave in each segment, one segment at time. Two vectors, Wr and Wl, representing the energy traveling to the right and to the left in whatever is the current segment, F must be defined. The number of elements in each of these vectors is equal to the number of time samples in the impulse response. That is to say, element Wr(i) and Wl(i) are the forward and reverse energy waves in the current segment. And i is the number of time samples since the stimulus first arrived at this segment. Initialize the system by setting each element except the first, in Wr, to zero. Set the voltage of the first element of Wr to 1—the applied step is normalized to one. Initialize all elements of Wl to zero. Now, from the second element to the last, Wr, the value is initialized according to this next equation.

$$Wr(i) = (Sr(i-1) - Sr(i)) / (2\sqrt{Z_s})$$

Here Sr(i) is the measured step response at time slot i at the port of the device under test. It is the data set that came out of your TDR machine or that you generated from applying the IFFT to your frequency domain measurements.

As each layer is peeled off, the first thing needed is the reflection coefficient at the right side of the segment. Note that in this one instance, $r(n)$—the reflection coefficient at the right of segment n—equals the voltage of Wl(2). If that equivalence looks a little like smoke and mirrors, more detail should help clarify this step. Initially the DUT is idle, dead, with no forward or reflected waves. Then at some time ($t0$), a unit step is applied. A forward wave of unit amplitude is injected into the initial segment of the transmission line. To easily envision this action, presume that the initial segment is a section of a 50-ohm transmission line. Presume a reflection coefficient of –0.25. This is shown in Figure 4.4.

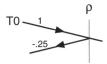

Figure 4.4   The First Reflection

The voltage measured at the first node at time *t1*, the sum of the forward and reflected waves, is 0.75 volt. The voltage applied is still one volt. So there must be a negative quarter volt being reflected. The difference between the voltage at time zero and the voltage at time one is the reflection coefficient. Look at it from the perspective of the current. The driver puts out the current required to make one volt at its output. In reflecting 25 percent of it, the load sees 0.75 volt. The difference in voltage between time zero and time one shows what the forward and reverse waves must be in that time interval. Repeat the process for each time interval, using the complete set of voltages making up the step response. The situation at the first time intervals is depicted in Figure 4.5.

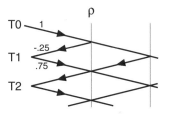

Figure 4.5   Initializing the Vectors

So, the measured impulse response is given, and we need the forward and reverse energy in the first segment of the transmission line. To find these vectors, take the differences of the applied voltages between the time steps. The voltage at *t2* cannot yet be predicted, nor can the reflection coefficient be calculated from *t1* or *t2* data because a reflection from further to the right may have added to this voltage. Only the first step can guarantee that there is no impact from further right, so only the first two elements can be used to calculate the reflection coefficient. All the remaining forward and reflected elements are calculated by taking the differences, and the system is initialized, ready for peeling.

Peeling requires two relationships. First, you need the sum of the energy waves approaching the right side reflecting boundary, which equals the sum of the energy waves moving away from that boundary. Second, you need to know the reflection coefficient for waves from the left. Name the energy components involved at the reflecting position as shown in Figure 4.6.

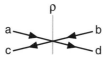

Figure 4.6   Naming the Components

The reason that we assert that the sum of waves coming in must equal the sum of waves going out is that the segment is presumed lossless. Though this presumption is never strictly true in any real system, it is close enough for use. In a real system, the sum of all the energy reflected out of any junction will always be less than the sum of the energy inserted. It will be less by the amount of energy lost to resistance and to radiation. You must weigh the impact of that presumption to determine when peeling is appropriate for the particular system you are designing.

The conservation of energy gives one of the two required equations; the definition of the reflection coefficient gives another. In combination, they yield all the information needed to derive all the wave elements in the next segment to the right from those in the current segment.

The reflection coefficient for a wave approaching from the right does not equal the reflection coefficient for a wave approaching from the left. When you examine the equation, you see that though the two differ, they differ only in sign. Trading places between Z1 and Z2 only changes the sign.

$$\rho = \frac{Z1 - Z2}{Z1 + Z2}$$

The reflection coefficient from the left is the negative of the reflection coefficient from the right. Due to conservation of energy, what doesn't get reflected goes through. The transmission coefficient is one minus the reflection coefficient. For me it works best to use the convention that, in all cases where the reflection coefficient is used, the value is as seen by a wave coming from the left. So, with knowledge of the forward and reverse energy left of the boundary and knowledge of the reflection coefficient at the boundary, you can calculate the forward and reverse energy at the right side if the boundary.

These are the Wr and Wl elements in the next segment. And it is again true that the top, or the first, reflection from the right for this segment involves no reflected wave from further out and so can be used to calculate the reflection coefficient at the right of this segment. That reflection reconstitutes from this segment all the information needed to calculate the next segment, and so on. That is why we call it peeling.

The result of peeling can be a list of reflection coefficients or a list of impedances, one for each time increment. All the rest of the information about forward and reverse waves can now be discarded. It is known that the system starts with a 50-ohm driver source resistance, so the next impedance is calculated from this impedance and the reflection coefficient, the next from that, and so on.

$$z(n+1) = z(n)\frac{1-\rho(n)}{1+\rho(n)}$$

That step reconstitutes the impedance profile of a lossless transmission line equivalent to the original data. Here is a simple example. This SPICE code is for a simple lossless transmission line with varying impedance through its length. You can use this model in two ways. You can send a voltage step into it and record and peel the reflected wave, or you can do a frequency sweep of it, use the IFFT to convert that to time domain, and implement the peeling. The following examples show both.

Examples

Given this SPICE circuit:

```
r1 1 2 50

t0 2 0 20 0 zo=50 td=0.2n

t1 20 0 10 0 zo=30 td=.1n

t2 10 0 11 0 z0=60 td= 0.2n

t3 11 0 3 0 zo=45 td=2n

r2 3 0 50
```

The first example using this code results in the graph of Figure 4.7. For this case, the circuit was analyzed in the time domain. The step response was calculated by SPICE. An extremely fast edge-rate on the step results in nice square corners.

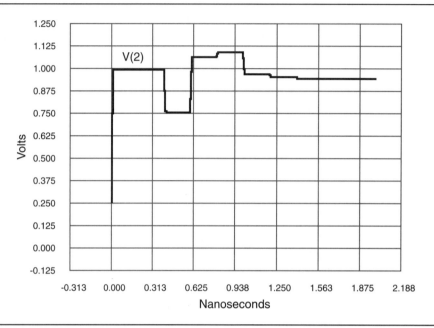

Figure 4.7   SPICE Step Response

The next step would be to peel that reflection profile to recover the original impedance profile. But that would be too easy. We'll do it later. First, let's look at the same model in the frequency domain. The SPICE model was frequency swept and S11 was calculated. The objective now is to take this calculated S11 and attempt to reconstitute the original waveform shown in Figure 4.7. From that reconstituted wave, we'll apply peeling to regenerate the transmission lines in the SPICE model. In examining this loop from SPICE model to S11 to step-response to SPICE model, numerous issues are uncovered and insights become available.

Creating S Parameters

At this time, only S11 is used. As an example, a lossless, non-uniform, single-ended transmission line is modeled in SPICE. A *lossless* transmission line is used because the accuracy of the method decreases as loss is introduced. For now we go lossless and minimize these complications. The example is a *non-uniform* transmission line because the characteristics of a uniform transmission line can be calculated by hand in moments, so are uninteresting. Also, note that it is the impedance that is non-uniform. The transmission medium is presumed linear. *Single-ended* circuitry, as opposed to differential, is used for simplicity.

As the above SPICE code shows, the DUT consists of a section of 50-ohm transmission line followed by a section of 30 ohms, a section of 60 ohms, and a final section of 45 ohms. S11 will be generated totally by hand; that is, by use of only fundamental SPICE operations to make it clear how you generate S parameters. In application, you would use whatever facilities your version of SPICE has to simplify this step.

To generate S11, you need to drive the DUT with an AC source that has a series resistance of 50 ohms. The far end, or the receive end, of the DUT is terminated with 50 ohms to ground. Analysis is in the form of an AC sweep of the DUT. The data you need to acquire is the voltage and current at the input node of the DUT. An important point to note is that, since S parameters are complex numbers, the complex voltage and current must be used. Most versions of SPICE, possibly all versions, default to outputting voltage and current magnitudes. Magnitudes are not adequate for the calculations. Print out the real and imaginary parts of the voltage at the input of the DUT, and the real and imaginary parts of the current through the AC source.

Looking forward, the S11 is used to calculate the impulse response through the inverse fast Fourier transform (IFFT). That procedure requires many values evenly spaced in frequency—a harmonic sequence. That spacing translates to a requirement that the AC sweep be a *linear* sweep. SPICE can also do others. "Many" translates to a number in the range of 2,000 to 5,000. Thus, the analysis line in the SPICE file might look something like:

```
.ac lin 5000 1 2e10
```

You should sweep to go to quite high frequencies because the rise-time achieved is determined by the highest frequency in the sweep. It is desirable to go to quite low frequencies if the DUT responds to DC. In this example, the frequency sweep starts at one, which is a good starting point because it is near zero. SPICE cannot sweep from zero. Yet, a true harmonic sequence would start at zero. To get a reasonable approximation to a harmonic sequence, start at a frequency that is low or small compared to the frequency steps in the sequence.

One more important point to which many might say "well of course" and others will spend a week scratching their heads is why SPICE errors out on such a simple program, as shown. To avoid this error, insert a SPICE line such as:

```
.option limpts=15000
```

Many versions of SPICE default to presuming a programming mistake if you attempt to print out more than a few hundred data points. You need to print out thousands. The `limpts` option enables you to print out those thousands. The numeric value you use is unimportant as long as it is big enough. The only reason this option defaults to a small number is that back in the early seventies when SPICE originated, printers were slow and printer time was expensive.

Generation of the Impulse and Step Response

The next procedure is to generate the impulse response and the step response from the S11 data. You can do this step with various tools such as Matlab or Octave. If you simply take the S11 values and run them through IFFT, the result is a set of complex numbers. What you need is a set of real numbers. The impulse and step responses are real, not complex.

When you take the FFT of a real function, the result is a set of complex numbers from zero to some maximum frequency, and then a mirror image of that data set extending again as far. The S11 parameters consist of only half of this set. The required set needs to be formed from the S11 data. This is done by mirroring each data point across the maximum frequency value. In implementing this step, note that the mirrored value is not precisely equal to the original value. Rather, the mirrored value has the same real part and the negative of the imaginary part. It is the complex conjugate. In Matlab code, this might be:

```
Se=S11;
```

```
Se(n+1:2*n)=S11(n:-1:1)';
```

When this is done, applying the IFFT to the `Se` vector can result in a real, rather than complex, impulse response. The step response is the integral of the impulse response. Of course, to get a step response that looks like the step response of a TDR, it is necessary to add an integration constant of one to each value. However, when that has been done, except for possibly the rise time, you can expect to see the exact same step response as would be seen if a transient analysis had been done in SPICE. If the same step response is not seen, check the source amplitude used in generating the AC sweep.

The first 100 points of the impulse response calculated according to the above procedures looks like this:

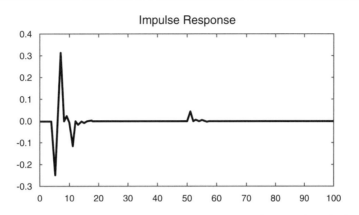

Figure 4.8   Peeled Impulse Response

It appears in this graph that the values from 20 to 50 and from 60 to 100 are all zero, but they are not. This difference will show up when the impulse response is integrated to yield the step response. At that point, it shows:

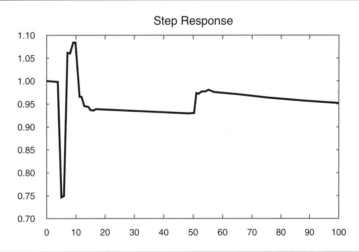

Figure 4.9   Peeled Step Response

The details to the twentieth time increment of this graph are expanded for comparability to the SPICE simulation shown above. Figure 4.10 shows just the first 20 samples of Figure 4.9.

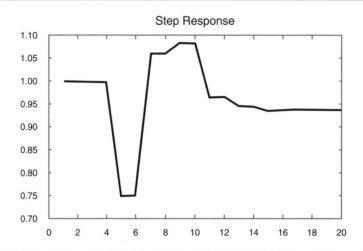

Figure 4.10   Expanding the First 20 Samples

The SPICE time domain simulation graph is repeated in Figure 4.11 for convenient comparison.

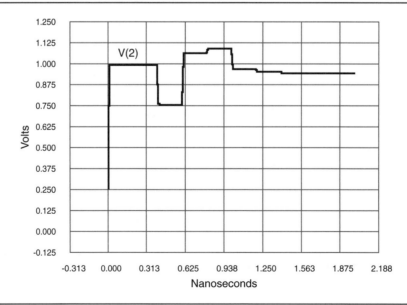

Figure 4.11   The Original for Comparison

Comparing the S11 derived plot to the original SPICE time-domain plot of the network, it is clear that they are similar, but the rise-times are much slower in the plot we derived from the S11 data. You might be tempted to say they are identical except for the rise times. That wouldn't be precisely true. Careful examination shows that regions that were totally flat in the original simulation now have a very slight slope to them.

The graph corresponds quite well to what SPICE showed for the step response, but the rise time is too slow because the frequency sweep used to generate the S11 values was only swept out to 5 gigahertz. The same procedure with the maximum frequency extended to 50 gigahertz yields Figure 4.12.

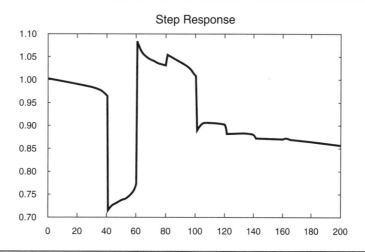

Figure 4.12   A Failed Attempt

Now the edges are sharper, but the flat parts are badly misshapen. What was done in SPICE was to change:

```
From    .ac lin 2000 1 5e9

To      .ac lin 2000 1 5e10
```

The impact of this change was to increase both the highest frequency and the spacing between measurement points by a factor of ten. Increasing the highest frequency yielded sharper transitions, as desired. Increasing the spacing between data points had the undesirable impact seen in all the low frequency components of this graph. Yes, we could, and should, change from 2,000 data points to 20,000 data points. But what would you learn if we did it right?

As a compromise between adequate rise time and massive quantities of data, the next attempt uses the SPICE analysis line:

```
.ac lin 5000 1 2e10
```

This compromise, sweeping to 20 gigahertz and acquiring 5,000 data points, yields an improvement and serves to show how the data parameters interact for this problem.

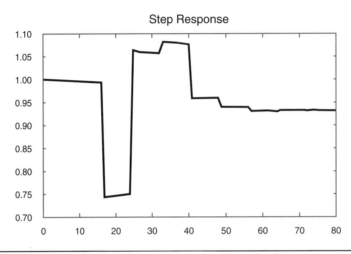

Figure 4.13   A Better Compromise

This result looks fairly good, perhaps good enough for an example. The next step is to run the peeling algorithm and see the results. Certainly this diagram is not "as good as it can get", but it does exemplify the impact of trade-offs. I have no doubt that clever engineers will make further improvements on such trade-offs by *interpolation* or *extrapolation* from data sets. Beyond just showing the procedures, these diagrams show some of the issues you encounter when you put these procedures into practice.

Figure 4.14 shows the result of peeling the data set of this example. Two things should be clear at this time. First, the result of this peeling is not a perfect reproduction of the original transmission line. Second, any desired degree of perfection can be achieved by adding more data points.

Recalling that the original model was 50, 30, 60, and 45 ohms, it is clear that the procedure is converging toward that result. It is also clear that with this fast a rise-time, a lot of data is required to get good results.

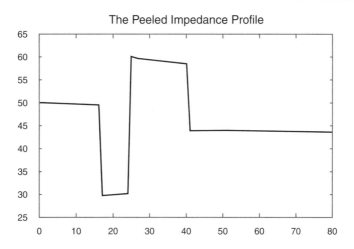

Figure 4.14   The Impedance Approximation

It isn't necessary to start with frequency domain data to do peeling. Frequency domain data is used in this example only to make it clear that you can do peeling whether you start in the frequency domain or the time domain. You need to understand what characteristics make a good dataset for this type of application. Certainly, if you have time-domain data in the first place, use it.

You also have undoubtedly noticed that Figures 4.8 through 4.14, with a single exception, use sample numbers rather than time in the horizontal axis. For the points that needed to be made in that section, time was irrelevant. One point is worth mentioning. The timing of events you observe in a reflected signal includes both the time to the feature and the time from the feature. Thus, the width of features in reflections appear to be twice their actual width. This time doubling has various implications. For example, if you observe a reflection that has a 50-picosecond rise time, the actual point of reflection saw a 25-picosecond rise time.

This example and Figure 4.14 show an impedance profile derived from S11 data. There are other possibilities. Often your interest is in what signal makes it through to a second port rather than what gets reflected back at this port. A typical case is a two-port device in which the signal observed at port two, resulting from the signal applied at port one, is of interest. The signal that gets through is quantified as S21 data. Generating an equivalent S11 data set and applying the peeling algorithm to that S11 set can model this.

In a lossless system, energy is conserved so S11 can be fully determined by S21.

$$S11 = \sqrt{1 - S21^2}$$

When the peeling algorithm was described, a key step was enabled by the presumption of a lossless system. Here again the statement was made that S11 is fully determined by S21 in a lossless system. Real systems are never lossless. Real systems have resistive losses, dielectric loss, perhaps radiative loss, and maybe others. In a real system, loss causes a difference between the total energy injected into a system and the sum of energy that is transmitted and reflected. As the portion of total energy lost in the device increases, the deviation from that predicted by this equation increases. The peeling algorithm is useful, even in lossy systems, but you must be aware that accuracy decreases as loss increases. Yet, in a lossless or effectively lossless system, since S21 is totally determined by S11, if you generate a model that gets S11 right, it must as a consequence also get S21 right.

So, even in a lossy system where S11 cannot be derived from S21, the peeling algorithm can be useful. In practical applications, peeling would not be used on the bulk transmission lines across the board, but rather on connectors and similar devices. These are usually selected to be minimal loss in the first place, so peeling works well.

Loss

A reasonable question to ask at this time is how severe is the loss of accuracy that results from the presumption of losslessness. To present a graphical answer to that question, we modeled a transmission line with frequency-dependent loss, using the HSPICE W model. The W model does a fairly good job of correlating to the losses measured on an FR4 circuit board. Physical and electrical conditions other than loss were similar to the lossless system that has been analyzed here, but lengths were made larger. The result of peeling this model is displayed here.

The most obvious observation is that transitions are crisp at the beginning but become increasingly rounded with distance, and the largest step shows some numerical instability. The experienced signal integrity engineer would look at this curve and recognize that it represents, at about 6 inches of FR4 trace per nanosecond, more than 6 inches of lossy trace. Most objects, such as connectors, that you might need to model in this manner are likely to be significantly smaller than this. Also, FR4 is probably one of the most lossy materials you will have to work with.

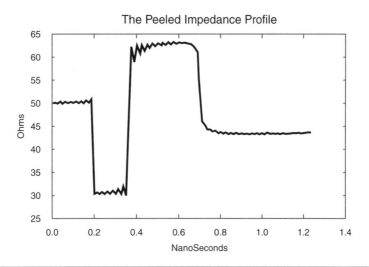

Figure 4.15 Same Profile, Very Lossy Lines

You can draw several conclusions. Foremost is that, though the procedure is not perfect, it is going to be useful in many applications. A second conclusion is that, in any attempt to measure and model a device such as a connector, minimizing the loss between the test equipment and the device being measured enhances accuracy. This conclusion is valid and important whether data acquired is intended for peeling or not.

More Fourier Transform Considerations

Many presumptions can be hidden in such developments. In doing the Fourier transform and its inverse, where the data came from can make a difference. Consider the discrete Fourier transform itself. Evenly spaced samples in one domain are translated to the complementary domain. As was seen above, that could turn out to be a lot of data points. Consider the frequency domain. In SPICE, a frequency sweep can be done in various ways. It is instructive to perform a wideband frequency sweep of a device, such as a resistive divider, that is simple and easy to examine. For a real simple example, try an analysis line such as this:

```
.AC lin 10 40 100
```

This line asks SPICE for a linear sweep of 10 evenly spaced frequencies starting at 40 hertz and ending at 100 hertz. To implement this sweep, SPICE divides the difference (60) by nine, to achieve 10 evenly spaced frequency points. The separation will be 6.6667 each. Using that spacing, a Fourier series would also have had several points at frequencies below 40. This simulation does not provide values for several data points at the low end of the frequency spectrum. Therefore, as it stands, it is not suitable for use in the inverse Fourier transform. It is not a harmonic sequence.

In a SPICE simulation, this seems easy to remedy: start the sweep at a lower frequency. If 40 is replaced by two, the range is large enough; there are almost enough data points, but it still is not right. What a Fourier transform would have provided would have been the frequency sequence: 10, 20.... What this simulation provides is 12.9, 23.8.... To actually get it right, the sweep has to start at zero. SPICE cannot do a frequency sweep that starts at zero.

In SPICE you could get it nearly right by starting at a really low frequency, but other cases are not so easy. Many network analyzers have minimum frequencies that are fairly high. The same problem exists, but not the same solution. The obvious solution to both situations is to mathematically resample the data set, interpolating the data to evenly spaced intervals that fit the sequence:

$$f(n) = fo * n$$

where: $f(n)$ is the individual frequency sample
          fo is the constant frequency separation value
          n is the series of integers, starting at zero.

Another problem remains. Neither SPICE nor the network analyzer can provide the frequency response at zero, but this problem need not become too serious an issue. The component at zero frequency has the impact of setting the DC offset in the time domain. Usually, the circuit conditions make it obvious what the right value should be. For example, if the through response of an AC coupled link is being computed, the frequency response at zero must be zero.

In Figure 4.15 above, an oscillation in the response near a sharp transition was observed. This ringing, called the Gibbs Phenomenon, can happen any time there is a large step in evenly spaced data points.[1] In fact, any time you have a step or a transition in a single time or frequency

---

[1] Search the Web for "Gibbs phenomenon" for plenty of details

increment, the Gibbs Phenomenon can occur. In fact, the ringing will have a magnitude of about 18 percent of the step size, which is not reduced by taking more data points in the same range. But, ah the glories of math! The Gibbs Phenomenon can be tricked largely out of existence. If more data points are taken, the magnitude remains the same, but the distance to which the ringing extends from the transition is reduced. As long as the data is going to be resampled to place it on the correct frequency domain locations anyway, you might as well resample to many data points and then use a filter to filter off the Gibbs Phenomenon. If the number of data points is raised high enough, the filter has arbitrarily small impact on the overall circuit response.

At this time, I'm not going to cover the subject of how many points are adequate to provide a specific level of error or what form of filter is most suitable. The Web has a lot of literature on the Gibbs Phenomenon and ways of dealing with it. For circuit design purposes, it is sufficient to know that you get greater accuracy when you use slower calculations. The computation time involved is not minutes but seconds, so the pain level is not sufficient to justify an extensive study of the trade-off.

Actually, the benefits are better than might be expected from the above information alone. If the simulation or measured frequency data is going to be resampled anyway, it need not be evenly spaced in the first place. If it doesn't have to be evenly spaced, the SPICE simulation can use one of the nonlinear sweeps to get much better frequency coverage at lower numbers of points. Summarizing all this, time is lost in the post-processing end of the procedure, but time is saved in the simulation end.

So far, a short refresher of mathematics was presented in the previous chapter and scattering parameters were presented. This chapter has explained how interchanges between time domain and frequency domain are possible and how peeling allows the extraction of models from either time-domain or frequency-domain data. This development covers a significant portion of the mathematical information you need to begin working with data moving at microwave data rates. At least one important subject has not yet been examined. You saw in the material above that reflections take place and that they transport energy away from the desired end point, the data receiver. In a realistic system with packages, traces, connectors, and passive components in the signal path, there are numerous interfaces where reflections take place. Sometimes a bit of energy is reflected back at one interface and then a bit of that is reflected to the original direction at another interface. The question is, what procedure can be used to calculate what gets through to the receiver? The answer comes in the section on Mason's Rule. First let's examine crosstalk.

Crosstalk

You can generate a SPICE model directly from measured data in either time or frequency domain, but crosstalk is at least as significant a factor as is the through-loss, particularly in economical multi-line connectors. A model is not complete until it can handle the crosstalk.

Frequency factors

Various design situations generate various opinions on what is the right way to handle crosstalk. What is actually right depends on how you will use the model you build. Here are several views on how you might handle crosstalk. You can read these and decide if one of these views fits your needs, or you may devise your own view.

The Flat Response Theory

The flat response theory holds that the peak amplitude of crosstalk is the only important parameter. The frequency profile is irrelevant. How important is the frequency response of the crosstalk path? This theory holds: not very. Because you can seldom guarantee any phase relationship between the aggressor and the victim signal, a realistic handling of crosstalk requires that you slew the phase of the aggressor over the entire time interval of the victim pulse. But this is equivalent to converting the aggressor to an equal amplitude low frequency signal. So the solution is to handle crosstalk as frequency independent, but be sure to get the peak amplitude right.

Microwave frequency transmission lines on lossy media (FR4) exhibit great loss for the high frequency components of the signal, but only little loss for the low frequencies. Thus, the low frequencies required to achieve an equivalent to slewing the aggressor phase are already there in the aggressor signal. You just need to couple the signal across to the victim at the right amplitude.

The theory works fine if the aggressor is in a line that has low loss. But it is a poor solution for an aggressor that has encountered high loss. Crosstalk starts out always looking capacitive. The coupling at DC is zero. The coupling profile looks like a high-pass filter. In a high-loss case, the high frequencies encounter more loss than the low frequencies, but a flat-response model treats them all equally. As a result, this model can produce crosstalk that is much too high for the case of a lossy aggressor.

The Capacitive Response Theory

This theory starts with the observation that crosstalk at zero frequency is usually zero. A look at the frequency response of the crosstalk path looks very much like a capacitor except at the high frequency end. You can model the crosstalk as just an R-C high-pass filter. For this model, you would choose a resistor that is large compared to the impedance of the aggressor line and then calculate the capacitance that yields the desired frequency response. You would then isolate this circuit from the victim, using an ideal current source.

The only unknown is the value of the capacitor, and you can calculate that once a frequency is specified. A good way to choose this frequency is to use the frequency where the *transfer function* is at half its ultimate response. Given this frequency and the resistance you choose, you can write a formula that specifies the capacitance. You now examine the frequency response of your crosstalk path and find the frequency where the response is either half of its ultimate value or where it is half of the response at the highest frequency you care about. Observe both the frequency and the amplitude of response at that frequency. Use the frequency to calculate the capacitance. Use the amplitude to set the gain of the mechanism you will use to couple to the victim line.

Of course, if you have more than one aggressor or if you have time-domain information only, then it isn't quite this simple. If you have more than one aggressor, another solution is to add the responses of all aggressors together to build a single equivalent or generate a separate coupler for each aggressor. I prefer the former.

If you have only time domain information, you could use an FFT on the response to find the frequency domain equivalent or you could fake it. Faking it consists of choosing a frequency, typically half of the data rate, and trying various coupling factors till the simulated response best matches the measured waveform.

The Perfection Theory

This theory holds that the only adequate model is one that perfectly mimics all internal and external electrical characteristics of the device. Perfection is a theory—in reality there is no such thing. You can spend 10 minutes generating a model with a method like one of those described above, or you can spend an extra two months trying to exactly match every nuance of the crosstalk response profile; over the range of manufacturing variables, you will still only achieve the same 95 percent accuracy. Models are models; they are based on measurements that will always have some error. Models run in tools that always add some error. Much more importantly, they model performance in circumstances that never exactly match the measurement conditions. These methods may not be adequate for you, but before you chose a path that will add a lot of work, convince yourself that there will actually be a measurable improvement in the final product.

My Approach

My approach is to get it right at the ports and forget what goes on inside. You can do this by using peeling for the signal paths and capacitively driven directional couplers for the crosstalk. The advantage of this method is that it is very easy to automate the process of generating this model, and the model can be very accurate in its response.

Limitations of this model include the fact that it won't give you any insights as to how to tweak the device to improve its performance. If you are designing the device being modeled, use a geometry-based model. If you are using an existing device in a circuit, use my approach.

Directionality

You could couple the crosstalk signal in by using a high-impedance source, such as a current source. The problem with doing this is that the injected signal would travel in both directions down the victim net, preventing you from being able to get both the forward and reverse crosstalk components right—they contaminate each other. Nor does it work to enforce directionality by inserting a series amplifier. That would only allow signal waves to travel in one direction. The model has to be able to transmit in both directions, handling both forward and reflected waves. What is needed is a directional coupler, a device that allows signals to travel in both directions but couples in a signal in only one direction.

The Directional Coupler

Ideally, the directional coupler would have no bandwidth limits—DC to light. As long as we are talking about blue sky, limit the forward-to-back ratio only by the numerical accuracy of the machine. In other words, the ratio of injected signal traveling in the intended forward direction to injected signal traveling in the wrong direction is limited only by the numerical accuracy of SPICE. The numerical accuracy of the machine would be something like 12 orders of magnitude, maybe a bit more. And why not require the coupler to have no through delay, zero, no picoseconds? Try this: require the same model to be able to automatically adapt to any characteristic impedance. If you want it to work at 50 ohms, just terminate at 50. If you want to use it at 85 ohms, terminate at 85.

If you had such a device, one could be placed at each end of the peeled model and it would be totally transparent to signals traversing the model. Yet, forward crosstalk would appear traveling in the forward direction only, and reverse in the reverse direction. The big question is, how much of this can be achieved in practice? You could achieve all of it if you could find or model an ideal transformer. This is SPICE. Of course you can model an ideal transformer! Keep reading, I'll show you how.

Figure 4.16 shows the schematic of an ideal directional coupler as implemented in SPICE. Signal passes through at ports A and B. That is, if this device is to substitute for a wire, one end of the wire is port A and the other end is port B. Crosstalk is injected at port C. Each transformer has an N1:N2 turns ratio, which sets the coupling coefficient of the coupler. In the figure, the ratio is 1:N. Note that N need not be an integer.

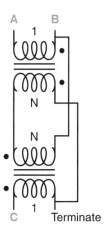

Figure 4.16   The Ideal Directional Coupler

Observe that the turns ratio is the same on each of the two transformers, and that there is a terminator on the lower right corner. My personal preference is to implement the coupler as a SPICE subcircuit and include the termination resistor inside it. Port C needs to be driven with a source resistance of this same value, so I include that inside the subcircuit, too. Any impedance value that is used for this terminator is the value that will provide an impedance match for ports A and B. This part is really simple. Some types have a primitive for the ideal transformer; if your does, you are done. If yours does not, you need to generate one through use of controlled sources. I will give you equations, but will not explain how and why the ideal transformer and the directional coupler work.

Turns Ratio

The coupling coefficient is the value that relates the amplitude of the output signal to the amplitude of the input signal through the coupling path. In Figure 4.16, that would be the ratio of signal at port B to the signal that is injected at port C. This coefficient can be expressed in at least three ways. The easiest is to simply recognize that a turns ratio of one to 10 yields a coupling coefficient of 0.1. Often the coupling coefficient is expressed in decibels rather than as this ratio. This is slightly tricky because you need to know whether the coefficient is expressed in terms of voltage or of power. Here we are concerned with voltage ratios, so this coupler will be called a 20-decibel coupler. In some instances, couplers are specified in terms of power. That would make this a 10-decibel coupler. Again, here we are interested in voltage ratios so our decibel expressions must reflect that. You set your directional coupler to whatever coupling value floats your boat by specifying the turns ratio.

The Transformer

When you have chosen a turns ratio, the next step is to implement a transformer that expresses that turns ratio. The transformer is a little trickier than the directional coupler. All you need are voltage sources, current sources, and resistors. You may want to refresh your memory on the SPICE syntax of the independent voltage source (Vxxx) and of the current-controlled current source (Fxxx).

The current source is controlled by the current through some specified voltage source. You implement this voltage source, used only to measure current, like any other voltage source, but the voltage is set to zero. Figure 4.17 shows the schematic of this ideal transformer. It is simple, containing only six components, two of which have a value of zero. You are free to choose the value of R1 and the turns ratio. Your choice of these two fixes the value of all the rest. So, here are the equations you use to build this ideal transformer:

$$Turns\ Ratio = N1 : N2$$

$$V1 = V2 = 0$$

$$F1(gain) = N2 / N1$$

$$F2(gain) = N1 / N2$$

$$R2 = R1(N2 / N1)^2$$

If your version of SPICE has an ideal transformer primitive, use it. If it doesn't, use these equations to create your own. Peculiarly, this transformer is so ideal that it actually works at DC.

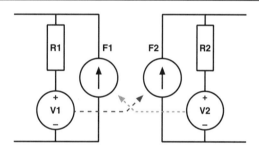

Figure 4.17   The Ideal Transformer

The components used to implement this transformer are fast and are available in Berkley 2G6 SPICE, and so should be available to anyone who has almost any version of SPICE.

To use this technique, place one directional coupler at each end of your transmission line model, and inject the appropriate crosstalk at each end. Since all ports on the coupler are at your Zo impedance, it doesn't work to directly tie the C-port to the aggressor line. Couple the aggressor to the directional coupler by use of an amplifier. SPICE provides the voltage-controlled voltage amplifier, the E element, for this. It gives you unlimited bandwidth and infinite input impedance. Set its gain so that, in combination with the coupling coefficient, it gives you the right crosstalk values. When you are done, your model looks like Figure 4.18

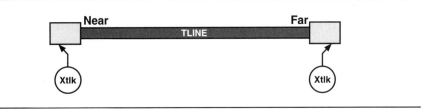

Figure 4.18 Block Diagram of the Model

By using subcircuits to implement the components of this model, you can achieve a very compact and high quality model of your device.

Differential

At microwave frequencies, differential lines are used. One way to make a differential model with this is to start with the differential TDR data for the device you are going to model. Use peeling on this to generate an equivalent single-ended variable-impedance transmission line; place an ideal transformer at each end of the model to do the single-ended to differential conversion. This method will not correctly account for common mode, but the reality is that, when we are doing our simulations, we seldom have enough information about the circuit board to realistically model common mode, anyway. Perhaps it would be better to use two transformers.

If you don't have a differential TDR machine, an alternative is to measure the device with a network analyzer and calculate the differential characteristics. Another alternative, one I don't recommend, is to use a *balun*. The word balun is a contraction of the phrase "balanced to unbalanced converter." The contraction, balun, has been used for about as long as there has been radio. It is often very difficult to get good measurements with a balun. It is too easy to get measurements that look OK but aren't. Often these devices work well when terminated into their target characteristic impedance but not so well when they are not. Now, if the device you were trying to measure was precisely 50 ohms throughout its frequency range, you probably wouldn't need to measure it anyway. If, as is typical, your device is not precisely 50 ohms throughout its frequency range, then what you measure with the balun is the combined characteristics of both the balun variations and the device.

In an attempt to reduce the impedance-dependent variations of the balun, people typically put a wide-band attenuator on each output port of the balun. Minimum value for this is about 10 decibels of attenuation. Though this attenuator does not totally eliminate impedance variations at the ports of the balun, it reduces them at the expense of an equal loss in measurement resolution. Because of all this, I recommend against making measurements with a balun.

In making time domain measurements of your device, take care to maintain the highest rise time achievable. The model you get has the measurement rise time built into it. So rise time gets double counted when using this model. The model's through response reacts for any signal as though its rise time was slower than it actually is, slower by about 30 percent of the measurement rise time. For example, if the TDR wave arriving at the DUT had a 45-picosecond rise time, then the peeled model will respond to a signal with a 100-picosecond rise time as though it had a 115-picosecond rise time. It doesn't add this time to the wave, it just responds as though the harmonic content had been a little lower. The overall impact is typically negligible, unless the original measurement was made with too slow a rise time.

To test this, create a connector model in SPICE and run a transient simulation to get the TDR response for whatever rise time you want. Then run the result through the peeling algorithm and create a model. Now run the same waveform through each, adjust for timing offsets, and compare output wave forms. The result shows how good a model your system is generating.

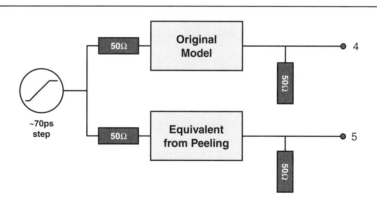

Figure 4.19   Testing the Model

So now you have all the information you need to generate functional models directly from measurements. The procedures would usually be implemented with scripts rather than by hand. The entire process of peeling the data and generating a SPICE file with the directional couplers in place can be done in less than a second once you have the appropriate scripts working.

T Lines vs. L-C

Up to this point, development proceeded from device measurements to the equivalent transmission line model. You could simply take the peeled impedance profile and implement it as a series of short SPICE T lines. That would work and would yield a good simulation of the device. Yet, you might not be altogether happy with the results because short sections of T lines tend to run slow in SPICE. A solution that runs faster can be made out of equivalent L-C sections.

Recall that the impedance of a lossless transmission line and the velocity of signals in it can both be expressed in terms of L-C sections.

$$Z = \sqrt{\frac{L}{C}}$$

$$v = \frac{1}{\sqrt{LC}}$$

The impedance equals the ratio of inductance and capacitance where each is expressed as a per unit length. Similarly, the velocity, in terms of the units of length, can be expressed as a function of the inductance and capacitance per unit length. When the peeling algorithm has completed its job, you are left with a list of impedances and time increments. From these you need to generate inductances and capacitances. You can rearrange that to express inductance in terms of impedance and capacitance.

$$L = CZ^2$$

Now all you need to do is find capacitance per unit, and the problem is solved. The impedance equation has already been used, so capacitance has to be somehow extracted from the velocity equation. Velocity is distance per time increment. The distance can be normalized to one, so velocity in this case becomes simply the reciprocal of the time increment. Rewrite the velocity equation like this:

$$v = dx / dt$$

$$dx = 1$$

$$v = 1 / dt$$

$$dt = \sqrt{LC}$$

Now everything is in terms of quantities you know—impedance and time increment. The rest is just mix and match to yield equations for inductance and capacitance.

$$LC = dt^2$$

$$L = \frac{dt^2}{C}$$

$$So:$$

$$Z = \sqrt{\frac{dt^2}{C} * \frac{1}{C}} = \frac{dt}{C}$$

$$C = \frac{dt}{Z}$$

That's it. To generate L-C segments from the impedance and time-increment data, use the one equation to get the capacitance, then the other to get the inductance.

From here you could proceed in either of two ways. The easy way is to just put down: series inductor, capacitor to ground, series inductor, capacitor to ground, and so forth. Some people prefer to split each inductor in half and place the capacitor to ground between the two halves. The advantage of this is that it makes the segments symmetrical.

When you make your measurement of the device you are going to model, you will likely acquire hundreds of data points. You may even acquire thousands of data points. You could turn these into a model with hundreds or even thousands of tiny little segments. Don't do it! This subject is one of my pet peeves. Is a model with thousands of tiny little features better than a model with only a few? The answer is usually a resounding no! Simulation tools are usually iterative in nature. Iterative numerical methods are often very sensitive to derivatives. When you add an excessive number of steps in the model, all you are doing is adding a lot more derivatives for the algorithm to deal with. You are only slowing the machine down. So how many increments is reasonable? One engineering rule of thumb is that the time increment should be kept less than a fifth the period of the highest harmonic at which you need accuracy. Some say a fifth, some say a tenth, some a twelfth—it depends on how much accuracy you need. You have the device measurements, so you know how long it takes a signal to traverse the device. Divide that time by this time increment, and limit your number of model segments to the resulting number.

That pretty much exhausts what needs to be said about peeling. You have a lot of choices and decisions to make about how to handle crosstalk, how to implement the algorithm, how to make the measurements, and so on. Overall, you should find it a good tool in your kit.

Mason's Rule

In a system dominated by loss and widely separated discontinuities, energy reflected at a particular discontinuity traverses a substantial loss as it travels to the next discontinuity. Energy redirected back to the original direction again traverses a substantial loss as it returns to the point of the original reflection. This loss might be great enough that the energy returning to the original discontinuity is too small to significantly impact the remaining forward signal. Such a system is said to be *loss-dominated*, and only limited error results from treating all reflected energy as totally lost at the first reflection. The total link-loss can be modeled by adding up a list of losses through sections and losses at reflections between sections.

In links that are not loss-dominated, following energy through multiple reflections can become difficult. Nevertheless, signal quality at the receiver can actually deteriorate as loss decreases because of multiple reflections in the link. In such an instance, it becomes important to examine the actual impact of all these reflections.

The simplest way to deal with a net that has multiple reflections is to model the link in SPICE and examine the transient response. The alternative is initially more difficult to set up, but once done, you can reuse it for various systems. This alternative will run much faster than the SPICE simulation and it will yield important insights; you can check the results by running SPICE.

A few decades back, people designing amplifiers with multiple feedback loops encountered the problem of how to predict the transfer function of such an amplifier. The solution they generated is called *Mason's Rule*. This procedure is fascinating in that it can accurately deal with feedback loops that intertwine and interconnect in arbitrarily complex ways. Professors love Mason's Rule because it is often exceedingly tricky to apply correctly. The trickiness makes it easy to create challenging problems on tests.

Here is Mason's Rule.

$$M = \frac{\sum_J M_j \Delta_j}{\Delta}$$

Where:

■ *M* is the transfer function or gain of the system.

■ *Mj* is the gain of an individual forward path.

- *J* is the count of all possible forward paths in the system.

- Delta-*j* is delta not touching path *Mj*.

- Delta, without subscript, is one minus the sum of all loop gains, minus the sum of all non-touching-loop gains, taken two at a time, plus the sum of all non-touching-loop gains taken three at a time, minus ...

$\Delta = 1 - \Sigma$ (all individual loop gains) $+ \Sigma$ (loop gain products of all possible

combinations of 2 nontouching loops) $- \Sigma$ (loop gain products of all possible

combinations of 3 nontouching loops) $+ \ldots$

The precise details of all this are not important for the discussion here because things get simplified when this equation is applied to a point-to-point circuit interconnect.

To apply Mason's Rule to an interconnect, treat the forward wave as the forward path and the reverse wave as a backward path. Then, loops are formed at interfaces where forward and reverse energy are reflected. The flow graph of a typical signal path is depicted by Figure 4.20.

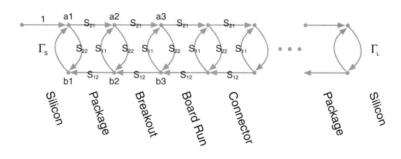

Figure 4.20   Flow Graph of an Interconnect Circuit

The flow diagram of Figure 4.20 shows that each reflecting interface forms a loop, and there is only one forward path. In this diagram, an individual component makes a contribution whose elements correspond to the scattering parameters of the device. The individual element through the center sections of this graph is depicted in Figure 4.21. The numerical components are the fundamental scattering parameters of the device.

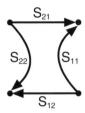

Figure 4.21   Flow Graph of an Individual Component

Applying Mason's Rule to this interconnect, the one and only forward path is removed, leaving the "non-touching" loops as depicted in Figure 4.22.

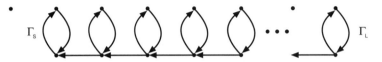

Figure 4.22   Flow Graph, Forward Path Removed

Thus, for this type of application Mason's Rule simplifies to a new standard form:

$$M = \frac{M_1}{\Delta}$$

In this form, M1 is simply the loss of the forward path. The total loss of the link, M, will be increased by the components of the divisor. In the divisor, all remaining loops are non-touching, resulting in no difficulty in identifying what are loops and which loops touch each other. The loop gains are the products of the S11 and S22 elements that make up each loop. The smaller each of these products is, the less impact that pair will have on the overall divisor. Of course, these values are not expressed in decibels when the products are made. Requiring small products is equivalent to requiring a low magnitude of return loss at interfaces.

The question is occasionally asked, how good is good enough? Among other things, Mason's Rule allows you to quantify how much signal loss will result from a specified amount of return loss. Much more could be added to the discussion but will be skipped here. This book is an introduction. A great deal of information is available on the web if "Mason's Rule" is used as the search keyword. However, I advise you to skip over any responses that refer to people who wear funny hats or drive tiny cars in parades.

Chapter 5

The Mathematics of Fields

Now the subject shifts to the mathematics of electric fields and waves. Maxwell's equations will be introduced and explained in enough detail to allow an introduction to tools that calculate fields. The fundamentals of one type of field solver will be explained as an example that introduces issues and requirements involved in choosing and using field solvers. An objective of this chapter is to help you recognize how and why field solvers differ and how they fit with various engineering requirements. When you were working at a few hundred megahertz, almost all the simulations you did could be done with nothing more than a good copy of SPICE. At microwave frequencies, you must to be able to run a field solver, too.

Since the mathematical derivations flow in that direction, they will be followed through the development of the wave equation, the telegrapher's equation, and then the reflection coefficient. By that point the topic diverges somewhat from fields and field solvers, but that's life.

Maxwell

In 1873, James Clerk Maxwell published a set of four equations that have since come to be known as Maxwell's equations. Later analysis has shown that the set can be reduced to two equations, the other two being redundant. I will approach fields from the perspective of Maxwell's two curl equations. One of the two is based on an equation known as

105

Oersted's law, the mathematical formalization of the physical principle that every electric current is accompanied by a magnetic field. A mathematical formulation of what Oersted discovered is:

$$\oint H.dr = \frac{4\pi}{c} I$$

The closed line integral around a path equals a constant multiplied by the current enclosed by that path. The current in this instance is static, or perhaps only slowly changing. The precise value assigned to these symbols depends, of course, on the system of units you are working with, and for our purposes is unimportant. What is important here is to understand that this says the magnetic field integrated around any path is proportional to the current enclosed by that path. This characteristic is quite different from the static electric field where integrating along any closed path always yields zero.

The *dr* in this equation is the increment of distance traveled along the chosen path. The shape of the path need not be circular or any other particular shape. The only thing that counts is the current it encloses. Of course, if a path is chosen that is farther away from the current, say a path at a greater radius, the magnetic field will be proportionately less because the length of the path will be proportionately greater. Consider, for example, a single straight wire and the magnetic field around that wire. For a path, choose a simple circle, a circle of radius R. If R is measured from the center of the wire, the magnetic field *H* could be expected to remain constant along the path, so *H* could be pulled outside the integral. What remains, the integral along the circumference of the circle, is well known to be *pi* times the diameter. In this case, the evaluation becomes:

$$2\pi RH = \frac{4\pi}{c} I$$

$$H = \frac{2I}{Rc}$$

That is, for this geometry, the magnetic field around the wire, at any distance (r) is linearly proportional to the current in the wire, and inversely proportion to the distance from the wire. We show you this example to help give a feel for the meaning of Oersted's discovery. What about that constant *c*? Hold that constant for a moment, it comes up again in another fundamental equation.

What Oersted probably didn't know, and can be of significant importance at microwave frequencies, is that the formation of this field is not instantaneous. It was stated that the equation applied to static, unchanging current. Today, time intervals have shrunk to the point that picoseconds can count. The field at a point is not, as Oersted claimed, proportional to the current, but rather is proportional to the current that can be observed by that point at that instant in time. If the current cannot yet be observed at a particular point in space due to the speed of light, the field at that point cannot yet be dependent on that current. At high frequencies, there is a difference between *quasi-static* field solutions and what are called *full-wave* field solutions. Quasi-static solutions do not take into account the speed of light.

Maxwell's equation for the magnetic field is based on Oersted's and is identical to Oersted's in the static case. Maxwell transformed this integral equation to a curl equation by application of Stokes's law. The formulation is different, but the mathematical statements are equivalent.

Maxwell's very important contribution was in recognizing that current can take place in forms other than the movement of charges. To exemplify this, consider current through a capacitor. The region between the plates of a capacitor can be totally empty space, yet current can flow. This current, sometimes called displacement current, creates a magnetic field just as does the movement of physical charges. Adding this factor to Oersted's equation results in the first of Maxwell's curl equations. It states that the magnetic field is generated by the sum of these two types of current.

If you calculated the kinetic energy of a moving mass of electrons, you would find that there is not nearly enough kinetic energy present to account for the energy transported by the current. The great majority of the energy transported by a current is in the fields themselves. Similarly, currents pass through a capacitor, but charges do not bridge the gap— only the fields do. Again, it is evident that the field transports the energy, not the charge carriers transporting it. Maxwell incorporated this realization into Oersted's equation to form his first curl equation.

Maxwell based his second curl equation on Faraday's law, the physical principle that a voltage is produced by a changing magnetic field. More specifically, in 1831, a little over 40 years before Maxwell published his equations, Faraday discovered that a current exists in any closed wire circuit whenever a nearby magnet is in motion, or when the magnet is stationary but the wire loop is in motion. From this discovery, he formulated what is now called "Faraday's law of induction." It is stated as:

$$IR = -\frac{1}{c}\frac{d\Phi}{dt} = -\frac{1}{c}\frac{d}{dt}\int B_n dS$$

In this equation, I and R are the current and resistance in the wire loop. Their product is a voltage. The constant c is the same as that found earlier in Oersted's work. The reciprocal of c gets multiplied by the time-rate of change of *phi*.

Geometric Shapes as Symbols

Phi is that Greek character that looks like a circle with a vertical line through it. This symbol is not to be confused with theta, a circle with a horizontal line through it, or sometimes with a diagonal line through it. Also recall omicron, a small circle with no lines through it. Ancient Greeks, it would seem, really liked circles. They apparently liked triangles, too. One of those is also found in their alphabet. Of course it is an equilateral triangle, never a right triangle. Mathematicians, who discovered that even the combined Greek and Roman alphabets don't contain enough symbols, have been known to turn this Greek triangle symbol upside down to form a new symbol. That one will show up later in this book. It doesn't work to turn phi, omicron, or theta upside down. The proof of this is left as an exercise. Neither the Greeks nor the Romans seem to have liked squares. No squares are found in either the Greek or Roman alphabet. Some alphabetical evidence exists that Koreans may like squares. My own culture, German-Russian, seems to primarily like sauerkraut.

Back to Faraday, *phi* is the magnetic flux density in a given area. It is obtained by integrating the flux passing through a surface, over that surface. As shown, phi can be expressed as an integral of the component of magnetic flux in the direction normal to the surface being integrated. The time rate of change of this flux density equals the voltage in the wire loop. Again, this integral equation can be changed to a curl equation by applying Stokes's law, and so yields the second of Maxwell's equations.

Stokes's law, or Stokes's theorem, describes how the line integral of something around the opening in a surface equals the surface integral of the curl of that quantity. It yields a way of converting a closed line integral into a curl equation. Operating with Oersted's and Faraday's equations in the curl formulation is useful here. The third and forth of Maxwell's equations are not used here so they are not detailed. Here is the entire set:

$$\nabla \times H = \partial D / \partial t + g$$
$$\nabla \times E = -\partial B / \partial t$$
$$\nabla \bullet H = 0$$
$$\nabla \bullet D = \rho$$

The first two of these, the curl equations, are described in detail in this chapter. To make these equations useful, you need to add a small set of auxiliary equations, sometimes called the *constitutive equations*. These equations are closer to definitions of terms than to mathematical procedures.

$$D = \varepsilon E$$
$$B = \mu H$$
$$g = \sigma(E + E_e)$$

In the first constitutive equation, the quantity, epsilon, is the electric field constant. The electric field constant is often described as the product of two parts:

$$\varepsilon = \varepsilon_o \varepsilon_r$$

That is, the electrical constant is the product of the dielectric constant of free space and the relative dielectric constant. This approach has the advantage that we need only the relative dielectric for a particular material. The numerical value of the dielectric constant of free space depends on the units of measurement. It doesn't have the same value in various measurement systems. This statement is like saying the volume of a lake will have a different value in gallons than in liters. On the other hand, the value of the relative dielectric constant does not depend on the units of measurement. Specifying the electric constant as a product of two parts allows us to clearly express it for any material without needing to specify the system of units, such as cgs or MKSA, in which it is valid. If the relative dielectric constant is two, for example, the total dielectric constant in this material is two times the dielectric constant of free space. The units of the result are equal to whatever units were used for the dielectric constant of free space.

You can handle the magnetic constant, mu, in the same way—a free-space constant and a relative multiplier. Sigma, which is electrical conductivity, is not independent of measurement units. Unlike free space, we do not have a global reference material for conductivity. Combining these constants with the two curl equations yields the form that is detailed here:

$$\nabla \times H = \varepsilon \partial E / \partial t + \sigma E$$
$$\nabla \times E = -\mu \partial H / \partial t$$

See how clean these equations have now become? H is in terms of E; E is in terms of H. For each field quantity, the curl of the quantity is expressed in terms of the time derivative of the other. Already it can be seen that if conductivity, sigma, is set to zero, radio waves in free-space, or in any other material, are described.

Yes, you, being exceedingly clever, have already realized that a term was dropped in forming that upper curl equation. Sigma-E-sub-e (σE_e), which was in the original statement of Maxwell's equations, is missing here! Well, it wouldn't have been used for anything done here anyway. That term was only there for completeness in the first place. What it represents is some guy walking by with a slightly charged chunk of metal in a pocket. Yes, such an event would technically be a current. No, that form of current won't be included in any further developments here.

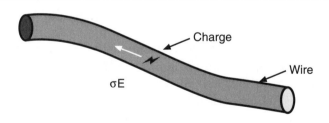

Figure 5.1   Normal Definition of Current

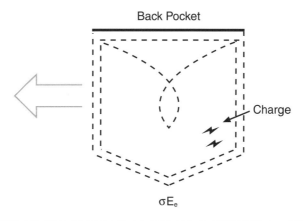

Back Pocket

Charge

σE_e

Figure 5.2   Ignore This Current

Deconstruction

Those two curl equations can be taken apart and examined in excruciating detail. First of all, the two quantities, E and H, are *fields*. That is to say, they each have a value that is specific to each position in space. The equations describe the forms that those values can take. The value could vary with time. Absolute understanding of these equations is so important that we will break them down symbol-by-symbol and examine each. First, we need to reemphasize that the word *field* is used all over this description. A field is simply something that has a value that depends on the position in space. Maxwell's equations are field equations. They tell the value of something at positions in space: the value of the electric thing, the value of the magnetic thing.

Del

Each equation begins with a symbol called "del." Del is a three-dimensional partial differential operator on a position in space. It is the symbol that looks like a capital Greek delta, turned on its head. The argument del accepts is a position in space; the story it tells is the rate of change of the field at that position, as position in space is changed. Del is defined:

$$\nabla \equiv \vec{x} \partial / \partial x + \vec{y} \partial / \partial y + \vec{z} \partial / \partial z$$

In use, it appears as below:

Del   Argument
of del

Figure 5.3   Del and Argument

This concept needs to be clear in your mind. Del is an operator; of it-self it produces nothing. It only produces something when applied to a function in space. Consider, for example, that you have some function that produces a value for any set of x, y, z coordinates you give it. That is a function in space. This, then, is a function that could be operated on by del. On the other hand, if you had a function of time or a function of pressure that was independent of position in space, del could not be ap-plied to that function. Del operates on a function of position and pro-duces the rate of change of the function, as position in space changes. Del answers questions such as: "How fast does it change if you move an inch to the right?"

Saying that something changes by 10 percent with each inch of dis-placement doesn't indicate any actual value. Only when the thing is de-fined with specific starting value does this 10-percent change yield another value. As an example, consider a function, $G(x)$, that produces a value at each position along an x axis. The values that $G(x)$ produces can be graphed as below.

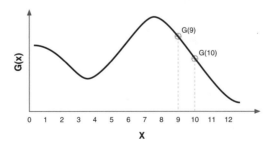

Figure 5.4 $G(x)$ at Two Points

Two particular values of $G(x)$ are marked on the graph: the value at x = 9 and the value at x = 10. Clearly, the two values are not the same in this graph. Since they are different, you need some way to express the difference. One way is to say how much the value of $G(x)$ changes as x changes at this point in the graph. In this example, del is called the operator and $G(x)$ is called the operand. Applying del to $G(x)$ produces a value that is this rate of change of G as x varies. X is position along an X axis.

This example is one-dimensional. In general, applying del to a three-dimensional function of position produces a result in three dimensions: x, y, and z. The magnitude of the x component of that vector equals the rate of change of the operand function in the x direction. The magnitude of the y component equals the rate of change of the function in the y direction; the same applies for the z direction. In the diagram above, $G(x)$ is depicted as varying only in the x direction. You can apply del to a one- or two-dimensional space by simply treating the remaining dimensions as producing a value of zero. Applying the del operator to $G(x)$ produces a vector whose value in the y direction and the z direction are both zero. Consider applying del to a function, $H(x,y)$, defined in a two-dimensional space. Here it produces a vector whose magnitude in the x direction equals the rate of change of H in the x direction, and whose magnitude in the y direction equals the rate of change of H in the y direction.

In the above definition of del, the letters x, y, and z all appear with an arrow above them. These, the letters with arrows over them, are unit vectors and have the effect of assigning a direction to each of the partials that follow them. So del produces the direction and rate of change through space of any function on which it operates. It produces not a single value, but a specific value at every point in space.

The Cross Product

In Maxwell's equation, del is not directly operating on a function, rather it is being combined with a second operator, the cross-product operator, designated by a plain x. This combination of operators is to be interpreted as the determinant of the particular matrix shown below. In the matrix, the unit vectors are the first row; the three partials are the second row; and the x, y, and z components of the function F being operated on are the third row.

$$\begin{vmatrix} \vec{x} & \vec{y} & \vec{z} \\ \partial/\partial x & \partial/\partial y & \partial/\partial z \\ F_x & F_y & F_z \end{vmatrix}$$

This is a determinant. The equation below expresses this determinant in full algebraic form, using the *H* field as the target function, the function above called *F*.

$$\nabla \times H = \vec{x}(\partial H_z / \partial y - \partial H_y / \partial z) + \vec{y}(\partial H_x / \partial z - \partial H_z / \partial x) + \vec{z}(\partial H_y / \partial x - \partial H_x / \partial y)$$

The equation shown here is mathematically identical to the determinant shown above. These two forms are shown because, for many, it is easier to remember the determinant form than the algebraic form. This operation—del operating on the cross product—is called the "curl" of *H*. One way of understanding this is that the curl measures the tendency of the field to rotate around the coordinates of the argument. The equation says that the curl of a function, in this case *H*, consists of three components, one in each of three directions. These three begin with the letter x, y, or z, each with the small arrow over it. These designate the direction of the component.

In each direction, the curl produces the difference between two parts. In the example above, in the x direction, the first part is the rate of change of the z component of *H*, with variation of position in the y direction. The second part is the rate of change of the y component of *H*, with variation, as you move in the z direction. At any point in space, *H* has a magnitude and a direction. Its direction is separated into three parts, one part in each direction: x, y, and z. The curl of *H* has a direction that is separated in similar manner. The components of *H* are designated by subscripts. The component of *H* in the x direction is designated by *H* with the subscript x.

For example, if the z component of *H* is measured at a particular point in space and then the measurement point is moved slightly in the y direction, a new value of the z component is measured. Thus, there is a change of the z component as the measurement point is moved in the y direction. The change could be zero. The first partial derivative in the curl equation produces the rate of change of the z component as the measurement point moves along the y axis. Similar notation applies to all the other components of the curl operation.

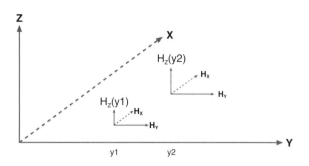

Figure 5.5   H at y1 and y2

Displacement Current

Maxwell's first curl equation asserts that the curl of the H field depends on two currents: the displacement current and the current produced by the movement of charges. The displacement current is a constant times the rate of change of the E field with time, at this point in space. The ordinary current is simply the conductivity multiplied by the E field at this point. The constant for displacement current, called the dielectric constant, is designated by the Greek letter epsilon (ε).

Examining that first curl equation, here reproduced, the displacement current is the first term to the right of the equals sign.

$$\nabla \times H = \varepsilon \partial E / \partial t + \sigma E$$

The concept of displacement current was Maxwell's contribution. This concept accounts for current flowing through a capacitor. Before this equation, there was no real explanation for current through a capacitor. If current is thought of as the motion of charges, and it is clear that charges do not flow through the insulating layer of a capacitor, you would have no explanation for current through a capacitor. On the other hand, if current can consist of nothing more than a change in the intensity of the E field over time, then the operation of the capacitor is explained.

That first curl equation should by now be making sense. You should now be able to look at it and say that the tendency of the H field to flow around a point in space equals the total current at that point in space.

$$\nabla \times H = \varepsilon \partial E / \partial t + \sigma E$$

The final term at the right side of the equation is the plain, ordinary current—the movement of charges. Sigma is the conductivity at this point in space, so sigma times the electric field describes the current at this point in space. This last term describes what Oersted discovered, that the motion of charge—current—produces a magnetic field. Together, these two terms describe the two sources of magnetic fields. One of these was known well before the time of Maxwell. The other was observed but not explained till Maxwell.

Rounding all that up, Maxwell's first curl equation simply describes how the *H* field, or the magnetic field, varies in space as a result of current and of variation of the *E* with time. Or, alternatively, how current and variation of the *E* field with time produces the shape of the *H* field. By similar scrutiny, Maxwell's second curl equation describes how the change over time of the *H* field produces the shape of the *E* field.

The Second Curl Equation

Maxwell's second curl equation is repeated here for your convenience:

$$\nabla \times E = -\mu \partial H / \partial t$$

The tendency of the *E* field to curve around a particular point in space is proportional to the rate of change of the magnetic field, with time, at that point in space. The constant of proportionality (mu) is the magnetic constant. Faraday made this discovery. In his terms, a change in the magnetic field produces a voltage in a direction perpendicular to the magnetic field and perpendicular to the direction of the rate of change. The curl equation models this result. The intensity produced in each direction is a function of the other two directions.

Curl and Divergence

At any point in space, any field can be described in terms of two concepts: curl and divergence. The curl is the tendency of the field to rotate around the point. The divergence is the tendency of the field to flow toward or away from the point. These concepts can be viewed in terms of a bottle of water. When water is poured into the bottle, there is divergence where the stream joins the water in the bottle. When the bottle is full, you could insert a stick and swizzle it around. Water is not being added so there isn't divergence, but curl is taking place. As used here, the curl of a field is the cross product of the del operator with the field function. The divergence, not used here, is the dot product—also not described here—of the del operator with the field function.

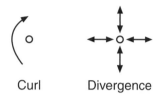

Curl   Divergence

Figure 5.6   Curl and Divergence

It may be tempting to question how knowing the curl of these fields can produce actual field values at any particular point. Consider taking a trip in a car. Someone gives you directions: go a mile north, then a half mile left, then two more north. These directions could lead to anywhere or nowhere—until a starting point is given. These directions, like the curl, only tell you the shape of the path you are to take. Adding a starting point forces the rest of the path to take on specific locations, specific values. The math guys, in speaking of the starting point, use the term "boundary conditions." When boundary conditions are specified, all the rest snaps into place.

E Field

A valid question at this time might be, what is the *E* field? A field, as a concept, has already been described as a function that has a value at every point in space. The *E* field is a field; it has the name *E*. Clearly, neither of these statements is satisfying. The *E* field is the mathematical construct that specifies a force, direction, and magnitude on a unit charge at any point in space. If charged bodies exist in space, there is a force either of attraction or repulsion between them. This force is given the name of *E* field. If another charge is placed in this field, as depicted in Figure 5.7, that charge will experience this force. The *E* field is said to originate and terminate on charges. In a static field, this is true.

Figure 5.7   *E* Field Pushes a Charge

H Field

The *H* field also describes a force on a charge at any place in space. Yet it is not the same as the *E* field inasmuch as the *E* field describes a force on any charge that is present. The *H* field only produces a force on charges that are in motion. In fact, the force it produces is at right angles to both the field direction and the direction of motion. *H* field lines form closed loops; they don't originate on objects. No magnetic monopoles are known to exist. Figure 5.8 depicts an electric charge traversing an *H* field. The impact of that field is to deflect the path of the moving charge. If that charge were not moving, the *H* field would do nothing to it.

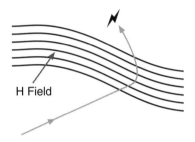

H Field

Figure 5.8   *H* Field Redirects a Moving Charge

A Simple Field Solver

With the material so far presented, it is possible, maybe even easy, to create an iterative field solver. In doing so, you will encounter some of the issues and problems that all field solvers must deal with. How these problems are dealt with is often a key to where a particular type of field solver is a good or bad choice. You can build a field solver by a mechanism as simple as discretizing the two equations. The first step is to examine the definition of the derivative itself. The derivative of a function, *U*(a), is defined like this:

$$\lim_{\Delta a \to 0} (U(a + \Delta a) - U(a))/\Delta a$$

As the distance between here and there gets very small, the derivative is the limit of the difference between the value of a function here and the value of the function there, divided by the distance between here and there. It is the slope of the function at a particular point.

It can be envisioned as this:

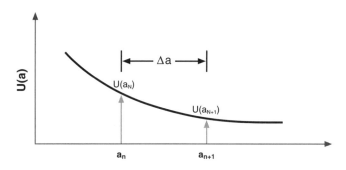

Figure 5.9   Two samples of *U*

A derivative is made discrete by simply fixing Δa, the distance between the two "a" values, at some small value. In that case *U*(a) is a sample at some point in a grid. *U*(a+Δa) is the value at the next adjacent point in the grid. So, in this gridded space, the derivative is approximated by this equation:

$$\delta U \, / \, \delta a \cong (U(a_{n+1}) - U(a_n)) \, / \, \Delta a$$

Where:
   $U(a_n)$ is the value of *U* at some grid-point n,
   $U(a_{n+1})$ is the value of *U* at the next increment, *n*+1,
   Δa is the step size, often called *h*.

In these terms it is possible to describe or approximate the entire curl equation in terms of function values at grid points in space. Doing so is the first step in generating a numerical method of solving the fields around objects in space.

Unfortunately, it is necessary to break the train of thought here. Those familiar with numerical analysis will now jump up and say that equation for the derivative is a very crude approximation and we could do much better. That is true, but it wouldn't make the point of this exercise any clearer, so I will leave it with this simple form.

The Discrete Curl

The method that will now be described is the basis of some commercial software packages. Numerous other ways also exist, but they will not be detailed here. This method is described to give you a point of comparison for other methods and a feel for what field solvers are about. Start by going back to the curl equation and also casting it in discrete form. That is to say, limit the position in space to points on a grid. Here is what the curl of U looks like:

$$\nabla \times U = \vec{x}(\partial U_z / \partial y - \partial U_y / \partial z) + \vec{y}(\partial U_x / \partial z - \partial U_z / \partial x) + \vec{z}(\partial U_y / \partial x - \partial U_x / \partial y)$$

So when the curl of U is restricted to a three-dimensional grid, or discretized, it looks like this:

$$
\begin{aligned}
Curl \quad U = [&\vec{x}(U_{Z_{(y+1)}} - U_{Z_{(y)}} - U_{Y_{(z+1)}} + U_{Y_{(z)}}) \\
+ &\vec{y}(U_{X_{(z+1)}} - U_{X_{(z)}} - U_{Z_{(x+1)}} + U_{Z_{(x)}}) \\
+ &\vec{z}(U_{Y_{(x+1)}} - U_{Y_{(x)}} U_{X_{(y+1)}} - U_{X_{(y)}})]/h
\end{aligned}
$$

This expression of the curl of U in terms of values at discrete points of a grid is an approximation, but it can be made arbitrarily precise by decreasing the separation between grid points, h. The equation describes some function U, where U was just pulled out of the air. For your purposes, substitute E or H when you apply this equation to either of Maxwell's equations.

Up to this point, development has been only on the left side of each of the two curl equations. The right side of the second curl equation will now be examined. Recall the curl equation:

$$\nabla \times E = -\mu \partial H / \partial t$$

The Discrete Time Derivative

The right side of the equation is a constant times the time-rate of change of the H field, at a particular place. But the rate of change over time is just the difference between two time samples, as explained above. Applying this equation results in a new interesting form.

$$\partial H / \partial t \cong (H_{t+1} - H_t) / \Delta t$$

That is, the partial of *H* with respect to time is approximately the value it was at the one time step, minus what is was at the next, divided by the size of the time step. Of course, more accurate ways of approximating this partial exist too, but that is not the point. What is needed here is a very simple form so you can concentrate on how this can become a field solver. In these terms, Maxwell's second equation becomes a new discrete equivalent.

$$\frac{\Delta t(\nabla \times E)}{-\mu} + H_t = H_{t+1}$$

This equation expresses the value of the *H* field at the next time increment in terms of the *E* and *H* fields now! Clearly, it is possible to generate a similar equation for the *E* field at the next time increment by similar manipulations. Once initial conditions are set up, it is possible to alternately apply these two equations over and over to all points in space and follow the development of the fields with time. This is a *field solver*!

The Questions of Practicality

All points in space constitute a really big set of data points. To be useful, this field solver, whose method is called finite difference time domain (*FDTD*), needs a more practical region of space. Consider a cube, one hundred increments on a side, defining the region that will be analyzed. That cube would be 10 times denser than Figure 5.10, but would be difficult to draw. That resolution might be acceptable for a small, not too complex device. It is only a million grid points.

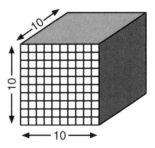

Figure 5.10   A Simple 10 x 10 x 10 Space

At each grid point, it is necessary to have the magnetic constant and the dielectric constant specified—two floating-point numbers. It is also necessary to have the three components, x, y, and z, of the *E* field and the *H* field—six more floating-point numbers. It might also be easier to reserve space for a second set of components as temporary storage for the field being computed on a given pass. You also need the conductivity, magnetic loss, and dielectric loss of each point—fourteen floating-point numbers in all, each requiring about five bytes of memory. So, the physical model of this space requires about 70 megabytes of storage. If a more complex object were modeled, perhaps one that required a 1,000 x 1,000 x 1,000 grid, 70 gigabytes of storage would be required.

A second matter to consider in this field solver is how time increments work. To speed the traversal of a given time interval, it is often desirable to make time steps large. There is a limit on how large time steps can be made in an FDTD field solver. If the time step is made larger than the time it physically takes a wave to cross from one grid point to another, the equations become unstable. A device that has fine detail not only requires a lot of memory, it requires a lot of time steps. For each grid point of the 100 x 100 x 100 example, the inner loop that calculates the next field value at that point must run twice. That comes out to two million passes through the inner loop per time step, one set for the *E* field, and one set for the *H* field. And that is for a mere 100 grid points per direction.

The Boundaries

Yet another matter is the question of what happens to a wave that encounters the edge of the gridded region. The easiest case is to say the boundaries are metal reflectors. Reflections are fairly easy to do. The harder case is that in which the boundaries are free-space. Implementing a boundary that yields absolutely no reflection for waves approaching from any direction is not easy. Many additional issues that are not necessarily difficult must be addressed to make this a useful tool. For example, how do you translate the description of the fields into capacitance and inductance matrices? How are impedances calculated? What of currents? How are discrete components, sources, and loads to be dealt with? Such questions will not be dealt with here, but you would need to answer them to make this into a useful tool.

The main reason for detailing the development of this field solver has been to convince you that creation of a field solver is not necessarily so esoteric a task as to be beyond comprehension. Many field solvers are quite easy to understand at the fundamental level. Yet a lot of details need to be addressed, and a lot of choices must be made by the designers in order to decide what approach best suits which requirements. The complexity of individual calculations can be fast, yet the sheer number of repetitions of each calculation, as in the example above, can become the limit of practicality for a given solver.

Perhaps the most important thing to take away from all this is that it seldom is practical for a commercial field solver to be totally general and totally valid. That is, although the creators of various commercial solvers know how to generate a solver that is mathematically rigorous and always yields "correct" results, it is seldom practical to do so. Most customers would not be anxious to purchase a tool that requires a supercomputer and still needs weeks to generate a single answer. To build a machine that is competitive in the market, the designers have to make compromises that increase speed or save memory. So, you must presume that every commercial tool uses shortcuts that work well in those applications for which the tool was intended. Unfortunately, they will likely work poorly if the tool is used in a way not intended. Your task is to determine how a particular tool is intended to be used and whether that corresponds to the use you need to make of the tool.

To choose a tool, you will have to consider what types of systems you will need to analyze in your applications, and then do a lot of talking to vendors of these tools. Seek out people who are working on problems similar to yours and ask what tools they use. Find out what they like and dislike about their tools.

A Field-Solver Sampler

A number of commercial field solvers are available to you, and choosing one that is optimal can be challenging. This section will briefly mention several of the terms and buzzwords you will encounter in making such a selection. There are valid reasons why more than one solution is available. Some of those reasons will be described next.

Finite Difference Time Domain

Finite difference time domain (FDTD) solvers are a good place to start since the underlying mechanisms have just been described. This method has several strong points. Because you can so easily understand this method, the probability of esoteric bugs is less likely for this method than it might be for some of the other methods. FDTD can be directly traced to Maxwell's curl equations and to the definition of the derivative, so the quantification of maximum errors can easily be performed and understood. The method is equally valid for all frequency ranges. Though the method was described for isotropic regions, it is clear that it could be extended to anisotropic regions. It is also evident that there are no limits on the number of dielectric and metal regions or values that could be handled. In fact, for a given grid and time-step size, the complexity of the physical object does not influence the rate at which the fields can be calculated.

Disadvantages of FDTD are primarily speed and memory requirements. The grid size must be based on the finest detail that the solver must resolve in the physical device being analyzed. It is difficult to implement variable-sized grids in this type of solver, so very small features will have huge impacts on time and memory requirements.

Some field solvers are designed primarily to produce electrical parameters such as the inductance and capacitance matrices of a device. Some solvers produce S parameters. Others are designed to measure and display emissions patterns, generating great graphics. If you are going to study emissions, you need to check that the solver does emissions. If you are going to study S parameters, check that it does S parameters. Some do all. Some do only a few.

SPICE

SPICE is not a field solver; it is a circuit solver. Yet, it is appropriate to mention it here. It, or one of its embodiments, is the tool that is most likely to be familiar to any circuit designer or signal integrity engineer. Many SPICE-based tool manufacturers have recognized that their customers need the ability to convert geometrical information into equivalent electrical parameters. To this end, field solvers are showing up in SPICE implementations. These solvers are usually two-dimensional solvers that do a good job of modeling any geometry that can be expressed as an extrusion. They calculate impedances and couplings, sometimes loss. This type of solver cannot deal with anything that varies in a third dimension. At microwave frequencies, through-hole vias in multilayer circuit boards are important features in traces. SPICE solvers are not capable of generating models of objects such as vias.

Speed is the reason for SPICE to remain an essential tool: compared to field solvers, it is incredibly fast. It also has no problems in dealing with discrete components and with non-linear components. In the future, I expect to see more need for collaboration between SPICE-based tools and field-solvers. The field solver can characterize components such as the through-hole via and the connector. That characterization is translated to a SPICE model, and the circuit analysis will, even as now, take place in SPICE.

SPICE was once said to be useful only up to 200 megahertz. Now it is found to be useful well into the gigahertz frequencies. There will be a point where SPICE or any other circuit-based solver will become obsolete. That point is reached when significant amounts of energy are carried in non-TEM (transverse electromagnetic) modes. At microwave frequencies, it is possible for energy to be transported in ways that are inconsistent with the circuit theory of traditional electronics. These alternate modes are usually inconsequential except at frequencies where wavelengths are short compared to the size of circuit devices. In the case of printed circuit boards, the circuit devices may not only be the traces used to transport signals around the board, but also the reference planes, power, and ground. They might even be such things as heat sinks and the gaps between reference planes. Circuit solvers such as SPICE do not recognize energy transported in such modes and so generate inaccuracy when such modes become significant.

That era when circuit solvers will be abandoned has not yet arrived for the small computer industry. When and if it arrives, SPICE solvers will finally become obsolete. In the meantime, these solvers are likely to remain the work-horses of this industry.

Finite Elements

Finite element methods are based on a classic method for numerical solutions of three-dimensional differential equations. The method involves dividing space into regions that are small enough that simplifying assumptions can be applied to those regions. Such a simplifying assumption might be that the solution is linear throughout the sub region and that a simple expression for the energy in the region can be found.

The finite elements method has the advantage that, where fields are more or less intense, the physical subsections can be easily scaled in size to maintain appropriate degrees of accuracy in calculations. To facilitate this, regions of three-dimensional space are usually broken up into quadrilaterals rather than cubes. The process is called *meshing*.

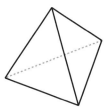

Figure 5.11   A Quadrilateral

Quadrilateral meshing yields a major advantage over FDTD for speed and storage requirements: the total number of regions is not tied to the size of the region of finest detail in the physical object being modeled. All that notwithstanding, this field solver is, for most people's needs, excruciatingly slow. It is not necessarily slower than FDTD, but still, it is slow. A moderately simple problem can often run days on a fast computer.

Other than that, this solver is usually capable of dealing with objects consisting of fairly arbitrary arrangements of various dielectrics and materials, just as FDTD was. This solver has the same issues with the boundaries of the region as FDTD and all other field solvers have. The range of applications where this solver is useful is often much larger than that of some other types that are much faster.

The use of quadrilaterals in the meshing allows fine detail where fields are expected to be intense and coarse detail in other portions. The tool does this by varying the mesh size in various regions of space. For the best speed in solving a particular system, mesh size is kept as large as practical. That minimizes the number of points where calculations need to be made. For accuracy, the tool needs to keep mesh size small compared to the minimum wavelengths of interest. That is why the tool will ask you for a maximum frequency before it generates the mesh.

Method of Moments

Many think of the method of moments (MOM) as the answer to all the world's problems. And, this is true, if you happen to live in that world. Although method of moments is indeed an excellent solution for many of the problems of finite elements and finite difference time domain, it can have problems of its own.

The Method of Moments is a different type of field solver. Instead of breaking space down into small elements, it works on alternative ways of solving equations. Some kinds of integrals can be set exactly equal to a matrix. Solutions of such an integral can be found by inverting that matrix. The solution thus found can be exact—not just an approximation. The integral that you can solve in this manner can be divided into two parts: a basis function and a Green's function. Two tricks are involved here. It is possible for a basis function to yield an exact correspondence between the field and the integral of desired form. It is also possible for a basis function to yield only a really good approximation. The bigger issue is the Green's function and how it is found.

The Green's function is the answer to the question, "What would happen if I took a hammer and hit the thing really hard once?" The mathematicians, who all gasped at that description, can now exhale. The Green's function is the response of the system to a unit impulse applied at all points. Once this is found and combined with the basis function, the matrix is built and inverted, and the fields problem is solved in one big step. Not only that, once the Green's function is found, various alternative stimuli can be applied to the system and responses calculated using that same solution. Thus when it works, it can work very fast. It can work exceedingly fast. It can work very exceedingly really fast.

There is more than one MOM implementation. A wide range of methods can all be classified under this category. Solutions can be implemented in the time domain or in the frequency domain. Each solution is usually limited to a very particular type of problem. This limitation is partly due to the difficulty of finding a Green's function for other types of problem. You might find a Green's function for layered media of infinite extent. You might find a Green's function for free space or for a circular region with conducting boundaries. The solver that is designed for a particular type of problem is not going to be useful for other types of problems.

Finding a Green's function for a particular assemblage of objects in a region of space is usually a daunting task. Thus, those actually used in MOM solvers may not be precisely correct for the actual physical device you are modeling. A common type of presumption is that reference planes in planar media are infinite in extent. Some electrical characteristics are not bothered by this presumption. Other electrical characteristics, such as reference plane resonances, cannot tolerate this presumption. So the question you need to ask is, "Does the particular problem fit the MOM implementation being used?" If it does, the MOM solver offers blindingly fast solutions. If it doesn't, you are likely to find a blindingly fast path to a wrong answer.

Transmission Line Modeler

The transmission line modeler (TLM) appears to be an interesting alternative. Since the core algorithm used is unconditionally stable, the stability issues associated with FDTD are inherently bypassed. This method can use an irregular mesh, as does the finite elements method, and so can be optimized for speed and storage requirements. The one implementation that is familiar to me qualifies for the description "blindingly fast." And finally, unlike MOM, it does not require a suitable Green's function.

The TLM usually is capable of being implemented with a quadrilateral grid. That makes it possible to keep the global mesh density independent of the local complexity of the device being modeled. In plain words, good resolution can be attained with limited memory requirements. Unlike FDTD, the fundamental method of the TLM is mathematically stable. Small time steps are not mandated simply for stability.

FastCap & FastHenry

You can find two free tools, FastCap and FastHenry, on the web; they are nicely suited to some kinds of problems. FastCap calculates the capacitance of an assemblage of objects; FastHenry calculates the inductance. Both are useful in particular types of instances.

FastCap is a multi-pole solver, a solver that uses a particular type of simplifying strategy. In an assemblage of objects, some nearby and some not so close, the response at any particular point is influenced by all objects, near and far. The impact of an object very near is likely greater than the impact of another that is far away. But the computational burden for calculating the impact of an object is the same whether it is near or far. The multi-pole algorithm takes on this dilemma and says: no, it is not. The multi-pole algorithm groups objects that are far away and uses an average position of the elements in the group *there*, to calculate the impact *here*. This strategy can significantly reduce computational complexity while only lightly impacting accuracy. The multi-pole algorithm itself is used in many other solvers beside FastCap. Yet the value of this particular algorithm is demonstrated clearly by this particular solver.

FastCap calculates the static capacitance between a group of objects and does so quite quickly. An advantage of this tool is that it can handle objects of totally arbitrary shape. A disadvantage is that it only sets up well in a region of uniform, or at least simple, dielectric boundaries. Perhaps a bigger issue is that, being static, it loses accuracy when object dimensions are a significant portion of wavelength at a particular frequency. FastCap does not of itself check or point out accuracy; it recognizes and points out some of the most severe failures. The only way to check whether the tool is producing a well-converged solution is to vary computational parameters such as the number of panels per area and then see whether the solution changes significantly.

FastHenry is an inductance calculator. It works well when the geometry of the object confines current to well-defined paths. It doesn't work in cases where the direction of current flow might be unknown. In any instances where these tools make sense, I recommend their use. It is always necessary to check the result of any field calculation to see if it has adequately converged or if it just plain makes sense, and that is especially true for these two tools. Neither of these tools knows if the presumptions built into them make sense for the particular problem you give them.

In addition, neither tool has a particularly good user interface, and additional utilities are needed to set up all but the most rudimentary input files. However, they are good tools.

Others

The list offered here is not exhaustive, but it is a reasonably representative list. Solvers can be classified in other ways, too. Most of the preceding descriptions have been from the perspective of the time domain. Some designers find it more productive to work in the frequency domain. Solution methods exist for both the time and the frequency domains.

Here is another common classification method. The discussion above made it obvious that speed and storage requirements are serious issues in all field solvers. If a particular tool is intended to be used for only one-dimensional problems, it would be nonsense to implement all three dimensions. Therefore, solvers referred to as two-dimensional (2D) are common. Two-dimensional tools work well for geometries that can be expressed as extrusions. For example, if a tool were intended for calculating the characteristic impedance of transmission lines, it would likely be implemented as a 2D solver.

In this context, it is clear what a 3D solver is. But what is a two-and-a-half-D solver? This classification describes a 3D solver that places restrictions on what variations can take place in the third dimension. The restrictions enable the solver to run faster or more efficiently. As has been pointed out several times already, such modifications make the solver work well for the solver's intended use, but poorer in uses for which it was not intended.

Yet another classification is used in describing field solvers. Some solvers are called *quasi-static* and others *full-wave*. The quasi-static solver calculates the static inductance and capacitance, presuming that they are constant over the frequency range of applications. This assumption is valid if all dimensions of interest are small compared to wavelengths you are concerned with. If an object is large compared to wavelength, the quasi-static assumption is no longer valid. In that case, you should use a full-wave solver. The full-wave solver accounts for the variations due to increasing frequencies. Actually, you have a midpoint between these two. One popular solver calculates the electrical characteristics at 100 megahertz. This strategy makes a good compromise between speed and accuracy, particularly in circuit boards.

The Wave Equation

If you work with signal transmission, you work with the wave equation and the telegrapher's equation. The forms that these equations take at microwave frequencies involve characters and terms you may not have encountered before. Now you will.

Question: what happens if you take the curl of the curl? Admittedly, you may find this less than interesting. You may even compare it to hitting yourself in the head with a hammer—it really feels good when you finally quit. Nevertheless, setting all that aside, here goes.

The original two curl equations are:

$$\nabla \times H = \varepsilon \partial E / \partial t + \sigma E$$

$$\nabla \times E = -\mu \partial H / \partial t$$

equivalently :

$$Curl H = \varepsilon \partial E / \partial t + g$$

$$Curl E = -\mu \partial H / \partial t$$

So, curling again :

$$Curl\, Curl E = -\mu\ \partial Curl\ H / \partial t$$

$$Curl Curl E = -\mu \varepsilon\ \partial^2 E / \partial t^2$$

Now, the product mu-epsilon ($\mu\varepsilon$) is related to the speed of light. The speed of light (c) is, in fact, the reciprocal of the square root of this product. And the curl of the curl is equivalent to del-squared, also called the Laplacian. Including these and substituting the first of Maxwell's curl equations continues the development to yield yet another equation:

$$\nabla^2 E = 1/c^2 \; \partial^2 E / \partial t^2$$

That equation is known as the wave equation. So now you know where the wave equation comes from. It is possible to set all y and z components to zero to express a one-dimensional version of this equation. It is also possible to substitute a voltage function of time and space for the E field. When that voltage function is expressed as a phasor, the result is known as the telegrapher's equation.

You may ask, why not just take it all on faith and skip this development? This math is not being recited just for fun. Follow this through: Several terms will be demonstrated, and those terms are used extensively in microwave signal literature. I could, for example, say that gamma is the complex propagation constant, but does that statement really mean anything at this point? When the development is complete, that statement will seem obvious. You might not know who Neper was, but after this development it will make complete sense that the real part of the propagation constant is measured in Nepers per meter. It will become clear that the real part should have a distinct and named unit of measurement.

The place to begin is in developing the one-dimensional version of the wave equation. To do this, simply set all y and z components of the expanded equation to zero and retain all terms that contain x. You then substitute a voltage function of time and space, $V(x,t)$, for the E field in the wave equation. Define that voltage function as a phasor. In this case, a phasor is not a science fiction weapon but rather the mathematical construct that electrical engineers have been using for decades.

When you have completed these steps, the equation becomes what is called the telegrapher's equation. Here is an example of this development:

$$\nabla^2 E = 1/c^2 \; \partial^2 E/\partial t^2$$

$$f(y) = f(z) = 0$$

$$\Rightarrow$$

$$\partial^2 V(x,t)/\partial x^2 = 1/c^2 \; \partial^2 V(x,t)/\partial t^2$$

Define :

$$V(x,t) \equiv \mathrm{Re}[v(x)e^{j\omega t}]$$

so :

$$\partial^2 v(x)/\partial x^2 e^{j\omega t} = v(x)/c^2 \; \partial^2 e^{j\omega t}/\partial t^2$$

$$\partial^2 v(x)/\partial x^2 e^{j\omega t} = -\omega^2/c^2 \; v(x)e^{j\omega t}$$

$$\partial^2 v(x)/\partial x^2 = -\omega^2/c^2 \; v(x)$$

Check these equations out. See that a voltage defined in space and time was substituted for the E field. See how that substitution limits the scope of the equation by defining voltage as a phasor, a function of position that varies in the sinusoidal manner described by a complex exponential. Note how the explicit exponential drops out of the equation, yet the sinusoidal presumption must remain. That is, though the complex exponential does not show in the final equation, the final equation is only valid for phasors.

Now, the really big leap takes place. The second derivative of the voltage equals a constant times the voltage.

$$\partial^2 v(x)/\partial x^2 = -\omega^2/c^2 \; v(x)$$

That constant is interesting—a negative frequency divided by a velocity, squared. This constant is given a name in the microwave industry. The name is somewhat arbitrary but you can guess how it came to be chosen. They could have called it Fred, but that doesn't sound very scientific. So they called it gamma squared.

$$\partial^2 v(x)/\partial x^2 = \gamma^2 v(x)$$

And science makes yet another giant leap forward, although I still think I would have preferred Fred. Getting back on track, since gamma squared is a negative number, gamma itself must be a complex number. In addition, solutions to this differential equation are going to be of the form:

$$v(x) = Ae^{-\gamma x} + Be^{\gamma x}$$

Gamma, a complex number having a real part and an imaginary part, can be divided into two parts, yielding the sum of two exponentials: one with the real part of gamma, the other with the imaginary part. Recalling fundamental mathematics, an exponential to an imaginary power produces a sinusoid. An exponential to a negative real power produces a decay envelope. So the constant gamma, known as "the complex propagation constant" in microwave signal literature, is itself divided into a real and imaginary part called alpha and beta. In combination they describe a sinusoid described by beta, with a decay rate described by alpha. An interconnect circuit described by this equation will have a loss factor that is described by alpha and propagation described by beta. Here is the standard definition for these three quantities:

$$\gamma \equiv \alpha + j\beta$$

Alpha, the loss factor, is quantified in units of Nepers per meter. In the MKSA system, beta is called the propagation constant and is measured in radians per meter. There it is. That is the conclusion it all came to. Well, not really. There is more. For example, the two parts whose sum make up $V(x)$ are interpreted as two waves, one moving to the right and the other to the left. This interpretation is the basis of most of what needs to be understood about how transmission lines operate at microwave frequencies or, for that matter, at any frequency where geometrical dimensions are large compared to wavelengths.

What are microwave frequencies? For me, they are frequencies at or above one gigahertz. Some people choose to consider them even lower than that. An alternative wording might be to say that microwave frequencies are any frequencies whose wavelengths are small compared to the physical size of devices and structures you are working with.

Reflection Coefficient

Although transmission lines are usually described in terms of a characteristic impedance, they don't always lend themselves to the types of calculations that apply to lumped impedances. When you work with transmission lines, you need to be able to deal with the peculiar impedance issues that show up at microwave frequencies. The problem is exemplified by the standard calculation referred to as the voltage-divider equation: given two resistors in series, the voltage between them is calculated by the voltage divider equation.

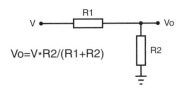

Figure 5.12   Another Voltage Divider

If R1 or R2 are transmission lines rather than fixed lumped components, the voltage divider equation may not work as expected. If *V* is a DC voltage and R2 is a lossless transmission line, the steady-state value of *Vo* will be zero. When transmission lines are involved, it is more convenient to use an alternate method of accounting for the voltages in this circuit. That method makes use of the reflection coefficient.

To set up a development of the reflection coefficient, start with a voltage source that includes a known standard output impedance. The most common value for the output impedance is 50 ohms. Early in the history of electronics, high-frequency signals usually were associated with radio. Radio signals in transmitters were usually transported through coaxial transmission lines. Clever engineers soon realized that the power that could be transported through a coaxial transmission line was a function of the ratio of inner conductor diameter to outer conductor diameter. In modeling this transmission line, they found that the solution of maximum power-handling capability showed a broad peak at about 50 ohms. Thus, the radio industry standardized on 50 ohm coaxial cables, and as a result, test equipment standardized on the 50 ohm impedance.

Equipment with 50-ohm output impedance best matches transmission lines with 50-ohm impedance. It is desirable, for reasons that will become clear shortly, to standardize such equipment in a manner that the voltage into a unit load, 50 ohms, is a unit, one volt. So the internal voltage, what is designated V in Figure 5.12, is actually two volts. It will produce 1 volt into a matched load. When R1 equals R2, Vo will be one.

$$Vo = 2(R2/(R1+R2))$$

Now Vo is the actual voltage measured out of the port; V is the voltage produced into a matched load, one. The difference between these two, or the voltage actually measured less the voltage that would be seen in a matched load, is called the *reflected voltage*. The ratio of the two is designated by the Greek letter rho (ρ). The reflected voltage is related to the matched-impedance voltage by calculating the difference between the two. That calculation yields the relationship:

$$Vo - 1 = \frac{2R2}{R2+R1} - 1 = \frac{R2-R1}{R2+R1}$$

But if we consider the output voltage to be the sum of a forward-traveling wave and a reverse-traveling wave, we get:

$$Vo = Vf + Vr$$

and

$$\rho \equiv Vr/Vf$$

so

$$\rho = \frac{Vo - Vf}{Vf}$$

Now if Vf is defined to be a single unit of forward signal voltage, the final form of the equation falls out:

$$\rho = Vo - 1$$

$$\rho \equiv \frac{R2-R1}{R2+R1}$$

This result is extremely important and is one of the few times that a formula actually should be memorized. Of course, memorize it in a format that makes sense for you. Here it is written in terms of the configuration in Figure 5.12. You will often see it in terms of characteristic impedance and load impedance. I have presented it in this form to emphasize that it is not peculiar to transmission lines or to test equipment. It is simply an embodiment of the standard voltage-divider equation.

The reflection coefficient can also relate to the wave equation. Recalling that a forward and a reverse wave were defined as having amplitudes A and B, well, the reflection coefficient relates B to A. If a signal of amplitude A encounters an impedance mismatch with reflection coefficient rho, a signal B is reflected whose amplitude is rho times A. Note that this works fine in the time domain but is a bit trickier in the frequency domain.

Numerous pieces of trivia can be associated with this concept. The voltage reflection coefficient of an open circuit is one. For a short circuit, it is minus one. For a matched load, it is zero. For a passive circuit, its magnitude can never exceed one. The current reflection is the negative of the voltage reflection coefficient. The coefficient at a junction is different when seen from the left side than when seen from the right. In fact, for the transient case, they are simply the negative of each other. But things really get good when steady-state sinusoids are considered.

Literature concerning steady-state sinusoids often uses the designation "uppercase gamma" for the reflection coefficient. This version of the reflection coefficient applies to the frequency domain. Recalling the wave equation solutions, if position x is referenced to a particular position such as the end of the line, which is often a load, the reflection coefficient at this position is designated gamma-sub-zero (Γ_0). At a terminator, and usually only at the terminator, gamma equals rho. The key point here is that rho is the reflection coefficient seen by the edge of a transient signal. Gamma is the reflection coefficient seen by a steady-state sinusoid. They differ because the transient sees no impacts from additional reflections further down the line. Mathematical development is shown next. Here A is the amplitude of a forward-traveling sinusoid. B is the amplitude for a reverse-traveling sinusoid.

$$v(x) = Ae^{-\gamma x} + Be^{\gamma x}$$

$$\Gamma(x) = Be^{\gamma x} / Ae^{-\gamma x}$$

$$= \frac{B}{A} e^{2\gamma x}$$

$$= \Gamma_0 e^{2\gamma x}$$

The details of how this impedance becomes a function of distance have already been presented and don't need to be repeated here. The equation that describes the impedance for steady-state sine waves, as a function of position, involves the hyperbolic tangent if the line has loss.

$$Z(x) = Zo \frac{Z_L + Zo \tanh \gamma x}{Zo + Z_L \tanh \gamma x}$$

Zo is the characteristic impedance of the transmission line, Z_L is the load impedance, and *x* is the distance from the load. Many more details could be explored, but this one is the most important. It asserts that the impedance measured on a transmission line is never a constant unless the line is terminated without reflections. In all other cases, the impedance varies with distance.

Some startling results come from this. An open circuit transmission line, viewed a quarter wave-length from the open, performs as a short circuit for that particular frequency. Similarly, a shorted quarter-wave stub acts as an open circuit at that particular frequency. At 10 gigahertz, a quarter wave in FR4 is about 0.15 inch. Traditional test points on boards often involve a via with a short stub to a test pad on the bottom of a board. Typical boards are about .06 to .09 inch thick. If the pad is about .04 inch square and the link to it about .04 inch long, it will present a virtual short to the 10-gigahertz component of any signal associated with that test point. In packages with high dielectric constants, the problem becomes worse.

Similarly, a half-wave section of line that is shorted on both ends can act as a resonator. You may occasionally see traces that were intended as shields shorted to ground at intervals. If the distance between these shorting points is not carefully chosen, such structures can become resonators.

Conclusion

This chapter refreshes the concepts of electric and magnetic fields in the context of Maxwell's curl equations and describes these equations in enough detail that you can understand them. A second objective of the chapter was to introduce some of the tools for finding solutions in the context of microwave electronics. No particular product was named as the "right" tool. Rather, the types of characteristics and buzzwords associated with such solvers were introduced so you can make sense of the claims made for various commercial products. You can find an immense body of information on these subjects. Those who sell field solvers will want to tell you every word of it, too.

I described the mathematical development of some key concepts required for understanding microwave signals. I sincerely hope that the material here will inspire you to study these subjects in much greater depth, and that the derivations included here are clear and accurate enough that you see there is no magic involved. The concepts and background for microwave signaling are within the abilities of most working engineers.

Chapter 6

Differential Signaling

The next wave of personal computer enhancements will include circuit interconnections running at microwave frequencies. Differential signaling enables these frequencies, making the subject of differential signaling important. It is critical that you understand what differential signaling, transmitters, receivers, and interconnect circuitry are all about. This chapter examines the meaning of "differential" in the context of transmitters, receivers, and interconnects. In the process, you will also examine common-mode signals and their impact. You will see why differential signaling enables microwave data rates.

It is tempting to ask a question such as, "What is differential signaling?" or "What is a differential driver?" Such questions are issues of philosophy, not of engineering. They are no more the realm of engineering than the question, "What is the meaning of life?" What *is* within the realm of engineering, are questions such as, "How is a system optimized for the transport of differential signals?" That is an engineering matter, that is the type of thing we are trained for, are good at, love to get our hands into. The distinction is important because "what is?" questions lead to endless discussions that seem to go nowhere, while "how is?" questions lead to engineering insights.

Definitions

To make the subject of differential signaling as concise as possible, I'll lay out a set of careful definitions. These definitions are intended as a reset. That is, what you may have read in the hobbyist journals about differential signaling is to be forgotten and ignored for the moment. Here, statements about differential signaling are to be interpreted in the terms defined here, and only in those terms.

Voltage

The potential difference between two points is called the voltage between those two points. I make this very obvious statement to emphasize the fact that voltage is always between two points. Everyday usage tends to ignore this in favor of the presumption that one of the two is always some fixed reference, ground. For everyday usage it is both convenient and appropriate to speak as if voltage is always so referenced. For engineering use, this presumption is inappropriate and leads to confusion.

When a manual says "measure five volts at this pin" it makes a difference whether that is five volts with respect to a nearby pin, the chassis of the device, or some wall outlet. When voltage is specified at microwave frequencies, it is critical that the reference point is well defined.

For a group of metal objects, the static voltage of each could be specified with respect to some external ground, or with respect to one of the objects, or perhaps with respect to each other in some other manner. You could make a list where the second element could be referenced to the first, the third to the second, and so on. In any of these methods, the voltage between one and any other could be calculated from the data provided.

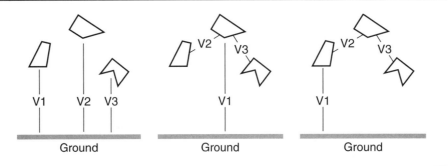

Figure 6.1   Voltage Measurements

Consider two objects and a reference called ground. One of the ways that the voltage of these objects could be specified is the average voltage of the objects with respect to ground. The average of any parameter on *n* objects is the sum of the individual values, divided by *n*. The average voltage of two objects with respect to ground is the sum of the individual voltages, divided by two. This is true for static voltage, and this is true at any instant in time for dynamic voltage.

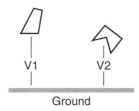

V1   V2

Ground

Figure 6.2   The Voltage of Two Objects

This value, the average voltage of the two objects, is referred to as *the common-mode voltage.* Common-mode voltage is the average voltage among a group of objects. The emphasis is on group. Common-mode voltage can have an AC and a DC component. The average voltage on an individual object is not a common-mode voltage. In Figure 6.2, the common-mode voltage is $(V1+V2)/2$. You occasionally see common-mode voltage described in terms of Vhigh and Vlow. Such terminology is wrong and needs to be discouraged, and the reason should be clear. These terms describe voltages on a single object.

If you want to express the precise voltage on either of these objects in terms that included the common-mode voltage, you can describe the voltage offset between the particular object and this average. That offset need only be expressed for one object because the other is forced by mathematics itself to have the same magnitude and opposite sign of voltage offset. If it did not, this would not be the average. In fact, this offset is always exactly half of the voltage difference between the two objects. This difference, $V1$ minus $V2$, is called *the differential voltage* of the pair of objects.

In knowing these two voltages, differential and common-mode, you can determine the precise voltage with respect to ground of either object. In reverse, measuring the individual voltages with respect to ground, you can determine both the differential and common mode components. An interesting property of common-mode and differential voltages is that they are orthogonal. Changing either does not force a change in the other. That property is one of the reasons that differential signaling excels.

I have just used a new term that I should define. Data that is encoded in the voltage difference between two conductors is referred to as *differential data*. Transporting such data through an interconnect circuit is referred to as *differential signaling*. A driver circuit that is designed to transmit differential data is called a *differential driver*. A receiver that is designed to receive differential data is called a *differential receiver*.

Those may seem like obvious statements, so obvious that they didn't need to be stated. The exact opposite is true. There have been prolonged, seemingly endless, discussions that included phrases such as: is this "really" a differential driver, is this "really" a differential transmission line? For purposes of this book, if that is what it is used for, that is what it is.

At the risk of sounding a bit preachy, one of the seven habits of "real" engineers is that they don't ask "is it really...?," they ask "how can it be optimized for...?" A joke that occasionally makes the rounds on the Internet says that the optimist sees the glass as half full; the pessimist sees it as half empty; the engineer sees that the glass is twice the size that is needed. That is to say, if you are an engineer, what you do best is make things as functional as possible given the constraints.

One final definition is needed. For the traditional digital transmission line—a single wire with a single driver and one input pin to the receiver—I use the term *single-ended*. This term is used to emphasize those cases where I describe circuitry that is not differential.

The Differential Receiver

The optimal differential receiver is a device that accepts two inputs. It has very low sensitivity to common mode signal on the two inputs. It has high sensitivity to differential signal on the two inputs. The two inputs usually provide equal impedances at the input pins. Typically, the receiver does not detect voltage with respect to some fixed voltage level, rather the receiver detects simply whether the differential AC component of the receive signal is positive or negative in sign. That is, the average becomes the reference for switching.

All real differential receivers have some limit on the range of common mode voltages over which they function well. This common-mode range can be small. Within this range, the receiver can be expected to show little output response to input common-mode signal. Usually you'll see some response to the common-mode voltage, and the parameter that describes the sensitivity to common mode input is called the *common-mode rejection*. To optimize common-mode rejection, design as much symmetry as possible into the receiver.

It is easy to envision a device that is sensitive only to differential signals. A simple example is an isolation transformer, which responds primarily to voltages that can produce a current in its input coil. Common-mode signals get through only by mechanisms such as capacitive coupling between the input and output coils. At microwave frequencies, transformers of adequate frequency response for digital signal use tend to be expensive, if they exist at all.

The advantage of a well-designed differential receiver results from insensitivity to common-mode noise. Much of the most serious noise that the receiver must deal with is in the common mode. Inside the device package itself, you will often find a lot of common-mode noise. One source is power supply ripple caused by variations in current demand. Another source is ground bounce caused by variations in input signals and variations in current through the active circuitry. These variations tend to couple equally to both sides of the receiver circuitry, so their impact is reduced by the common-mode rejection of the receiver. A similar situation exists for external noise sources. They tend to couple equally to both input lines and so are rejected as common mode.

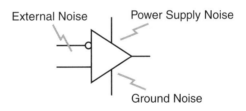

Figure 6.3   Common Mode Noise at a Differential Receiver

Recalling that package pins usually have a significant inductance and that voltage across that inductance is proportional to the rate of change of current through the inductance, you can see that higher frequencies result in greater noise across power and ground pins. This increase is countered by the use of carefully balanced currents in the differential receiver.

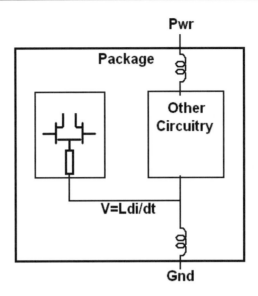

Figure 6.4   Package Noise, Common Mode at the Receiver

The Differential Transmitter

Many of the benefits described for the differential receiver also apply to differential transmitters. Careful balance in the design can minimize the current variations caused by data traversing through the transmitter, thus minimizing the common-mode noise in the transmitter circuit. All output parameters must have symmetry maximized, including the delay through the package to the pins. The quest for symmetry includes the output voltage swings; it includes the rise and fall times of the signal edges. And it includes the output impedance at each of the transmit pins. Imbalance in any one of these areas causes AC common-mode voltages and power supply current variations to form.

DC common-mode voltage is usually not a major concern. Unless the signaling scheme requires a DC component, the DC common-mode voltage can be handled by AC coupling, then by re-establishing the required voltage in the receiver itself. But AC common mode is much more serious, and you must minimize AC common mode conversions both at the source and throughout the interconnect circuitry. Figure 6.5 shows three voltage situations and their impact on common mode noise. At the left, rise-time, voltage, and timing are matched so no AC common mode is formed. In the middle, a difference in timing causes a common mode pulse to form. At the right, a difference in rise-time causes the AC common mode.

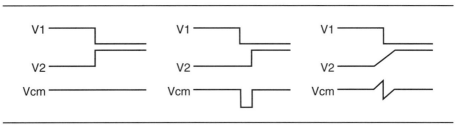

Figure 6.5   AC Common Mode

On an individual pin, the output voltage in digital bi-level signaling usually is specified at two levels. The output level that corresponds to a logic-true output voltage will be given a name such as *V*high, and the logic-false output level will be given a name such as *V*low. In an ideal differential driver, the difference between these two levels will be the same on each of the two pins of the driver. In practice, there are tolerances, so the levels at the two pins are never exactly the same.

One occasionally sees common mode voltage wrongly described in terms of the difference between *V*high and *V*low. This description is wrong because it presumes that the values are the same for each of the two pins out of the driver. The fact that this calculation yields a value for the DC common-mode component that is accurate within engineering tolerances is irrelevant. What is relevant is that common mode is the average among a group of conductors, not the average on a single conductor. Also relevant is that those who try to think in terms of *V*high and *V*low have a difficult time understanding the AC component of common-mode voltage, because on a single conductor there is no AC common-mode voltage. So, let me emphasize one last time that the common-mode voltage is the average at any instant of the voltages on the two conductors of the differential pair.

One way that a differential driver is sometimes implemented is through use of a constant-current source shared by two transistors coupling to two matched resistors, as shown in Figure 6.6.

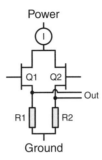

Figure 6.6   A typical Differential Transmitter

The two transistors are driven by complementary inputs. That is, when one is on, the other is off. They can be thought of as simply steering the current to one or the other of the two resistors. If the two resistors are well matched, the two output voltages will also be well matched. This circuit exemplifies several of the benefits and limitations of differential circuits.

Consider what happens when both transistors are partially off, in some intermediate moderately-high impedance state. If the dynamic range of the current source is great enough, the current remains constant. If the dynamic range of the current source is not great enough, the current may be reduced or increased. In all other instances, the total current from power to ground is constant. It is whatever current the source provides.

Compare that with the current from power to ground in a single-ended driver. When the single-ended driver drives high, the current at the ground side falls to zero; when it drives low, the current at the power side falls to zero. In an individual driver, as in Figure 6.7, this current pulse might only be 10 or 20 milliamps. In a wide bus, the current pulses for the cumulative switching of numerous such drivers can get into the range of amps. Attempts to switch amps with rise-times of less than a nanosecond, through the inductances of the power and the ground pins, causes large voltage transients on the power and grounds inside the package. The voltage produced is the product of the rate of change of current and the inductance. The voltage produced has been traditionally handled by adding power and ground pins to reduce the associated total inductance. This solution was useful but eventually got to the point that the circuits needed an individual power and ground pin for every output signal pin. Thus, every added signal required a total of three added pins.

The ability of differential signaling to operate with nominally constant power supply current results in much less need for extra power and ground pins in the package. Each signal added only increases the package pin count by about two. So, at high data rates, differential signaling actually can make more economic use of package pins than single-ended signaling does.

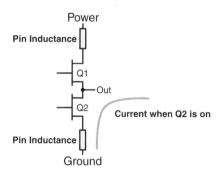

Figure 6.7   A Single-Ended Driver

Another benefit is in the nature of the power transients produced. Single-ended drivers produce current flow as long as the output remains in the same state. Their spectrum can go all the way down to DC. Differential transients tend to be produced mainly at the signal transitions; this can make it easier to control their impact through the use of small capacitors. Advantages such as these make it clear that differential signaling is a good engineering choice for data transport at microwave frequencies. To maximize the benefits of differential signaling, these obvious symmetries need to be preserved, as described above.

A final note is that the differential driver shown above, through use of a constant current source, yields another significant benefit. A current source tends to look like a very high impedance. When you look into the driver from the output side, you see the output resistor effectively in parallel with two series elements: the very high impedance current source and the variable impedance transistor. The result is that the output impedance tends to remain constant and dominated by the resistance of the output resistor. This situation is very good for termination of transmission lines. Even the driver transistors don't really have to be particularly well matched in impedance because they are in series with the high impedance of the current source. Capacitances should be well matched and, to provide wide bandwidths, should be kept very small. A 1-picofarad capacitor at 1 gigahertz has an impedance of 159 ohms. If that capacitor is across the output impedance of a driver, it significantly impacts the total output impedance at this frequency.

Differential Transmission Lines

As mentioned before, for the purposes of this book, any two lines that are used to transport differential data are a differential transmission line. The interest here is in how you optimize these two lines for this use, rather than the philosophical question of what is or is not a differential thing. This information is targeted at digital applications, and such applications have traditionally involved semiconductors and planar media. But semiconductors are not targeted here, so I will emphasize multi-layer planar media, also called circuit boards.

Geometrical relationships are among the various properties that might be used to describe a chunk of copper as a part of a circuit board. This makes a good starting point. From the geometrical relationships between this chunk and others around it, and from the physical properties of dielectrics in the region, you can calculate the capacitance and inductance of this copper object. Numerous books have already shown the derivation that the characteristic impedance of a transmission line is determined primarily by the inductance and capacitance.

$$Zo = \sqrt{L/C}$$

The characteristic impedance is an extremely important property of any transmission line. It is the impedance seen by a fast transient. It is not the steady-state impedance nor the impedance seen for a sine wave at any particular length of line. The differences between these have already been examined. Now about half the professors in the world just jumped up and shouted that that equation is wrong! It is only the characteristic impedance if the line is lossless. Well, that is true. The complete characteristic impedance also needs to recognize the copper and dielectric losses. And, when those are included, the actual characteristic impedance will differ from the prediction of this equation by a small fraction of a percent. Meanwhile, economic and manufacturability constraints limit the predictability of impedance to ranges of around 10 to 15 percent in boards intended for consumer applications. In short, this equation is easy to remember and more than adequately accurate for the use intended here.

This equation is acceptable for a single isolated transmission line. The impedance of a differential transmission pair is not equal to the impedance of a single isolated line. Neither is it strictly twice the impedance of a single line. Before going into details, I'll need to explain other concepts first. That is, how do the various transmission modes that can be imposed on two wires compare?

Transmission modes can be defined in various ways. Definitions have already been given for differential, common, and single-ended modes. Alternatively, the literature occasionally speaks of *even and odd impedances* or *even and odd modes*. Naturally, you may question how these fit together. That answer needs development.

Consider two signal lines, one terminated to ground and the other driven with some digital data pattern. The voltages of the pair can be calculated in terms of differential and common mode voltages, even though one of the lines is not being driven. Suppose the one line has one volt on it while the other has zero. Then the common-mode voltage, the average of the two, is one-half volt. Calculating the differential voltage, a similar result is found. Half the energy has gone into common mode, and half into differential mode.

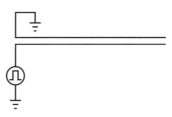

Figure 6.8   Single Side Drive of a Differential Pair

Again consider two conductors suspended in space. These two are the only thing in their universe and they have some static capacitance between them. If you change the voltage on one of them, a transient current flows between them, through this capacitance. If you shift both of them through precisely the same voltage pattern at precisely the same time, no current flows between them. You might say that in one case a shift in voltage produced a current and in the other the voltage shift did not. But impedance is the current-to-voltage ratio. Clearly, there were two different impedances. In fact, the impedance seen at one of the two was dependent on the voltage pattern on the other. The impedance seen by the common-mode signal was different than the impedance seen by the differential component. Look Figure 6.9 over and reread that last sentence. It is one of the really important concepts in differential signaling.

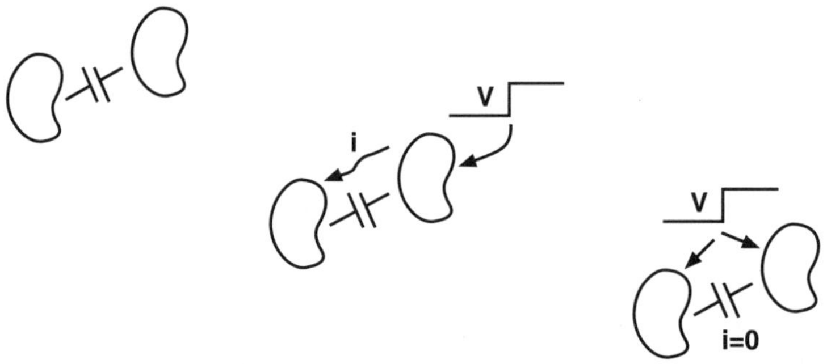

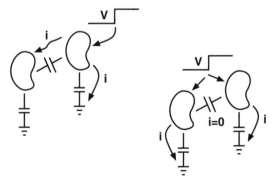

Figure 6.9   Current Depends on Voltage Mode

Real transmission lines exist in proximity to other conductors; they don't exist in an isolated universe. Typically, they have a significant capacitive component to ground or to other nearby conductors. Yet, a capacitance always exists from one line to the other, and the common-mode signal component does not cause current through this component. The differential component does cause current in this capacitance. And so, the impedance is different for the common-mode and the differential-mode components of any signal. The impedance for either of these signal components is also, for the same reason, different from the single-ended impedance.

Figure 6.10   Including Ground Coupling

The impedance seen by the common-mode voltage component in an isolated pair of transmission lines is called the *even-mode impedance*. The impedance seen by the differential voltage on an isolated pair of transmission lines is called the *odd-mode impedance*. Again, you have noticed that there has been some deliberate, although perhaps awkward, wording used in those statements: "on an isolated pair of transmission lines." The concepts of even and odd mode impedances are only strictly valid for a single isolated pair, not three, not four. Yet, in practice, separation between pairs—not within pairs—is often kept great enough that it is a reasonable approximation to calculate in terms of even and odd parts.

Coupling

Next consider a small increment in the length of a transmission line that is being optimized to transport differential signals. That increment, as in Figure 6.11, will be examined in isolation. In isolation, the AC component of signal on the pair makes this increment look like a di-pole.

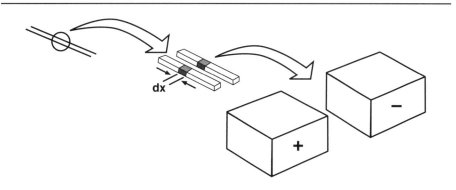

Figure 6.11   Viewing a Small Increment of Length

Recalling those fundamental physics classes from long ago in engineering school, fields around a di-pole diminish at a rate $1/r$ times faster than fields around a monopole. That applies when r is normalized to the separation between the two elements of the di-pole. And again, this is not true; it is only sort of true. The truth is that the fields converge toward this rate, with distance. But it is a useful enough concept to expose some really good information about differential transmission lines.

Consider a pair, separated by 0.01 inch. An adjacent pair is spaced 0.1 inch from this pair. The field produced at the second pair by the first pair is about one-tenth the field that would have been produced by a single-ended line at the same distance. But invoke reciprocity, the principle that what goes around comes around. That is, if the pair produces one-tenth the field, it is also one-tenth as sensitive to other fields at that distance. The result of this is another of the really big advantages that differential signaling produces. Differential transmission pairs can tolerate far closer spacing for a given crosstalk requirement than single-ended signals can. This is particularly important in enabling transmission of microwave frequency data on circuit boards that typically have very dense spacing.

An alternate advantage is the reduction of radiation at radio frequencies. The radiation at those distances specified by regulatory agencies is essentially negligible in terms of the differential component. In real circuit boards, various engineering requirements and manufacturing tolerances make it difficult to keep the common-mode component any lower than about 30 decibels below the level of the differential component. At distances specified by regulatory agencies, typically three meters, the radiation due to the common-mode component greatly exceeds that due to the differential component. It is commonly said that only the common-mode component radiates. In effect, this is true.

Image Currents

Some of the literature points to the fact that in differential transmission the reference planes need not be relied on for return currents; the complementary lines provide this service for each other. In any circuit, currents flow in closed loops. Single-ended transmission lines typically close this loop through the ground system. Ground systems are not always perfect, and discontinuities can alter the return path in ways that produce large amounts of radiation and other undesirable characteristics. Radiation is proportional to the area of a circuit loop. In a single-ended circuit, the return path is the image current in the reference plane adjacent to the signal trace. Thus, the loop area is the trace length times twice the height of the trace. A discontinuity in the return path forces the return current to deviate from the region directly below the trace and can cause major increase in the size of the total current loop.

Consider a trace 5 inches long and 5 thousandths of an inch above the reference plane. The total loop area is 50 square mils. Now consider a 0.1-inch wide by 1-inch long slice out of the reference plane below this trace. The return current going around this adds an additional 100 square mils to the area of the loop. The radiating loop is now three times the original, and the radiation produced will be approximately that, too.

When a charged conductor resides adjacent to a metal plane, certain rules can be applied to help visualize the fields. If the voltage is static, the *E*-field lines must enter and exit the metal surfaces in a direction that is precisely normal to the surface. If it were not, there would have to be some component of the field that was tangent to the surface. If the surface is conductive, and conductors are conductive, this tangent field must produce a movement of charge. Movement of charge violates the provision that the system is static. So, in the static case, *E*-field lines exit conductors in a perpendicular direction. In the dynamic case, this is nearly true, too.

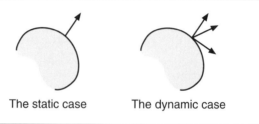

The static case   The dynamic case

Figure 6.12   Static and Dynamic *E* Fields

In objects whose size is very small compared to wavelength, that is at low frequencies, the shape of the dynamic fields are very similar to the shape of static fields. In fact, one of the classifications sometimes used for field-solver software is "quasi-static." Such a solver presumes that the shape of the static field is "accurate enough." So what happens to the field of a conductor over a flat reference plane? The *E* lines spread out and enter the reference plane perpendicularly.

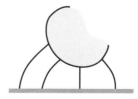

Figure 6.13   Field Lines Entering the Reference Plane

If the reference plane is removed and then replaced by a mirror image conductor, everything remains the same, except the charge in the image is reversed, as shown in Figure 6.14. The fields at this first conductor would be identical to the shape and strength that they had with the reference plane in place. The reference plane acts as a mirror. In that mirror image, real currents exist and, for single-ended drivers, provide the return path that closes the circuit loop.

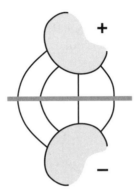

Figure 6.14   A Mirror Image

With differential circuits, these same images exist in the reference planes, but they are not needed to provide a return path. If there is a discontinuity in a reference plane, the image current for a single-ended circuit must find an alternate path around the discontinuity to complete the circuit. The differential case is much better. As shown in Figure 6.15, the differential image current only needs to flow across to the complementary image path to complete its circuit. This is not to say that discontinuities in reference planes can be totally ignored in differential signaling, but rather that they don't impact differential signals nearly as severely as they do single-ended signals.

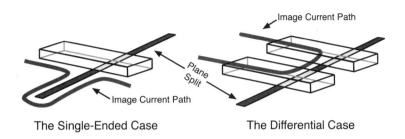

Figure 6.15   Single-Ended vs. Differential Return Currents

In any realistic differential-interconnect circuit, some level of common-mode signal will always be present. When this signal encounters a discontinuity in the reference plane, its return current always tries to find a path to loop around the thing and, in so doing, causes increased radiation. Careful design and planning to avoid discontinuities or to provide return paths for the common-mode are still a very good idea.

The bottom line is this: both single-ended and differential signals cause image currents in their reference planes. Single-ended circuitry usually uses the image currents as the return path. Differential circuitry usually does not. It is not a good idea to ignore discontinuities, but the reasons for this differ for either case.

Balance

To summarize in one word what is needed to optimize any circuit for differential transmission, the word is balance. Balance here means symmetry. A circuit that is truly optimized for the generation, transmission, or reception of differential signals always exhibits very great symmetry.

That symmetry minimizes current variations through the power supply of transmitters and receivers. That symmetry also produces precisely the same, although complementary, voltages and currents out of drivers. In impedance, symmetry of transmission lines produces equal currents in the two complementary signal lines and thereby maximizes field cancellations. Since trace impedances are established by the geometry of the trace, symmetry of geometry—both of the traces and of nearby metal objects—optimizes the trace pair for differential transmission.

One of the difficult symmetries to maintain is electrical length of the two elements of the differential transmission line. Consider two traces on the same routing layer of the circuit board, side by side. Such traces are said to be *edge-coupled*. If, as is often inevitable, the pair must turn a corner for some reason, the outside trace at the corner, as in Figure 6.16, traverses a greater distance than the trace at the inside edge.

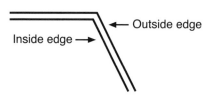

Figure 6.16   A Bend in an Edge-Coupled Pair

Having traversed a greater distance, the electrical signals on the two sides are no longer precisely complementary at any particular point after the corner, as in Figure 6.17. Part of the differential signal has been converted to common-mode signal by the corner. Among the results are increased radiation and increased crosstalk in this section. Another impact is due to the fact that, in a passive system, mechanisms that convert differential to common, equally convert common-mode to differential. As a result, such mechanisms add to the general noise on the wires coupled from noise on the reference planes.

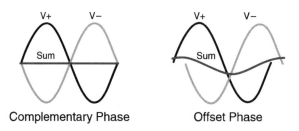

Figure 6.17   Mode Conversion

It is fairly easy to create plots that show this conversion. Just create two sine waves, amplitude one and minus one, and plot them from zero to two-pi. Now to one add a phase offset. A particular frequency has a particular wavelength in your transmission line. That wavelength corresponds to 360 degrees. An offset of, for example, one percent of a wave length between the lengths of the two traces corresponds to 3.6 degrees. Express the offset between the two traces as a portion of the wavelength for a particular frequency. Express that in degrees. Add that as the phase offset to one of the two when the complementary waves are added. The resulting sum shows the common mode conversion caused by that length difference for that frequency.

Conclusion

In the effort to design microwave-frequency interconnects, it is necessary not only to be clear about microwave frequencies, but also to be clear about differential signaling. Differential signaling works fine even without microwave frequencies. Microwave frequencies on circuit boards do not work well at all without differential signaling. Differential signaling yields more benefits than it imposes burdens. It reduces the crosstalk between signals and reduces radiation. At high frequencies, it reduces the number of pins per signal. It also reduces the noise generated inside packages as well as sensitivity of receivers to noise. Most importantly, it greatly increases the data rates that are practical on circuit boards.

Chapter 7

Modeling Issues

N ow it is time to consider some practicalities of how you will actually implement a design that transports data at microwave frequencies. This material will be more of the same old thing in the sense that those who have been working in the lower few hundred megahertz have mostly been analyzing their signal integrity with various SPICE implementations. As you now move into the gigahertz realm, you will still find SPICE the workhorse of signal integrity analysis. You need answers to three questions: When are SPICE simulations valid? What does a simulation tool need to yield good results? And, what do you do with problems that are outside the capabilities of SPICE simulators?

This chapter explores modeling alternatives and issues that cannot be directly resolved by a SPICE simulator, even though it is not yet time to abandon SPICE. Enhance your ability with SPICE tools by learning how to cast problems in terms that SPICE can simulate. The slow field solvers may be correct for some structures, but they can also be used to generate models that are useful in SPICE simulations. The underlying reality is that a simple problem, such as 10 inches of differential trace with a connector in the middle, can be modeled in seconds with SPICE, and can take hours in a 3D full-wave field solver. Real engineers need to be productive; you cannot afford slow tools in cases that don't mandate such.

Time Domain Analysis

Signal integrity engineers have good reasons for preferring to work in the time domain. There is no reason to abandon the time domain now, but there is good reason to add the frequency domain to your areas of competence. First we will concentrate on time domain, later we'll concentrate on frequency domain.

When functions are expressed as a function of time, they are said to be in the *time domain*. Examples are such things as voltage, v(t), or current, i(t). Similarly, an oscilloscope waveform is almost always a time-domain presentation. In SPICE, time-domain analysis is performed by the `.tran` statement. This statement tells the simulator to observe the circuit for some specified amount of time. The simulator is usually initialized at the beginning of this time period with a voltage step or a pulse.

SPICE

Whether recognized or not, SPICE simulators are at the heart of many or most circuit simulators. So the material that is about to be described can be of use to you if you use numerous other circuit simulators in addition to SPICE. A critical requirement of any simulator that qualifies it for use at microwave frequencies is that the simulator absolutely must have the capability of modeling transmission lines with frequency-dependent loss. Frequency-dependent loss is so pervasive at microwave frequencies that any tool without this capability will be of little use.

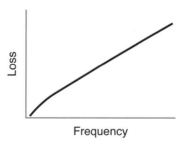

Figure 7.1   A Plot of Frequency-Dependent Loss

Unmodelable Features

Real interconnect circuits have numerous features that circuit simulators simply don't know how to deal with. The presence of such features does not render the simulator useless; rather, it usually means some other tool is needed to translate the feature into language the circuit simulator understands. Such an approach applies to things such as corners, end effects, bends in edge-coupled pairs, and vias.

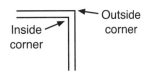

Figure 7.2   A Corner in an Edge-Coupled Pair

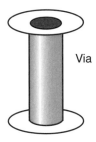

Figure 7.3   A Via

Other features are random in nature and deviate from the ideal characteristics that SPICE presumes. These features, such as roughness and etching variations, are modeled in SPICE only when the simulation deck is intentionally designed to include such characteristics. In some instances, the major loss mechanism is radiation. SPICE simulators do not know about radiation. Finally, there are solutions to Maxwell's equations that do not conform to circuit theory, and, in instances where these *higher order modes* become significant, the accuracy of circuit simulators decreases. The following few paragraphs describe several examples of such features and how they can be accommodated.

Differential and Common Modes

SPICE doesn't inherently understand the differences between and impacts of differential and common modes. If a pair of edge-coupled traces turns a corner, the trace on the outside edge will travel farther than the one on the inside edge. This causes a conversion of some of the differential energy into common-mode energy. This can be partially modeled by adding a section to the transmission line at the point in the model where the bend takes place, but this is only an approximation. In the real physical world, the subsequent trace will radiate energy much worse than did the section where the signals were matched. SPICE will not model this effect. On the other hand, the procedure of adding a section of transmission line for the corner is valid in that the SPICE simulation will likely accurately model the increased crosstalk caused by the added common mode. So it is recommended that this procedure is used.

Recall that a short segment of transmission line often has a disproportionate impact on simulation time. Where segments are short, as this would be, it is much preferable to model the segment as an equivalent L-C section. The equations to do this were presented earlier and will be again later. In this short segment, you can ignore loss.

With any instance where an edge-coupled differential pair is to make a bend, add a small segment of trace to the inside trace to account for the phase shift caused by the bend. It is true that in *broadside-coupled traces* this would not be necessary, but *layer-to-layer registration* is typically too poorly controlled to make broadside practical in commercial printed circuit boards.

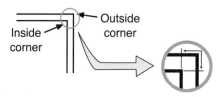

Figure 7.4   Detail of a Corner

At lower frequencies, it was acceptable to equalize line lengths by matching the total length of the net to the required value. At microwave frequencies with differential signaling, this procedure is no longer adequate. A definition is needed to describe the requirements. Define a *feature* as anything in the signal path that is not a simple, straight, isolated, plain old differential pair of traces. Look at Figure 7.5 for examples of features in a typical layout. In traversing a link between two pieces of silicon, there will usually be numerous features, such as packages, corners, vias, perhaps a connector, maybe a passive component like a capacitor. For purposes of this discussion, all these are features. The traces between features are defined as *segments*. So an interconnect consists of segments separated by features. With these definitions, the following statement is made: Within a differential pair, trace lengths are to be adjusted or equalized to maintain precisely complementary phase alignment, also called balancing, of the signals on a segment-by-segment basis. It is not adequate simply to match physical lengths at the end of the link; it is best done segment by segment. This ideal is not always practical in real layouts. Yet, even such a thing as a 90-degree bend in the traces followed a half-inch later by a complementary bend produces significant and easily measurable impact on the signal.

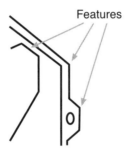

Figure 7.5   Examples of Features

The reason that this careful matching at the segment level is desirable is that now segment lengths are significant compared to wavelengths. The more significant portion of a wavelength means that these segments can become much better antennas radiating the common-mode signal. Similarly, the higher frequency produces much better coupling of the common mode into the *planar waveguides* produced by the reference planes and results in both additional radiation and coupling to the *resonant modes* of that waveguide. As will be detailed later, the common-mode portion of the signal produces crosstalk typically an order-of-magnitude worse than does the differential portion. The simplest way of viewing all this is that common mode is "bad" and differential mode is "good." Avoid making or transporting common mode.

Again, if a small section of transmission line is added to account for each corner, there is an impact on simulation time. Simulation goes much faster if you use an L-C equivalent rather than an actual transmission-line equivalent. The error will be small as long as the length of a segment that is represented by a single L-C segment is less than –one- tenth the wavelength of the highest frequency of interest in the circuit. This frequency will usually be about 1.5 times the data rate. If the data rate is 2.5 gigabits per second, this frequency should be at least 3.75 gigahertz. Wavelength in FR4 at this frequency will be about 1.6 inches, so no segment greater than .16 inch in length should be modeled as a single L-C section for that data rate. In most cases, a simple bend in a differential pair will not add this much trace, so there is no problem. The appropriate values for the elements of the L-C segment are easy to calculate. They derive simply from the two equations:

$$Z_o = \sqrt{\frac{L}{C}}$$

$$v = \frac{1}{\sqrt{LC}} = \frac{1}{\sqrt{\mu\varepsilon}} = \frac{c}{\sqrt{\mu_r \varepsilon_{r_{eff}}}} = \frac{c}{\sqrt{\varepsilon_{r_{eff}}}}$$

Note that stripline fields are totally immersed in the board material, so their effective dielectric constant equals the dielectric constant of the board material. This is not true with microstrip. The effective dielectric constant for microstrip will typically be somewhat less than the dielectric constant of the board because some of the field lines are in air.

That final equation presumes a non-magnetic material—usually a safe presumption in circuit boards. The trick is in selection of the units for the speed of light. The inductance and capacitance in the above formulae are always in terms of *per unit length*. The unit length is established by the units used for the speed of light (*c*) in the above equation. Light travels at about 186,000 miles per second. If you use that value in these equations, the capacitance and inductance will be per mile. A more reasonable light-speed value might be 3*10^10 cm per second.

With a typical dielectric constant for FR4 of about four, the signal velocity would be about half the speed of light. In that case, for a specified characteristic impedance:

$$\frac{1}{\sqrt{LC}} = 1.5 * 10^{10}$$

so :

$$L = \frac{1}{(1.5 * 10^{10})^2 * C}$$

but

$$Z_o = \sqrt{\frac{L}{C}}$$

so :

$$C = \frac{L}{Z_o^2} = \frac{1}{(1.5 * 10^{10})^2 * C Z_o^2}$$

$$C = \frac{1}{1.5 * 10^{10} * Z_o}$$

Recall the capacitance in these equations is capacitance per centimeter of trace. Substitute the capacitance back into the impedance equation to get the inductance. To get the inductance and capacitance values that are used in the SPICE model of the segment, multiply each by the length in centimeters of the desired segment. It is usual to model such a transmission line segment either as two half-inductances with a capacitor to ground in the middle, or two half-capacitances with an inductor between. Three ways that a segment of transmission line can be implemented are shown in Figure 7.6. Though the three act essentially identically at middle frequencies, they act very differently at very high frequencies. If you care whether the circuit presents an open or short at very high frequency, you choose which of the three on that basis. In a SPICE simulation, these models run a lot faster than a short transmission line segment runs.

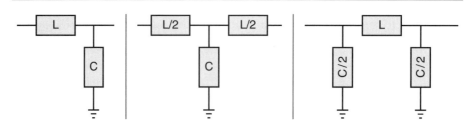

Figure 7.6   Three Ways for an L-C Section

One final comment on this procedure. Although it is simple enough that it could be easily programmed into a spreadsheet, the procedure isn't always quite as simple as has been shown here. In the case of stripline, the dielectric constant is that of the circuit board material, so the procedure is simple. It is simple because the signal velocity can be derived from the relative dielectric constant. Namely, the velocity equals the speed of light divided by the square root of the relative dielectric constant.

In the case of microstrip, it isn't that easy. There, the dielectric constant that you need to use is the *effective dielectric constant* made up partly of air and partly of board. In this case, the method might not work exactly as shown because the effective dielectric constant might not be known. One solution would be to let the simulator calculate the velocity for you and use that calculation with the two fundamental equations. Or, you can find one of the analytic approximation formulae for the values of L and C.

The point of all this is that SPICE simulations often go faster if discreet equivalents are substituted where there are very short sections of transmission line, particularly in the case of lossy transmission lines. Calculating the values of capacitance and inductance that simultaneously yield the right impedance and velocity is easy to do.

Return Paths and Image Currents

SPICE does not know about return paths and image currents. When the frequency of interest was a few megahertz, this was no big deal. When frequencies got up to a few hundred megahertz, it became a big deal. To get good correlation between simulations and measurements, it became necessary to explicitly model the return paths.

SPICE provides a node, zero, that is ground. At low frequencies, this is fine. It makes little difference that node zero at this end of the board is at precisely the same potential as node zero at that end of the board. It makes little difference that the signal into node zero at this end of the board sees absolutely no time delay in getting to that end of the board, as shown in Figure 7.7. At low frequencies, the distance from this end to that end of a board were small enough that the timing differences were imperceptible. They were inconsequential. It takes about two nanoseconds, maybe a little less, for a signal to cross a typical baseboard in a personal computer. The original personal computers had clock cycles that were over 100 times longer than this. Now cycle times are approaching an order of magnitude smaller than this, and the time required to cross a board is very significant. Even the time required for the signal to traverse a package and pin can be significant.

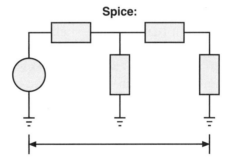

No time delay, no loss, no inductance, etc.

Figure 7.7   SPICE's Ideal World

To accommodate the reality that return paths are a part of the interconnect circuit, the return paths must be modeled in SPICE just as the signal path must be modeled. Unfortunately, the return path is often less conspicuous than is the signal path. As an example of this dilemma, consider an integrated circuit housed in a package with multiple ground pins. The ground pins may be distributed throughout the pin field. Some may be much nearer the signal pin than others. Some may connect through paths inside the silicon or the package that are not made public to the board designer. It has never been easy to generate a really good SPICE model of the return paths for many real circuits.

And now things are going to get even more complicated. Microwave signals respond to capacitances and inductances that are small enough to be nearly immeasurable. At microwave frequencies, components that were intended to be capacitors can look like inductors. Short stubs can look inductive at some frequencies and capacitive at others. SPICE programs can directly handle some effects, others it cannot. Features such as plane-splits and vias cannot be directly modeled in SPICE and so must be simulated in field solvers and then converted into SPICE-compatible formats—usually L-C equivalents. That is not to say that you have to throw your SPICE simulator away when you encounter these features. No, what it means is that you may need another tool to help you generate L-C equivalent models for these features.

Differential Transmission

Most SPICE versions are not optimized for the analysis of serial or differential signals. Certainly serial and differential can be handled by any SPICE simulator, but that is not the same as being optimized for such applications. When you need to measure the differential voltage at a particular point in a circuit, you are not yet likely to find a *"Vdiff"* function in your SPICE simulator. You are going to have to define this by hand. If you want to plot the common-mode signal, again you must define it yourself. Of course now that it is printed in a book, the programmers will put it in.

Differential signaling enables very high data rates on circuit boards. But traditional techniques for controlling skew and for distributing clocks run out of gas at these speeds. The answer is often *embedded clocks* and *de-skewing* inside the silicon. A typical embedded clock is implemented by encoding the data in such a way that there is a guaranteed minimum transition rate, or number of signal edges per unit of time. Then, a phase-locked loop can be used with this data to recover the clock.

In the days of parallel buses, the skew between the data lines and between the data and clock were a major concern. *Skew* is the difference in flight-time for the various individual traces. Even if the lines were all carefully laid out to be exactly the same length, variations in the dielectric constant in the board material caused skew. As bus rates increased, skew became a factor limiting the maximum usable bus rate. The reason was the way data was strobed into the receiver. The parallel data would arrive at each of the bit latches and when all had settled and were stable, the clock or strobe would trigger all the latches simultaneously to capture the data. If some were earlier and some later, all would have to wait for that last bit to be ready. The range of arrival times for the individual bits became a major limiting factor on how fast the bus could ultimately run.

In high-speed serial systems, de-skewing is done electrically rather than mechanically. De-skewing can be done by mechanisms such as measuring the time-offset of each input and selecting a particular clock phase that best matches it. It is fairly easy to generate a range of clock phases to facilitate this. This method in turn necessitates a *circuit training* plan in which the relationship between clock and data can be measured. As the arrival phases of the individual signals are identified, the optimal clock phase for each can be locked in. So, the issue of skew between differential pairs that are not within an individual pair has passed into the realm of non-issue.

Chapter 6 examined differential signaling in detail. Part of the objective was to clarify the concept of differential signaling so that you will be able to handle typical cases using the SPICE program, where a lot of hand manipulation is necessary. The SPICE tool will need help in dealing with differential signaling.

Because perfect components, components with no time delay and no parasytics, come naturally to SPICE, it is very easy to set up a differential driver—two outputs with complementary signals. Of course, there are a few standard warnings. As in any modeling task, be sure to include appropriate parasytics. For example, the tool can quite easily implement a behavioral driver that has no capacitance to ground. In the real world, such a thing will never exist. As is typical of driver models, the important things to get right are the output voltage or current swing, the rise and fall times, the impedance, and the capacitance. In addition, differential drivers have both common-mode and differential impedance, and these can be independent of each other. The point is, take care to get them right.

Differential Receivers

Just as SPICE doesn't inherently recognize differential drivers, neither does it recognize differential receivers. Again, you are typically going to have to build the model. It is fairly easy to do because primitives such as the voltage-controlled voltage source already embody most of the characteristics needed in an ideal differential receiver. All the model needs is appropriate parasytics, termination impedances, capacitance, and so on, and you can use it as your receiver. At this time, non-linearities and dynamic range will not be covered because the target of this book is the interconnect circuitry rather than what goes on inside the silicon.

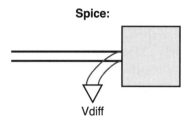

Figure 7.8   A SPICE Ideal Component to Monitor Differential Voltage

Signal level and phase arriving at the receiver are usually critical parameters in any high-speed link. Viewing the differential signal is easily achieved through use of an ideal voltage-controlled voltage source, as in Figure 7.8. In the case of using such a device to monitor a differential signal, all parasytics are left off so that the source produces infinite impedance at the point of measurement, and the gain is usually set to one. As such, it is possible to make measurements in SPICE that cannot be made in the real world. Alternately, many versions of SPICE have the capability to do math on signals, so the differential voltage can simply be defined as an equation. Placement of a physical probe on a line always adds parasytics. At microwave frequencies, the added parasytics, indicated in Figure 7.9, are usually far too large to ignore. That makes it difficult to measure waveforms that exist on the line when the test probe is not present.

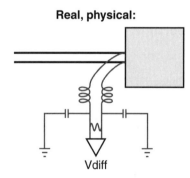

Figure 7.9   Parasytics Added for a Voltage Probe

Two solutions are possible. One is to get or generate a good model of the test probe, and run a simulation with the probe model in place to correlate what is measured with what is there when the probe is not present. An alternate is to use a receiver designed to measure the signal quality at its inputs. A third alternative that actually works well in the frequency domain is to electrically characterize the parts, packages, and so on and calculate the result.

Differential Transmission Lines

Almost everything can be modeled. Recall the "T" line that came with the original SPICE implementations. This was an *ideal transmission line*. It had no loss. When it was used, you did not have to calculate an inductance-capacitance ratio that would yield the desired impedance and velocity; the "T" model made that unnecessary. It simply asked for the desired impedance and delay. That level of support for differential transmission lines does not yet exist in most SPICE tools. Among the parameters that you might like to see in your modeling tool is the ability to accept a transmission line definition in terms of differential and common-mode impedance, loss per unit of distance, and delay. The fact that such facilities as these are not there does not stop you from performing simulations; it merely adds a bit more work to include them by hand.

Of course, eventually all of this work might be bypassed by the enabling of *S*-parameter models in SPICE. Again, in an ideal world you would work entirely in the frequency domain. Components would be characterized by their *S*-parameters, and the response of the entire circuit response would be calculated by applying chaining to the various elements of the interconnect. In this ideal world, circuit simulation would not even be needed. The response would be mathematically generated from measured or simulated frequency domain models—*S*-parameters—and no iterative procedures would be required. Rather than simulation, there would be an extremely fast mathematical procedure.

Unfortunately, that ideal is not the world as it is. The problem is linearity. You cannot presume that the voltage and current sources are linear. They are not. The interconnect circuitry might be reasonably linear, but the silicon at the ends is nonlinear, at least to some degree. That nonlinearity makes it inadequate to examine the response one frequency at a time. The actual response will have interactions between harmonics, and the response will be dependent on the amplitude and phase relationships between the harmonics. It becomes a modulation problem.

But the interconnect, the packages and circuit board traces, are likely to be linear in voltage response. The sort of thing that would make these parts nonlinear would be the presence of magnetic material. Without magnetic material, the parts are linear. That linearity makes it practical to solve the response of the interconnect in the frequency domain using very fast analytic procedures and then add the impact of nonlinear drivers in an iterative, time domain, analysis. The capability of using blocks defined with *S*-parameters in time-domain simulations is just beginning to show up in SPICE tools.

One reason for interest in the frequency domain is this: Time domain simulations often rely on iterative methods and so are relatively slow. Frequency domain solutions can often be achieved through analytic methods and can be extremely fast and not iterative. You can even see this in SPICE. Compare the time it takes SPICE to calculate the time domain response of a moderately complex L-C circuit with the time it takes to do a frequency sweep of the same circuit.

Corners and Bends

Corners and bends are unmodelable in the sense that SPICE does not have built-in mechanisms to deal with them. The handling of a corner in an individual trace is a bit more complicated than the handling of a bend in a differential pair. In the lower gigahertz frequencies, the impact of a corner in a trace is often so much less than the variability of the materials themselves—the manufacturing variables—that corners in traces can often be ignored. A square corner adds a small amount of capacitance; the amount can be calculated with a field solver—not by SPICE. The added capacitance is sometimes the combined effect of added physical area and the reactance of ephemeral modes produced by the corner discontinuity. The usual way of modeling a corner in SPICE is to add a small discreet capacitor at that point in the transmission line, add a small L-C-L segment, or ignore it.

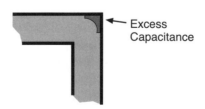

Figure 7.10 Capacitance Added by a Corner

Bends are another issue altogether. Here we are using the word "bend" to refer to a differential pair's corner. The handling of a bend has been already described, but more details may be useful. The main thing that a bend does, but is not recognized by SPICE, is increase emissions. Conversion of some signal to common-mode by a bend can cause loss due to radiation, and SPICE doesn't know about radiation. Usually this is not a major cause of signal loss, but it can be a major cause of emissions.

Planar Waveguide

The region between two metal planes can be described as a planar waveguide. Examples of this type of waveguide, shown in Figure 7.11, exist on most circuit boards in the form of the region between power and ground planes, or the region between multiple ground planes.

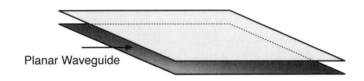

Planar Waveguide

Figure 7.11   A Planar Waveguide

Signals can be injected into this waveguide by applying a current that traverses the distance from one plane to the other. In other words, when the signal passes through a via that traverses this region, as in Figure 7.12, the signal couples into the planar waveguide, as in Figure 7.13. SPICE doesn't know about this. Though this phenomenon can couple resonances to the signal and cause signal problems, it also can usually be easily controlled.

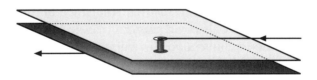

Figure 7.12   A Via Traversing a Planar Waveguide

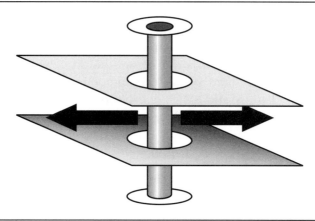

Figure 7.13   Signal Injected into a Planar Waveguide

The cancellation of radiation by the presence of a complementary signal, the other side of the differential pair, significantly reduces the coupling to this waveguide. Radiation into this waveguide is a significant factor in the total loss of a via, and, in the case of a single-ended signal, is the major cause of signal loss. The way to deal with vias is to calculate an appropriate L-C model through use of a field solver and import that model into SPICE.

When a planar waveguide has a lot of vias and holes in it, energy leaks out or is extracted fast enough that its probability of becoming resonant is low. However, if the waveguide has few holes and vias, it can become resonant. This can cause a problem. The mechanism that couples your signal's energy into the waveguide also couples energy out of the waveguide. The mechanism that converts part of your differential signal to common mode also converts common mode to differential energy. The end result of this chain is that if you have a plane that goes resonant, you are likely to see that resonance in the differential characteristics of the link. This is yet another reason why you need to take care to minimize mode conversions by maintaining symmetry within your differential pair, as much as you can.

Plane-Splits

As with many other things examined above, SPICE does not know about plane splits, shown in Figure 7.14. Signal integrity and the emissions impact will require a different tool if you are concerned. Emissions apply primarily to the common-mode component of a signal. The signal-integrity impact can be modeled by treating the gap as a *pi-network* of capacitors. But the value of the capacitors is found through use of a field solver. This is not too severe a problem if this rule is followed: never cross a plane-split with any high-speed signal.

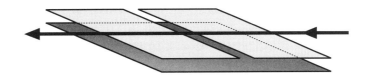

Figure 7.14 A Signal Crossing a Plane Split

On the other hand, the impact of a narrow, say 10-mil wide gap, on the signal integrity of a differential signal is not going to be very significant. If the particular design is such that emissions is not a big concern, crossing plane splits is not too big a concern either. One approach that can be used is to assign some penalty to crossing a plane-split and use that as a criterion to help minimize the number of plane-split crossings. That is, tell the architects and the layout guys that each plane split is equivalent to reducing the overall useful trace length by an inch. With features such as plane splits and vias, it is very hard to predict the precise impact. They will increase loss, crosstalk, and emissions—but how much? Assigning an overall equivalent impact, such as claiming an overall usable distance reduction of an inch per, helps clarify the need to minimize such features in a high-speed pair. In some designs, this might be overstating the fact. In others it might not.

Vias

A via has two main impacts at high frequencies: it can cause signal loss through injection to the planar waveguide and it can act as a resonant stub at microwave frequencies. The coupling to the planar waveguide is linearly proportional to frequency; that is why this phenomenon may not have been noticed by those working in the lower few hundreds of megahertz. As frequency increases, it becomes a much more serious issue. Again, a major advantage of differential signaling is that differential energy is far less impacted by this than is common-mode. When a differential signal traverses a planar waveguide through symmetrical and closely-spaced vias, it is almost exclusively the common-mode component that loses energy to the waveguide.

A good side to this is if a single-ended signal has to traverse the waveguide, and if the two planes are at the same potential, insert a second via near the signal, using it to short the two planes together. Image current will flow through the shorting via and largely cancel the fields of the signal via. Losses will decrease. Surprisingly, this works even with differential signals. Adding a shorting via will decrease loss in the signal vias.

A fairly good model of a via can be constructed by R-L-C components where there is capacitor for each surface and reference plane, and an inductor for each region between. Such models can even be constructed with reasonable accuracy through use of lookup tables. Of course, the entries in the lookup table are calculated with a field solver. Such a model may not show the impact of shorting vias, or their absence, but it can show the impact of resonant stubs in the via.

Electrostatic Discharge

It has already been pointed out that SPICE knows nothing about electromagnetic radiation. Neither does it know anything about electrostatic discharge (ESD). ESD typically involves non-linear phenomena and, though they can be modeled, they are seldom included in models designed for signal integrity applications. There is a very high significance for signal integrity in one aspect of ESD. Pins that are designed to withstand ESD typically do so through the use of current shunting devices, often diodes. These components typically add significant capacitance to the protected pin. That capacitance shows up in circuit models as a value in parallel with the termination resistor. This capacitance is often the biggest problem preventing really good values of return loss in microwave frequency ports. In typical systems, the better the ESD protection, the more capacitance. Because of this, very high speed ports often have very poor ESD protection. You need to keep this in mind whenever you handle these devices.

Modelable Features

Having covered a list of items that are not particularly well handled by typical implementations of SPICE, you now get the other side. Don't get the idea that nothing works in circuit solvers at microwave frequencies. A lot does work. As pointed out above, there are things that cannot be handled without the aid of field solvers, but the idea is to characterize features with the aid of the field solver, translate that characterization into lumped models that SPICE can deal with, and then do the signal integrity work with the SPICE tool. Any time such a translation is made, there is a frequency range wherein those models are valid. Any time such a model is generated, it should also have the frequency range of applicability specified.

Again, I want to emphasize that there are numerous tools—circuit solvers—which, at heart, are versions of SPICE. The one critical property that such a tool absolutely needs if it is to be useful at microwave frequencies, is the ability to work accurately with transmission lines that have frequency-dependent loss. Without this capability, it is very difficult to get useful information out of a simulation. That is not to say that without such capability you are not going to be able to work with microwave frequencies; rather, without that capability, reconcile yourself to working with some tool other than SPICE.

Frequency Dependent Loss

Frequency-dependent loss (FDL) is due primarily to two factors: *copper loss* and *dielectric loss*. The word "primarily" is used intentionally. Other sources, such as EMI, are important, even very important, from some perspectives. But, for the signal integrity modeling of transmission lines, these two are what will be covered by the description of frequency-dependent loss.

Numerous of the factors impacting the signal available at the receiver are functions of frequency. Examples are radiation reflections and crosstalk, all of which SPICE can be really good at. But these are not included in the meaning assigned here. Here, the words "frequency-dependent loss" mean resistive losses in the copper and dielectric losses. In fact, signal available at the receiver is often described in terms of *eye opening*, a concept that will be described later. In that sense, even crosstalk can be a major contributor to signal loss. But all that is yet to come. If you needed something to look forward to, there it is. For now, you need details about copper and dielectric losses.

Copper Loss

Copper has resistive loss as does any conductor. At high frequencies, the internal inductance of conductors pushes the current to the outer surfaces; this effect, shown in Figure 7.15, is called *skin effect*.

HF Current Distribution

Figure 7.15 Skin Effect

This phenomenon decreases the effective area available for current flow and so increases the effective resistance. It is as if there is only a thin layer on the surface of the conductor that is involved in high-frequency current flow, and the thickness of this layer is called the *skin depth*. As with many physical constants, mathematical operators, and similar scientific things, skin depth is designated by the Greek delta symbol.

$$\delta = \frac{1}{\sqrt{\pi f \mu \sigma}}$$

In this equation, pi has its usual meaning, 3.14 and so on, *f* is the frequency in Hertz, mu is the magnetic constant—usually that of free space, except when not—and sigma is the conductivity of the metal. In this list, the one that is often overlooked is mu. In copper, gold, silver, and such metals, the relative magnetic constant is unity so that of free space is correct. In metals such as nickel and iron, the relative magnetic constant can be very high. If you want to generate a low-loss conductor for microwave frequencies, magnetic materials are a poor choice. On the other hand, if you really want to have a lot of loss, such as in a chassis, iron might be a really good choice.

The loss due to skin-effect is high at microwave frequencies. Increasing the value of sigma can reduce it. If gold is substituted for copper, this loss will decrease by a couple percent. On the other hand, the loss is inversely proportional to the circumference of the conductor, so increasing the conductor size by a few percent can do the same. Decide for yourself which to do—which makes better economic sense for your design.

The current density decreases exponentially with depth in the conductor. The meaning of skin depth is that it is the equivalent depth if the current were evenly distributed in that skin layer. It is used to calculate the effective resistance of the conductor for a particular frequency.

As an aside, consider what might happen if the skin depth is larger than the thickness of the conductor. Consider this in the context of a reference plane. Fields will be attenuated, but not blocked, by the conductor. Can this be a problem? Consider one more situation. Your board has a switching regulator mounted on it. That regulator is running at 70 or 80 kilohertz and switching tens of amps. It is a very bad idea, a *very* bad idea, to run a signal trace under the switching transistor, even though there may be a reference plane between.

In printed circuit boards, conductor thickness is usually a constant, so loss in a trace is strongly dependent on trace width. If the impedance is to be maintained, increasing trace width requires greater dielectric thickness. That dependency often means that the total thickness of the board stackup is strongly related to the trace loss, and so can strongly influence the maximum frequency that can be transported a specified distance on a circuit board.

Although dielectric loss increases at a faster rate than does copper loss and at high enough frequencies becomes the dominant material loss, copper loss never becomes negligible. Dielectric loss is sometimes regarded as the only loss that counts. This is a mistake. In real circuitry, total loss is made up of numerous contributors and, while dielectric loss can become a major contributor at frequencies of one or more gigahertz, it is never the sole contributor. In fact, when package losses, impedance mismatches, connector losses, passives, and copper loss are all accounted for, dielectric loss seldom even contributes the majority of the loss.

Copper loss comes not only from the bulk resistivity of the copper, it also comes from surface roughness and from other materials used at the surface of the copper. Sometimes the copper has a solder plating on it—note that solder has a resistivity about five times higher than copper. Tin plating is often used. Tin has much higher resistivity than copper. When a fiberglass core is made, often the copper is roughened and coated with copper oxide to increase adhesion. That is unfortunate, but needed. It is always advisable to remove any metal coatings, except perhaps gold, that are not absolutely required for reliable manufacturing of the board. In short, make it as good as you can, but not better.

Dielectric Loss

In dielectrics, the relative dielectric constant is thought to be due to such things as the physical distortion of molecules, the reorientation of molecules, the changing of the shape of electron orbits, etc., as shown in Figure 7.16. Each case has a stimulus and a response.

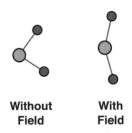

Without   **With**
Field   **Field**

Figure 7.16   Molecules in an Electric Field

In such systems, the response always lags the stimulus by some amount. The lag in response shows up in vector representations of the dielectric constant as an imaginary part. When calculating the response of the system to fields through this dielectric, the imaginary part of the dielectric constant shows up as a loss. It is typical that the delay in field response is somewhat constant. That is, the dielectric response to the imposed field lags by a small, fixed amount of time. In this case, the relationship between the real and imaginary parts of the dielectric response vector is linearly dependent on frequency of the imposed field. Thus, dielectric loss is approximately linearly dependent on frequency.

The dielectric loss is often specified by the angle of the dielectric vector, illustrated in Figure 7.17. The tangent of this angle—that is, the tangent equal to the imaginary part divided by the real part of the dielectric constant—is often published as the loss factor for the dielectric.

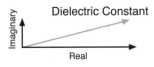

Figure 7.17   The Dielectric Constant

In another feat of scientific innovation, the ratio itself is designated by the Greek lower-case delta symbol. This is done, presumably, to maximize the probability of confusing the dielectric loss with the skin depth. Of course, there is no relationship between the two, but why miss such a golden opportunity to generate confusion? The dielectric loss factor is thus designated *tan-delta*, which delta is symbolically identical to the skin depth, but is physically unrelated in any way.

*in FR*4:

$$\tan \delta \cong 0.02$$

At low frequencies and in practical materials, copper loss dominates and dielectric loss is safely ignored. Depending on geometry, at moderate frequencies of about one gigahertz in FR4, dielectric loss catches up and becomes about equal to copper loss. At higher frequencies, dielectric loss dominates. The dominance of dielectric loss does not mean that copper loss has gone away. It is still there. It still is increasing as frequency increases. You will occasionally encounter the idea that changing the board material to one of the *low-loss materials* will reduce signal loss by an amount equal to the improvement in dielectric loss. This of course is far from true. To see for yourself, simulate your total link, silicon to silicon, and vary only the dielectric loss parameter.

When you are looking for a SPICE simulator capable of dealing with frequency-dependent loss, one choice is the W element available in HSPICE. This is not intended to be an endorsement of HSPICE, but rather a simple statement that it is an option, and it appears to work. Other options also appear to work; not all include the word "SPICE" in their names. The advantage of tools that include that word in their names is that they tend to be fairly standard in the code format that they accept. Other tools have other advantages and, as usual, you need to choose the tool that fits the job.

Drivers and Receivers

From the perspectives of circuit simulators, all drivers are essentially the same. Circuitry will vary, but it makes little difference to the circuit simulator whether that circuit is outputting microwave signals or lower frequencies. My own bias is to simplify drivers and receivers through use of ideal sources surrounded by appropriate parasytics whenever possible. The advantage of this method is that it typically runs a couple orders of magnitude faster in SPICE than do transistor-level models. Of course, some refuse to believe that this method could ever generate acceptable accuracy. To them I point out that even the transistors in the transistor-level models are themselves parametric models. Useful models are sometimes as simple as the one depicted here in Figure 7.18, but often need to be substantially more complex.

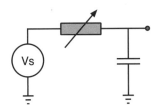

Figure 7.18 My Favorite Driver Model

Certainly there are cases where there is no choice available other than running the transistor-level circuitry. But avoid doing so when possible. Whether at microwave frequencies or not, these complicated circuits cause numerous problems in trying to get a simulation running. Such models are often automatically generated from the layouts of the driver or receiver circuit. When so generated, they often are found to include component arrangements that are physically possible but cannot be handled by SPICE. Most common is the situation where a node joins three capacitors, and nothing else. The DC solution at this node is indeterminate, so SPICE will fail.

It is my recommendation that a vendor should never release a SPICE model that has not been verified functional in a real simulation, and a customer should never accept such a model. Getting back to the real world, if you are stuck with such a model, the only choice may be to go through it line-by-line and modify it so it will work. Take that three-capacitor node and add a ten-meg resistor to ground.

Packages

At microwave frequencies, packages cannot be ignored. Nor is it likely to be adequate to model a package pin as a simple inductor or even a capacitor and inductor. The length and crosstalk of the trace in the package coupled, with the tolerance of the termination presumably on the chip, will result in a frequency-dependent impedance at the pins of the connector. An optimized board interconnect has to, absolutely must, include these factors. It would not be as bad if the termination could be relied on as being purely resistive, but the pin capacitance at the silicon will typically, at the very least, be significant, and sometimes even the dominant impedance at the high-frequency end of the spectrum. Also, crosstalk in the package will sometimes be a significant factor.

Even though signal characteristics may well be specified at the pin at the point where the package meets the board, it is not adequate to specify impedance as a single number at that point. Optimized board design will require that the impedance either be explicitly defined as a function of frequency, or be implied by specifying a transmission line model for the package.

Significant problems can occur when generating a model of a package. You might rely solely on simulations, but the real physical entity might not really hit the mark chosen for the simulation. Simulations are great tools, but measured values make a better basis for a working model. Note that there is not exactly universal agreement on that last statement, but authors get to state their opinion. The design of the package will have made good use of simulations, but the final characterization of the physical part should be based on measurement. Two measurements are available: time domain (TDR) and frequency domain (NA). In either case, SPICE models will usually be the translation of these into some form of transmission line model. This can be done by something such as the application of the peeling algorithm. If you are using such a model, you have the easy job. If you are the one who must generate this model, you probably already know that you have the hard job. The special mechanical requirements of packages make the use of field solvers unavoidable in many cases. Often the physical size requirements force the use of very thin conductors and result in the accompanying high loss. Mechanical requirements placed on the reference planes often result in geometries that cannot be accommodated by the 2D field solvers found in many signal integrity tools.

Recall that Figure 7.6 showed a lumped element transmission line model, and a single section was deemed adequate because the section was physically short. In the case of packages, the transmission lines are often not short enough to model with a single section. If you try to model a transmission line that is too long as a single lumped section, you'll get substantial errors at high frequencies. This can easily be seen by SPICE frequency sweeping the model with a single and with multiple sections. To model a line with n sections, simply calculate the inductance and capacitance values for a single section, then divide those values by n; repeat the section n times. Recall that knowledge of the dielectric constant and impedance of a line is adequate to calculate the inductance and capacitance per unit length. Scale those values to the actual length of the segment that is to be modeled.

I modeled an inch-long segment of transmission line with one, two, and three segments. The frequency response, shown in Figure 7.19, of each look good up to about a gigahertz. By the time you get to two gigahertz, the one-segment model begins looking inadequate. By the time you get to five, only the three-segment case looks usable. This illustrates the impact of using too few segments to model a section of transmission line for a particular range of frequency.

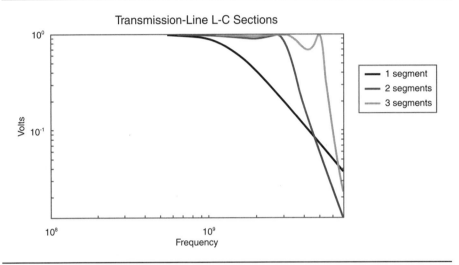

Figure 7.19 Three L-C models

Reference was previously made to a rule sometimes called the tenth-wavelength rule. It says something like, "Always keep segment size in your models at most a tenth wavelength of the highest frequency you are concerned about." Examination of Figure 7.19 can show just how much error would result from relaxing this rule in this case.

Let me climb onto my soap box: It is no worse to violate a rule of thumb than it is to use it without understanding what it does for you. Rules of thumb save us a lot of time. If used intelligently, they can even promote good engineering.

Breakouts

Breakouts, the circuitry that interfaces the package or connector to the circuit board, are problematic. The realities of snaking a trace through a pin field, or attaching a connector to a pad, often force significant deviations from the ideal geometries and impedances desired for the traces.

At microwave frequencies, the first half inch or so of trace can easily account for the majority of the near-end crosstalk. This much trace can easily be entirely in the breakout region. The breakout region is best treated as a distinct entity when you do your modeling.

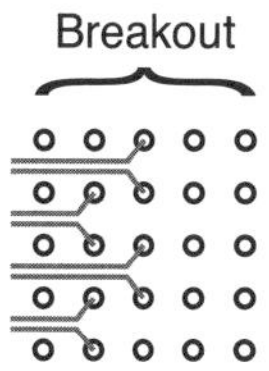

Breakout

Figure 7.20   The Break-Out Under a BGA

Sometimes the electrical characteristics of the package or connector itself are significantly influenced by the details of the breakout. In such cases, it makes sense to include some or all of the breakout on the circuit board as part of the package or connector, including it in the package or connector model. It makes little sense, for example, to characterize a connector that mandates use of a through-hole via of some size, without including that via in the characterization of the connector. The problem with this is that the model may then need to include a board-thickness parameter in some way.

For reasons of cost, packages are tending to finer pitches and closer spacings. At the same time, higher frequencies and the attendant greater losses call for wider traces. It is often found that traces in breakout regions simply cannot meet impedance, loss, and crosstalk characteristics desired for the rest of the board. In simulations, it is necessary to optimize the breakouts and then choose the remaining interconnect to accommodate what is left of the interconnect budgets. That is, it is much easier to limit crosstalk in the long trace run across the board than it is to do so on the breakout region. It is much easier to hit the precise desired impedance out in that open space than it is in the very confined regions of the breakout.

Interconnects

The interconnect circuit is the entire assembly of features and traces that connect a transmitter to a receiver, as seen in Figure 7.21. This often involves numerous discontinuities and variations that are difficult to reliably deal with in hand calculations. The sections above describe how to calculate impedance as a function of distance from a discontinuity, how to calculate the cumulative effect of multiple discontinuities, and how to do all sorts of things by hand. SPICE simulators do an excellent job of dealing with all those things for you.

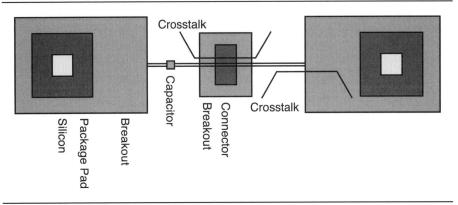

Figure 7.21   A Typical Interconnect Design

Having been told that, do not conclude that all the mathematical derivations have been for nothing. Without understanding the mathematics and physics behind what is happening, you would have no idea of how to make improvements when SPICE says that the interconnect link is broken. You may have little interest in working with things like hyperbolic functions to determine the impedance at a position in the line, when SPICE can do it easily. But now you know how it works and will have ideas of what to do when SPICE says your link is busted.

In modeling the interconnect, it is important to recognize that, unless you take steps to overcome it, all simulations treat the world as ideal. The transmission line in the simulator does not randomly vary in width. The transmission line doesn't encounter regions of varied dielectric constant as traces on FR4 really do. In a simulation, unless you intentionally model the variations, everything is beautifully perfect—and not very realistic.

Connectors

Connectors are a real challenge for measurements and modeling. But that is starting to sound like a mantra by now. What isn't a real challenge? The dominant thing you need to know about connectors is that they often will be major locations of crosstalk in the link. Assume you choose a connector that matches your line impedances. It is typical for the crosstalk of connectors to have a bigger impact on signal integrity at microwave frequencies than loss in the connector has. Never consider using a particular connector if its crosstalk is not well specified. Don't settle for statements such as a connector has such-and-such percent crosstalk. Drill down and find out what that statement really means. It is fairly easy to get good crosstalk from a single aggressor signal or a slow rise time. But what is needed is the total sum of the contributions of all nearby signals at an appropriate rise time or frequency range. Take a look at Figure 7.22. In some geometries there can be many more than just one or two aggressors coupling into a particular pin or pin-pair. You can't really blame a vendor if all they give you are accurate numbers, but not necessarily the numbers you need.

Figure 7.22   A Connector with Multiple Crosstalk Aggressors

If it is necessary to model this connector in a system simulation, who will provide the model and what type of model will it be? Every model for any device has a limited range of accuracy. Questions you need to ask about connector models include over what frequency range is the model accurate and what level of accuracy does it provide in that frequency range? Also understand the conditions under which the model is characterized. There have been cases where board features that were absolutely required for the connector were not included in the model because they made the connector performance look worse. A useful model is a model that accurately represents how the device will perform in a real application. Real applications often use board-to-board connectors actually mounted on boards.

Another aspect of connector selection you need to think about is the physical length of the path through the connector. Consider modeling an ideal lossless connector in SPICE. The only parameter you need to vary in this model is the length of the connector. As an example, make the impedance of the path through the model exactly 50 ohms. In a real implementation, the circuits that go to this connector may target 50-ohm impedance too, but there will be a real-world tolerance. So model the line in and out of the connector as 45 ohms and terminate both ends at 45. Now run frequency sweeps at various physical lengths in the connector.

If you do this experiment, what you will see is that the connector, even with ideal lossless lines, acts something like a low-pass filter. And you will see that the knee frequency depends on the length of the connector.

Cables

Cables are not all that different from what has been already covered. Losses in cables tend to be substantially less than in FR4. Some really good cables are out there, but even the mediocre ones that are practical for use in consumer electronics are really good compared to FR4. Expect losses in cables to be in the range of cable loss-per-meter equal to FR4 loss-per-inch. If microwave cabling is new to you, you should know some things. The first goes something like this: if you name a loss figure, a cable can be found that can meet it. This fact, that exceedingly wideband and low-loss cables exist, is not really relevant to the design of circuitry for consumer applications. It is not an exaggeration to state cables that cost over $1,000 per meter are readily available. I have some in my lab. For their application, they are the right choice. Their application is definitely not consumer electronics. The $600 and the $30 per meter cables also have valid reasons for existence. In consumer applications, what you need are the cables that are closer to the dollar-or-less per meter items. These too exist. In these, the connectors on the ends may cost more than the cable material itself. The nemesis of the engineer with a cable need is the vendor who claims to have a cable that solves all those problems, but the price isn't stated.

Besides that, one of the major differences between cable and trace is that it is quite difficult to get really good length matching on the individual conductors in a cable. As the number of pairs in a cable increase, this problem becomes worse. In traces on the board, matching lengths is fairly easy and matching velocities more difficult. In cables, matching lengths is the more difficult proposition. It sometimes is also useful to note that the common-mode impedance in a cable may be very different than that on the circuit board. This can be true even though both have precisely the same differential impedance.

It is significant to note that cables can present very severe ESD problems. Those center conductors in cables can sometimes support thousands of volts of charge. The *human body ESD model* includes a 1,500-ohm series resistor. But when that cable plugs in, the series resistance is in milli-ohms. So, at least in the lab, always put a terminator on a cable to discharge it before plugging it into your equipment. It is a good idea to lose sleep at night, figuring out how this will be handled by consumers if you have a cable that goes outside your chassis.

The same frequency-dependent-loss transmission lines that were used to model traces are used to model cables in SPICE. Of course, the loss tangents are quite different.

An interesting phenomenon has shown up in cable assemblies designed to meet specific interconnect standards. When the maximum loss allowed for a cable at a specific frequency is specified, all cables, independent of length, tend to have that loss. Consider a cable of some length and loss, cut it in half, and the measured loss will now also be cut in half. That is not what is happening here. When all else is the same, the cable loss tends to decrease as the cable diameter is increased; the cable cost increases as the cable diameter increases. If the maximum loss is specified, the manufacturer minimizes cost by decreasing cable diameter, increasing cable loss to the specified limit. So it is that in this circumstance, cable diameter tends to decrease as length decreases, rather than cable loss decreasing as length decreases.

Crosstalk in differential cables, both quad construction and twin-ax construction, illustrated in Figure 7.23, is typically dominated by the connectors. If the cable length is doubled, the crosstalk does not double, it may even show very little increase. Often an important cable parameter is the quality of the shielding. Again, it is possible for the connectors to make major contributions to EMI. If there was no common-mode signal entering the cable, radiation would not be a significant problem, but since cable lengths are difficult to match and connectors are not perfect, common mode can be generated by the cable connectors themselves.

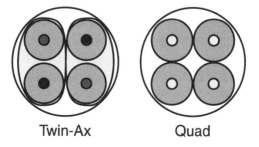

Figure 7.23 Quad and Twin-Ax Cable Constructions

Modeling Philosophy

At the beginning of the book, I said that engineers make poor philosophers and that there would intentionally be no philosophy in this book. By now you have read a fair chunk of this thing and suspect that sometimes I lie. With that said, it is time to plunge into philosophy, to boldly go where everybody else has gone before. And that philosophy is: how to model your circuit.

Monte Carlo

In a microwave interconnect, there are numerous segments of trace separated by features, passive components, connectors, vias, and such things. Each of these is likely to introduce new degrees of freedom. Each is likely to have an independent range of key parameters that characterize the feature or thing. The simplest simulation is one in which each parameter is set to its typical value, and a single run is made to determine the performance of the link. This is the simplest and always the right place to start. A link that does not work with typical values is broken. The next step is to model with variations of the parameters. Every parameter that is not fixed in value will have a maximum, typical, and minimum value. In most cases, it is not clear which combinations of parameters will result in the overall best or overall worst case. There are various strategies that can be used to try to identify the best or worst cases. One strategy that is often used is to run a large number of Monte Carlo simulations. After these are completed, the results are evaluated and you run another even longer simulation. You evaluate the output parameters of the run. If there is a significant change in the evaluation, repeat the procedure until no further significant change takes place.

This method has a few problems. One is that it gives no guarantee that the worst case or best case has actually been found. Another is that it can involve a very large number of runs of the simulation. Finally, perhaps the biggest problem is that it does not inherently include any indication of what to try next. A bunch of runs were made and perhaps the link is demonstrated marginal. What specific variables, changed in what direction, are likely to improve the result?

An advantage of Monte Carlo simulations is that they automatically generate the variations that are simulated. When you set up tests by hand, there seems to be a tendency to favor some scenarios and ignore some that are thought unlikely to happen. Yet, it could very well be that the failure takes place under a scenario that was ignored. Monte Carlo methods can help avoid this inasmuch as they are not likely to have the pre-conceived notions that people have.

Experiment Design

An alternative is to operate in a more systematic manner. Plan experiments that allow you to minimize the number of runs needed to calculate the sensitivity of the output parameters to variations of input parameters. When the sensitivities have been calculated, they can be used in a maximization or minimization problem to solve for the likely best or worst cases. This approach also directly yields information as to what parameter changes are likely to best improve the output.

Note that this line of approach usually presumes that the parameters interact in a fairly consistent and predictable manner. It has more difficulties when something happens that you didn't expect. An interaction that was modeled by a linear equation may change drastically if, for example, a resonance comes along. It is this type of event, the unexpected resonance, that Monte Carlo is more likely to catch. A good compromise is to start simulations with a few Monte Carlo runs, and then shift to the curve-fitting methods to refine the design.

Communications Theory

In testing a data link, often a significant issue is the *inter-symbol interference*. In fact, at high data rates, this interference often becomes the limiting factor establishing the maximum data throughput. The mechanism is the result of the previous data bit not having totally settled before the current data bit begins. This causes the waveform of the current data bit to be somewhat dependent on the previous data bit. The previous data bit was dependent on the one that preceded it, and so on. When an effort is made to achieve the absolute maximum data throughput on a link, the speeds can be such that the current waveform could be dependent on data patterns that extend back dozens of bits. In this case, a common response of the signal integrity engineer is to measure the response to numerous variations of data patterns and search for worst-case conditions.

There is an alternative to this, and that is to measure the pulse response, as shown in Figure 7.24, of the interconnect circuit and calculate the worst-case response. Consider for example, a pulse that is one unit interval wide in time. This pulse settles to a steady-state condition in some number of additional unit intervals. If the transmission medium—the circuit board—is mathematically linear, as it probably is, then the voltage at any point in time is the sum of the present response and the time-shifted responses of all the previous pulses.

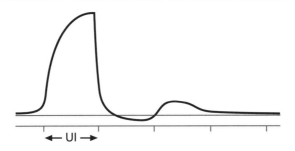

Figure 7.24   Pulse Response

When the negative parts of all previous pulses are added up and combined with the current pulse, as depicted in Figure 7.25, the result is the worst case of minimum height for the current time interval—the worst case one. Similarly, if the positive parts of the pulse response for all previous pulses, not including the pulse itself, are added to a zero that takes place in the current interval, the result is the worst-case low level that can be achieved—the worst case zero.

The point is that judicious use of the information describing an isolated pulse can yield the worst-case high, the worst-case low, and even the worst-case data pattern for a particular link. This information can be a powerful tool in the analysis of a link. In practice, you would perform a SPICE simulation of an isolated pulse and save the data in a file. You would then write a script in your favorite computer language to divide the response into unit intervals of time and add the appropriate portions together.

Advantages of this method are that it can eliminate numerous SPICE runs searching for worst-case patterns, and it yields a waveform that can be confidently identified as worst case.

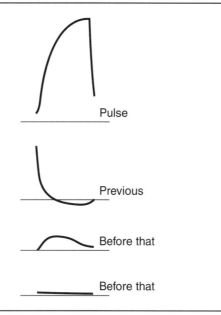

Pulse

Previous

Before that

Before that

Figure 7.25 History of Responses

Impulse Response

The response of a system to a pulse that is of unit area and infinitely short in time is called the *impulse response* of the system. This is not to be confused with the pulse response. The impulse response is only of mathematical significance and so is very important in some applications. Particularly, the inverse Fourier transform of the S11 data yields the reflected impulse response of the system, or at least the impulse response limited by the bandwidth of the data in frequency domain.

Step Response

Summing all the samples of the impulse response yields the step response of the system. This one is of more significance, in that it is measurable in real laboratories with real test equipment. Time domain reflectometry (TDR) looks at the step response of a system. Some people say that the pulse response of a system can be obtained from the step response by delaying a second copy of the step response one unit interval of time, then subtracting from the step response, as in Figure 7.26. This is almost true.

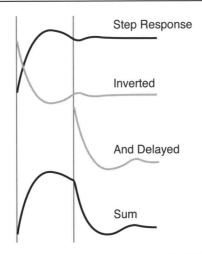

Step Response

Inverted

And Delayed

Sum

Figure 7.26   Step Response to Pulse Response

Why, you ask, is it 'almost' true? Well, it would be true if the driver had the same strength, edge rate, and so on, in both the positive and negative directions. In a real application, it makes sense to account for these differences. But for the passive part of the interconnect itself, the assertion will be true.

Worst-Case Response

So this is the recommendation for the way to obtain good confidence that actual worst-case signals are really identified and to do so without excessive simulations: Simulate the pulse response and mathematically manipulate it to extract worst-case-eye measurements. Examine the pulse response; make sure you get the entire pulse response, not just the first few unit intervals. Divide it into unit intervals according to the pulse-width of the data of interest to you and calculate worst-case responses by addition of the appropriate sections of the response.

This procedure is valid as long as the transmission medium is linear, allowing total response to be validly characterized as the sum of its parts. In the drivers and receivers themselves, in the silicon, this may not be valid. But in the interconnect circuitry, it probably will be valid. The dielectrics are not likely to vary in value as a function of voltage. The copper resistance is not likely to be voltage sensitive to any significant degree. The most likely place to find an amplitude dependency in a passive circuit is in a magnetic component. Though microwave magnetic components exist in forms such as isolators and circulators, they tend to be narrow band and are not much use in circuits of interest here. Similarly, isolation transformers are occasionally used at lower data rates but are not particularly practical for consumer electronics in the microwave frequency ranges.

Spreadsheets and Mathematics Software

Much of the above work can be very nicely done in mathematics packages such as Matlab or Octave. Much can even be done in such simple and inexpensive tools as spreadsheets. A spreadsheet program that can output a text file can even be used to write code for the SPICE simulator. An advantage of this type of approach is that input parameters for the simulation can be conveniently grouped and displayed. Comments can be added; calculations can be made. This is not to say that much of this cannot be done by directly writing the SPICE code, but often it cannot be done as well. When a particular code file is viewed and inputted to SPICE, it is seldom conveniently readable. It is organized to be read by the machine rather than by a human. A spreadsheet interface makes it convenient to organize material for viewing by humans. Colors can be used to group and designate particular types of data. Boxes are available to further organize it. Fonts and highlighting add further clarity. These things are not available in the SPICE file. Tastes vary. You may prefer a version of Basic, C, or even Perl.

Sometimes we get the idea that we are stuck with the user interfaces provided with our simulators. Often these are not all that good. The programmer that is very skilled at writing a particular type of simulator is likely not going to be very good at writing user interfaces. Sometimes the analysis mode that is required or desired for a particular problem is not available in the user interface at all. Many SPICE implementations won't display an eye diagram without a whole lot of work. You don't have to be limited by the limitations of the user interface. Import the data to an alternative tool and display it there. Use Matlab, a spreadsheet, or Perl; write a short C program. Similarly, most SPICE implementations provide very limited facilities for generating serial bit streams. It is not difficult to write a script that writes the code to generate a specific or a quasi-random bit-stream in SPICE.

Frequency Domain Analysis

Though long experience with time-domain analysis has made many of us prefer that domain, there are very good reasons to also be competent in the frequency domain. The most obvious advantage is measurement capabilities. In the frequency domain, measurements can be made over a dynamic range of about 80 to over a 100 decibels. The high end of frequency available for typical network analyzers is in the range of 20 to 50 gigahertz. By comparison, the time domain reflectometer is capable of about a 30-decibel dynamic range and about 6-gigahertz equivalent frequency response.

Conversions between Frequency and Time Domains

In Chapter 2, methods to convert between frequency domain and time domain were presented. The main procedure in this conversion, is the Fourier transform and its inverse. These are usually implemented in the form of the fast Fourier transform, FFT, and its inverse, the IFFT. These are not perfect tools inasmuch as they make the presumption that the data being analyzed is actually a portion of a repetitive wave and that presumption introduces undesired artifacts. Dealing with those artifacts sometimes requires procedures that are unpalatable to purists. It was suggested that faking data could be made more palatable by assigning an alternative name—completing the data set—to the procedure.

In this section, applications and uses of frequency domain data will be discussed. There are some aspects of frequency domain data that are so obvious that, when you see the graphs, you will immediately recognize the utility of this data format. After all, there is no inherent information in the one format that isn't present in the other. It is just that different uses benefit from the particular manner of information presentation.

Why Frequency Domain?

I've already explained that measurements in the frequency domain can be made with great precision, dynamic range, and frequency range. These are adequate reasons to justify getting familiar with the frequency domain. There are additional benefits from working in the frequency domain. The frequency domain can be very powerful in projecting or extrapolating characteristics beyond the bounds of measurements, as in Figure 7.27. Of course, if there is a resonance just outside the range you measured, this can get you in trouble, too. Frequency is also the natural domain for studying the quality and range of applicability of models.

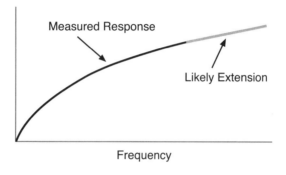

Figure 7.27   Projecting the Frequency Response

Measurability

Consider the possibility of designing a better time-domain reflectometer. Presume that you are given the task of designing a TDR that can match the performance of a relatively inexpensive network analyzer. For example, a network analyzer that measures out to 20 gigahertz, with a dynamic range of 80 decibels. The first task will be to design a step generator that can deliver a 25-picosecond rise-time step to its test head. The frequency-dependent loss that will be present in the interconnect between the physical step generator circuitry, and the actual test point will likely require that the step generator be capable of internal rise-time of 10 or fewer picoseconds.

Eighty decibels corresponds to one part in 10,000. To generate accuracy at that level, the output pulse will need to be calibrated and compensated by some sort of automatic mechanism. That implies a way of measuring the voltage with about 14-bit accuracy. This measurement sounds like an analog-to-digital converter: 14 bits and perhaps 10 picoseconds settling time. As Shakespeare would have said, "Now there's the rub." It is not to say that this is the only issue, nor that this is insurmountable. The point is that it is likely easier to design the network analyzer than the TDR when frequencies become high.

This higher level of measurement accuracy and range come at the cost of equally greater care required in making the measurements. The requirements include such things as the need to calibrate the equipment at regular intervals. This is typically facilitated by pre-programmed routines; calibration routines are usually built into the test equipment. Usually they also provide precision calibration standards with the machine. All this is used in conjunction with test structures that you need to place on the device under test. In short, the network analyzer requires you to have a new set of skills even though you may be proficient at making measurements with the time domain reflectometer. The return for those new skills are high-quality measurements. More on measurements follows in Chapter 9.

Qualification of Models

The bane of signal integrity is the unreliable model. A significant portion of most signal integrity efforts goes into verifying the accuracy and range of applicability of models. The network analyzer is very useful in solving this problem. It can provide an accurately measured characterization of a device. Meanwhile, SPICE itself can be used to generate S parameter data that corresponds to the provided model. Comparing the measured data with the SPICE data then shows how accurate the model is and how the accuracy varies with frequency.

Through the peeling algorithm, you also can often directly generate SPICE models from network analyzer data.

Equalization

Equalization, extending the useful range of an interconnect circuit by manipulating its frequency response, can be done with the aid of network analyzer data. In most microwave-frequency data interconnect circuits, frequency-dependent loss is the major cause of signal degradation. The three main methods to deal with this problem are:

1. Manipulate the transmit spectrum to complement the frequency response of the channel, or pre-emphasis.

2. Manipulate the receiver frequency response to complement the channel frequency response, or adaptive equalization.

3. Use passive filtering techniques to complement the frequency response of the channel.

The first two seldom employ network analyzer data, but the third usually does. You measure the channel frequency response and then design a circuit that complements that response to yield an over-all frequency response that is suitably flat. This method can be called passive equalization.

Pre-emphasis vs. De-emphasis

Manipulation at the transmitter can be implemented in various ways. This activity usually involves manipulating the transmit signal amplitude on a bit-by-bit basis. One common method is to set the amplitude of the first bit of any series of equal-logic-value bits to a level higher than the remaining bits in the series. There are two ways you could do this: boost the leading bit to a higher level, called pre-emphasis, or reduce the level of the bits subsequent to the leading bit, called de-emphasis. From outside the package, they probably look the same.

If a current driver is used, pre-emphasis or de-emphasis can be achieved by manipulating the current of the current source. This is both fairly easy to do and fairly economical of silicon area, so some variation of this is likely to be found in most high-speed drivers.

Adaptive Equalization

Adaptive equalization usually refers to manipulations of the data inside the receiver. There are several ways of achieving this, and none of them is the right solution for all cases. One way is to track the history of past bits and offset the input signal to compensate for the part of the input signal that is actually the remainder of past bits, as shown in Figure 7.28. This can be very effective. It requires more high-speed circuitry than the simple receiver does but, that trade-off is available to the silicon designer.

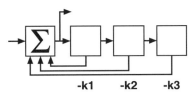

Figure 7.28   An Adaptive Equalizer

One problem related to such receivers is that they can make it difficult to measure signal quality at the input of the package. In a receiver without internal equalization, the usual measure of signal adequacy is the eye opening at the pins of the receive package. In a case where adaptive equalization is used, there may be no eye opening at the input pins. In this case, you may not be able to measure signal quality with an external tester. The answer may be that the transmitter and receiver must be able to work together to measure and quantify channel margins. If, for example, the transmitter can reduce the transmit signal by some amount, and the receiver can then verify that the error rate is still acceptable, then that can indicate a level of loss margin.

Radiation

Radiation tends to be more serious as frequencies increase. When circuit boards were running at speeds of tens of megahertz, finding a trace or any other structure that was as long as a quarter-wavelength was rare. At multiple gigahertz, all sorts of structures can become efficient radiators. At tens of megahertz, signals traveled down wires. At microwave frequencies, signals can travel quite well down the gap formed by the edges of two adjacent planes. What we used to think of as a plane-split, the microwave people call a *slot-line*. At the right length, it can make a nice antenna. A signal can travel around the outside edge of an isolated plane. If that periphery is the right length, it can make another nice antenna. The microwave guys call it a *patch antenna*. The point here is that structures that were of little interest at lower frequencies can become very interesting and perhaps troublesome at microwave frequencies. These transmission lines that SPICE doesn't know about can provide many of the same services, crosstalk and such, that good old wires used to provide.

Circuit solvers such as SPICE do not know anything about radiation. Any time it is necessary to model radiation, expect to be using a 3D full-wave field solver.

Of course testing real boards is an important part of studying emissions. It often is not practical to build a full 3D model of a circuit board with all the components, heat-sinks, cables, chassis, and so on that comprise the end product. Sometimes the right answer is to take it to the lab and make measurements. But you need to know the buzzwords so, when a region starts radiating, you know that it might be acting as a patch antenna or a slot antenna. That is, so you know what to look up for answers.

Crosstalk

If you look at a broad definition, radiation can be a contributor even to crosstalk in the circuitry. If a signal gets launched into the dielectric region between two reference planes, that signal can get reflected by various structures, and standing waves can develop. Those standing waves can cause enhanced crosstalk between the circuitry that inadvertently launched the wave and the circuitry that intercepts it. A similar situation could exist for things like slot-lines. The first line of defense is to minimize the amount of signal that is launched into such structures. Again, this usually corresponds to minimizing the common-mode component in the differential signals.

Planar Waveguide

One structure that can nicely transport a microwave signal is a planar waveguide. This device is a dielectric that is bounded top and bottom by a conductive plane. When a signal is introduced to this waveguide, it travels radially outward from the point of introduction. At frequencies and dimensions that are found in the printed circuits of computer systems, it will be a TEM wave. TEM waves follow all the capacitance, inductance, and velocity equations that have been described in previous chapters. The significance of this is that, at the edge of the plane, there will be a sudden drop in capacitance so there will be a sudden increase in transmission line impedance. There will thus be a reflection in the signal. If the overall planar structure has low enough loss, it will be a resonator.

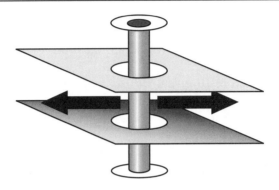

Figure 7.29   A Dielectric Resonator—Less the Dielectric

The way you launch a signal into this structure is to run a current between the planes in the direction normal to the two planes. A way of looking at it is that the magnetic field surrounding this current propagates out through the waveguide, carrying energy with it. However you choose to view it, the simple mechanism of running this current from one side to the other is an effective way of injecting a signal to this waveguide. To physically accomplish this, you would make a small hole in each plane and then run a wire through that hole. Current in this wire would then inject or extract energy from this waveguide.

Since the edges of this waveguide are typically open circuits, while some of the energy gets reflected, some gets radiated and becomes radio interference. There are several mechanisms that can extract energy from this waveguide. Energy will leak out through holes, if there are holes in the planes. Energy will be coupled into other wires that happen to pass through the planes. Energy will be lost in the dielectric and the copper losses of the planes themselves. To make this structure resonate well, you would minimize the number of holes through the waveguide and the number of wires through it. Then you would make it small so signal doesn't have to travel through too much loss before it gets reflected. Of course, to minimize the resonances, you would do the exact opposite. This isn't only of theoretical interest. Many power fills and such structures on multi-layer circuit boards fit very well the description of a really good microwave resonator.

Vias

What has been described above, signal insertion to a planar waveguide, is precisely what many signal vias do. So the via can be a good mechanism for inserting or extracting signal. Note that it is not the fact that the via passes through the planar waveguide that injects signal, it is the fact that the signal current passes through that injects the signal. A good way of minimizing the energy that is coupled into this waveguide is to always use well-balanced, closely-coupled differential signals where signals must pass through such a structure. If the signal is a closely-coupled differential signal, it becomes nearly true that only the common-mode AC part of the signal couples into the waveguide. For engineering purposes, it can be considered true.

The energy coupled into such waveguides can be the major part of the loss in high-frequency vias. Keeping differential signals well balanced helps to minimize the loss through vias. Another way to reduce signal injection and so minimize loss is to short the two planes surrounding the waveguide together at a point near where the signal passes through. If both the planes happen to be grounds, this is practical and is recommended.

Modeling of a single via in a particular application is not too difficult on a 3D field solver. The problem is that, though the via geometry may remain the same in various instances of its use, the model and the response for the case of a signal flowing from one surface to the other will be very different than the model and response for the case of a signal flowing from one layer to another nearby layer. When viewed this way, you can see that a single via geometry may require dozens of variations in the simulation and the model.

One solution is to solve a bunch of cases and form a look-up table that can be interpolated. Reasonable results can be achieved by this method. The via can be decomposed to geometrically simple primitives, as depicted in Figure 7.30, and multi-dimensional tables generated of the electrical characteristics of those primitives. Through scaling and table lookup, this makes it possible to generate a spreadsheet that can generate a reasonable SPICE model of the via, given only the geometric description of key parameters. This method can reduce the time required to generate acceptable models, from weeks to minutes.

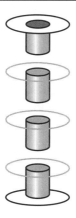

Figure 7.30   Simple Primitives that Model a Via

Patch Antennae

You need to be familiar with the concept of a patch antenna—an antenna that can be fabricated as an integral part of the surface of a printed circuit board. Occasionally you will find that things you intended as plane-fills act as patch antennae. You get the subject of the patch antenna here because you need familiarity with the term. The subject is too complex to be reasonably covered within the scope of this book. The patch antenna is the answer to the question: "How can I build a good antenna on planar media, or circuit boards?" An antenna is not necessarily a big tower or a long pole extending into the air. An antenna might be as inconspicuous as a square of copper on a circuit board, especially at microwave frequencies. The point is this: if it looks like a patch antenna and signal is injected to it, it is going to radiate.

Submit the phrase "patch antenna" to a favorite search engine on the web and you will get thousands of responses.

Slot Antennae and Hole Size

This subject is introduced much like the patch antenna was introduced. A slot antenna is simply a hole in a conducting surface. If it is the right size, it can be a very good antenna. Many of the connector holes found in the chassis of older personal computers are, at microwave frequencies, really good slot antennae. As frequencies increase, the size of holes in the chassis, both intentional and inadvertent, must proportionally decrease.

Recall that free-space velocity is a little less than 12 inches per nanosecond. A 6 gigahertz harmonic will have a free-space half wavelength of one inch.

Common-Mode on Cables

The shielding on inexpensive microwave-frequency data cables can be quite good. Usually a very significant proportion of emissions comes from the connectors or from the way the connectors are mounted. The most important source of emissions is the common-mode signal that leaks onto the outer surface of the cable shield. It is estimated that somewhere around 2 to 5 micro-amps of signal on the shield of a cable is all that is required to fail FCC emissions standards.

It is a very good idea to carefully model the entire cable connector region to examine the leakage characteristics. This includes not only the electrical connections of the signal lines, but also the connections of the ground pins, the shell to the chassis, and anything else that is involved in maintaining proper shielding.

In the past it was seldom necessary to specify the electrical connectivity of the connector shell-to-chassis path. Simulation will show that at microwave frequencies this can be a major source of emissions. You will want to examine this characteristic of connectors and their shell-connections to the chassis.

Conclusion

This chapter has not been about how to use a particular simulator—the vendors provide extensive literature and classes to cover that. Rather, this chapter has presumed that you are already familiar with the basic tools but need information as to how those tools can be applied to digital interconnect design at microwave frequencies. I wouldn't expect you to be able to smoothly transition to ever higher frequencies without aid. This chapter addressed various issues that you may never have seen unless you spent time talking to microwave engineers. Sure, eventually we would all have heard of slot lines and patch antennae, but here is a leg up. Many of the subjects introduced here are also covered in tomes of mathematics and theory. This book should not be the final look you take at many of these subjects. On the other hand, not everyone has the time to read a dozen microwave books to discover the source of that peculiar resonance on the new circuit board.

Chapter 8

Board Layout

We standardize board design rules or procedures or practices to increase the likelihood of success in a design. It is common practice to analyze various situations and identify solutions that are relatively safe—that is, have a high probability of succeeding. Then we codify those solutions, calling them design rules. This chapter presents a list of board layout rules. Such sets of rules are seldom absolutely optimal for any particular design but, if followed, yield a high probability of success. Perhaps it would be better to think in terms of guidelines, since these are not instructions to be blindly followed against all contravening evidence. Rather, they are recommendations that are deemed reliable in cases where full analysis is for some reason impractical. You should keep yourself informed and should always be willing to break such rules; you also should always be prepared to justify having broken such rules. These guidelines are presented to help fill in gaps that occur when you don't have enough resources, or not enough time to do a full analysis of each and every situation.

Fundamentals

In the design of buses, the layout must meet certain objectives. It is not enough to simply connect point *a* to point *b* to point *c*. The design must guarantee that the time required for the signal to become valid at particular endpoints satisfies timing requirements. Voltage requirements, maxima and minima, must be satisfied. Rise and fall times must meet specifications, and so on. In designing high-speed differential interconnect circuitry, the objectives are both similar and different to those you encountered at lower frequencies.

To have a successful design, you need clear understanding of the objectives, so this chapter starts with objectives that apply to circuitry interconnecting high-speed-differential transmitters and receivers. Terms that have grown up around differential signaling are introduced. It is expected that some may read this chapter and largely ignore the rest of the book, so there may be some repetitions. Some terms will be very similar to those used in design of classic bus systems. Because of the similarity of many concepts, it is necessary to clearly understand the concepts and terms. Pay particular attention to instances where the same word is used to describe different concepts in the two domains. Sometimes the differences are very subtle, yet critical.

The primary objective of any high-speed-differential interconnect circuit is to provide signal that can be reliably recovered at the receiver. Numerous factors combine to make this difficult. The biggest factor at microwave frequencies is usually loss—primarily frequency-dependent loss. At times, especially in short links, the biggest factor is the reflections caused by impedance mismatching. Often crosstalk is a significant factor. Sometimes common-mode conversions play a role, and sometimes unintended couplings play a role. It is the job of the layout engineer to find ways to connect point *a* to point *b* while minimizing the impact of all these factors.

Eye Diagrams

How do you know that the solution is good enough? The most common measurement used to qualify the virtue of the interconnect is the receive eye diagram. An eye diagram is what is seen on an oscilloscope if the voltage on the transmission line is measured while the oscilloscope is being triggered by the data clock. It is usually viewed while the scope is set up for long persistence; while either random data or specifically-designed test data is being transmitted while adjacent traces are sending their normal data—to include crosstalk.

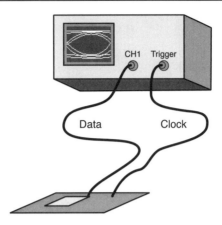

Figure 8.1   Scope Setup for Measuring the Eye

An eye may be measured in single-ended or differential manner, but you must distinguish which is which in specifications and in verifying that signals meet specifications. One important duty of the layout engineer is to design an interconnect that provides the greatest available eye opening. Note that in some types of adaptively equalized circuits, there may be no eye opening except inside at the silicon level. For our purposes, this material is presented as though a measurement point is available where the eye pattern can be measured.

The significance of the eye opening is that it displays the signal quality at the point of measurement. That is, the vertical opening displays the voltage difference between a logic one and a zero. The receiver presumably requires some minimum voltage difference between a signal that will be interpreted as a one and a signal that will be interpreted as a zero. The minimum voltage that the receiver needs is the minimum acceptable vertical eye opening at the receiver. If the eye has no opening, or an opening smaller than specification, the receiver may interpret some one-bits as zeros and zero-bits as ones.

Similarly, an eye has a horizontal opening. This is usually specified as a percentage of the unit interval, the clock-to-clock width of a data bit. The difference between the unit interval and the eye opening is called the *timing jitter*, or just plain *jitter*. The horizontal eye opening required by a particular receiver corresponds to the setup and hold time that the receiver needs, combined with clock uncertainty. If the horizontal opening closes too much, a bit from an adjacent time cell may be interpreted as belonging to this one. These eye parameters are illustrated in Figure 8.2

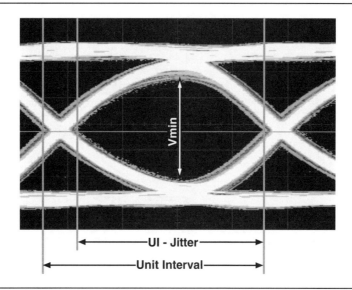

Figure 8.2   The Eye Pattern

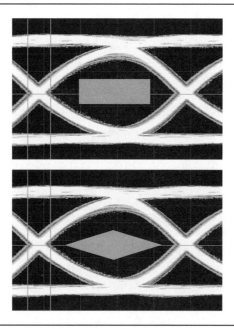

Figure 8.3   Examples of Two Types of Eye Masks

The required eye opening is often specified in terms of a mask, a geometric shape that must be capable of being fitted totally inside the eye opening. If no part of the measured eye at the specified location falls within the mask area, the signal is acceptable. If any part of the traces that compose the eye fall inside the mask area, the signal is unacceptable.

Numerous factors on circuit boards contribute to the closing of the receive eye. These include frequency-dependent loss, reflections, crosstalk, ground-plane resonances, common-mode conversions, and so on. The layout guidelines in this chapter are specified to help reduce these impacts. In no case can they be made to totally disappear, and in most cases careful analysis of some particular feature will yield more optimal results than will general purpose guides such as these. Yet, often it makes more sense to follow a guideline than to perform weeks of analysis that only gets you a few percent improvement over the guidelines.

The biggest contributor to closure of the receive eye is often, although not always, the signal loss in the trace itself. Signal loss is the first subject to be examined in any prospective board design. But we will first briefly examine that eye and its measurement.

Test Patterns

Numerous factors combine and contribute to the eye pattern observed. It is important to understand these, because they will have great impact. Consider as an example a test that is made with all adjacent channels turned off. The impact of crosstalk will not be seen, and the eye may look better than on the real device in real application. Consider a measurement that is made with the data sequence "101010101010…" repeated continuously. Since harmonic content doesn't change, the impact of frequency-dependent loss will largely be absent, and the eye will probably look very much better than it will be in a real application. Choosing the right data pattern for making a measurement of eye opening is not a simple task, and it needs explanation.

The fascinating subject of test patterns, is expanded in the measurements section of Chapter 9. This chapter, what you are reading right now, targets layout issues rather than measurement issues. However, you cannot totally ignore structures needed to measure the eye. A board that cannot be adequately tested fares poorly in mass-production environments. If part of the board test is going to be measurement of eye patterns, the layout must include viable facilities to enable such measurements. The details of these facilities are expected to be designed by the board-design engineer or the signal-integrity engineer.

The need for symmetry and the elimination of stubs are the most important issues to be noted in layout. If a test point is placed on one side of a differential pair, put another test point at the same place on the opposite side of the pair to maintain symmetry. Maintaining symmetry turns out to be one of the most important tasks in creating good high-frequency differential traces.

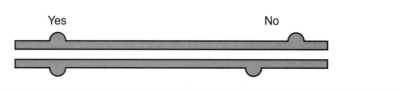

Figure 8.4   Right and Wrong Placement of Test Points

It is also important to know that stubs can easily cause circuits to fail. Any connector or test point that forms a stub in the test configuration or in the operational configuration should be vigorously avoided. Depending on the requirements of your design, you should consider any stub whose length is greater than a tenth wave-length, or sometimes even a twentieth wavelength, to be a potential problem. The wavelength of concern is the wavelength of the highest frequency you feel is important in your circuit.

Recommendations

- Maintain symmetry.
- Vigorously avoid stubs.

These two lines form an example of how this chapter is structured. A discussion of key points that define the issues and recommendations is followed by a concise statement of the key message. The objective is that you will be able to very quickly review or even list particular points that should be checked in reviewing the layout of a board. The format of the key message will be as the above recommendations. It is strongly advised that these recommendations are not treated as an alternative to reading the chapter. Read the chapter to understand the meaning of these recommendations. And it is always true that in any particular design situation, some of these recommendations will be less than optimal. There is nothing wrong with not complying with a recommendation as long as you have a valid reason backed up by analysis.

Frequency-Dependent Loss

Two factors make up the majority of frequency-dependent loss in an interconnect: copper loss and dielectric loss. Both are significant whenever frequencies reach into the gigahertz range and are somewhat dependent on choices that you make. Dielectric loss can be reduced by selection of low-loss dielectric material for the circuit board. Making traces wider can reduce copper loss. These simple-sounding solutions need to be expanded; they are not always as simple as they might sound.

The most common material used in circuit boards is FR4. It has low enough loss that loss was almost never an issue when signals were restricted to a few hundred megahertz. At microwave frequencies, voltage loss is often an issue. The loss factor of readily available versions of FR4 ranges by at least two to one, so it is important to know the quality of material that you will use in your application. Ask the vendors. They know what their numbers are.

The total loss in decibels of a simple straight piece of trace is approximately linearly dependent on trace length and on frequency. If the data rate is doubled, the high-frequency loss approximately doubles. If the trace length doubles, the loss again approximately doubles. Since loss can be a major factor in closing the receive eye, always minimize loss. Since loss is proportional to trace length, always minimize the trace length of long high-speed signal traces. So, why did I use the word "long" there? For short links, sometimes jitter is the biggest problem. Sometimes jitter is actually reduced by adding a bit of length to the trace. That brings us to the next layout recommendation.

Recommendation | Always minimize trace length of long high-speed signal traces. Vigorously avoid stubs.

By similar reasoning, always use the lowest-loss board material that is practical for a particular design. Though easily said, this is not always easily evaluated. There are materials that have much lower loss than does FR4. The use of such materials is not always optimal. Some of these materials do not laminate well. Some are expensive. Some do not drill well and so harbor hidden costs. If your design will sell a few million boards, material availability may be an issue. Use of low-loss materials is always preferable but needs careful examination for hidden costs. Again, ask your vendor. It is likely the vendor will be very familiar with the hidden costs.

An often-seen alternative is use of low-loss material on only some layers of a board. These layers are primarily reserved for the high-speed signals in a particular design. Such a solution is an excellent engineering compromise. On large boards, it needs to be analyzed for the possibility of causing board warpage.

Recommendation | Always use the lowest-loss board material that is practical for a particular design.

Even after the best practical board material is used, copper loss remains. The resistivity of copper combined with high frequencies and surface roughness cause significant signal loss. At microwave frequencies, signal flows through only a very thin "skin" on the surface of the conductor. Total resistance seen by the signal depends on the thickness of the skin, the width and length of the conductor, and the conductivity of the copper. If copper is relatively smooth, little can be done about the thickness of the skin, but the width of the conductor is an engineering choice. As the trace is made wider, loss decreases. The obvious recommendation is to always make traces as wide as practical.

The downside to this is that, when all else is equal, congruent trace geometries have equal characteristic impedances. Note that the congruence includes ground. Trace geometry here is intended to refer to the geometry of the view perpendicular to the axis of the trace—the view seen when the board is sliced open perpendicular to the trace direction. It is the reversal of this that is of concern. If characteristic impedance is to be maintained, congruence must be maintained. That is, if the trace width is doubled, dielectric thickness must be also doubled. Often numerous different types of signal traces must share the same routing layer; usually most of them have impedance targets, too. So if the trace width is doubled, for example, the dielectric thickness must be doubled. That means that to maintain their impedance targets, all the other traces on the layer need to be doubled in width as well. Thus, achievable routing density is impacted by the choice of trace width for the high-speed signal lines. Even in cases where layers can be dedicated to high-speed signals, the choice of wide traces can impact total board thickness.

Each of these factors needs to be evaluated in light of the system requirements of a particular design. Having said that, if traces can be made wider, widening them is the right thing to do.

Recommendation | Always make high-speed traces as wide as practical.

Loss establishes the vertical eye opening. But it also impacts the horizontal eye opening. Both are to be maximized at the receiver. The closure in the horizontal direction is due to timing variations. These variations in the time at which the receive signal edge crosses over from positive differential to negative value are called jitter.

To help visualize this, Figure 8.5 shows a step response seen at the output end of a fairly lossy link. Tick marks show where each unit interval of time ends.

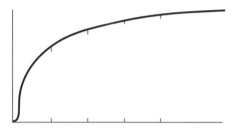

Figure 8.5   Lossy Channel Step Response

Now consider inserting a single isolated zero bit at one of these tick marks. The size of the pulse that results is the same, independent of which tick mark you place it at, but the same relative to where it starts. Figure 8.6 illustrates this concept. Depending on which tick mark the next pulse starts on, the minimum voltage it can reach changes.

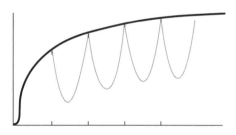

Figure 8.6   Four Places the Next Pulse Could Be

Now if an eye were generated that included examples of each of these pulses and their complements, you would see something like Figure 8.7.

Figure 8.7   The Resulting Eye

It is clear that if the step response didn't have that long slope, if the single-bit pulse reached the same total amplitude as the five-bit pulse, the eye would be open much wider. That slope in the step response is caused by frequency-dependent loss. That slope is also a cause of inter-symbol interference, something that you, as a signal integrity engineer, are surely familiar with. The lower frequencies see less loss than the higher frequencies. It is clear that the closure in amplitude and width are both due to this same mechanism.

Jitter

Yes, jitter is strongly tied to frequency-dependent loss. In a well-designed long interconnect, the majority of the jitter introduced will be due to this loss. There are other contributors that also need to be understood and minimized. The second major contributor is crosstalk, depicted in Figure 8.8. Control of crosstalk is one of the major reasons for the use of differential signaling in the first place. Consider a fairly long link that has lost 75 percent of its amplitude by the time it arrives at the receiver. Now envision 5 percent crosstalk from a transmitter adjacent the receiver. The loss of the receive signal means that the crosstalk signal is now at 20 percent of the amplitude of the receive signal. Note that crosstalk is always referenced to the receive signal level.

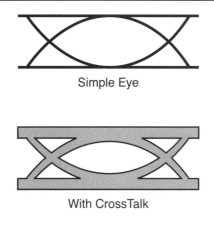

Simple Eye

With CrossTalk

Figure 8.8   Crosstalk in the Eye Pattern

The total timing budget is typically divided into three approximately equal parts. The transmitter is allowed to use one third of the unit interval, the interconnect circuitry gets to use one third and the remaining third is reserved for eye opening at the receiver. Given this, a 20 percent contribution is a substantial chunk. Careful layout can improve the situation.

The relative spacing of traces strongly impacts crosstalk. The critical number is the ratio of within-pair spacing to spacing to other traces or pairs. You minimize crosstalk by closely coupling the traces of the differential pair. Of course, this coupling impacts trace impedance and must be included in the calculation of the differential impedance of the pair. Due to the crosstalk, it is not a good idea to widely space the differential traces that compose a pair.

Recommendation | Minimize spacing between traces within a differential pair.

As always, weigh that recommendation in the light of your impedance requirements or you might find yourself adding jitter through impedance mismatches, while trying to reduce jitter from crosstalk.

Another factor contributing to the crosstalk at the receiver are features such as connectors. Such features have crosstalk factors built into them, and often those factors are not as good as might be desirable. Keep in mind that the proportional voltage coupled onto the receive line is what is important. If the connector is positioned very near the receiver, the signal coupled from any nearby transmitter will be stronger than if the connector is positioned at a further distance where the transmit signal will have encountered some loss, too.

Recommendation | Don't place connectors unnecessarily close to receivers.

Note that a major advantage of using differential signaling in the first place is that it produces less crosstalk as an aggressor, and is less impacted by crosstalk as a victim. Thus, for a given crosstalk limit, spacing can be closer if the aggressor is a differential pair than if the aggressor is a single-ended signal.

Recommendation | Space single-ended signals farther from differential signals than required for differential-pair to differential-pair spacing.

Planning the Stackup

Planning the stackup is one of those chicken-and-egg—which comes first?—sort of things. Often there is a prescribed board thickness, and all stackup choices must fit it. In such a system, you may not be free to make high-speed traces as wide as desirable nor as well separated. On the other hand, the more restrictions on the form of the stackup, the easier it is to plan the stackup. That is not to say that the end product will be globally optimal, but rather that fewer degrees of freedom result in fewer choices that must be made.

In planning a stackup, the first thing to consider from the point of view of high-speed signaling is that it is always desirable to minimize layer-transitions—shifting from layer to layer—of the high-speed signals. Different layers will have somewhat different impedances. Every time a signal transits from one impedance to another, signal is lost due to reflections. There is also additional loss in the via itself, but that will be covered later.

Recommendation | Minimize the number of layers used by any individual high-speed interconnect.

If it is possible, and if the trace must change layers, it is preferable that it change to a layer that shares the same reference plane. This reduces the loss of changing layers but does not eliminate it. Another savings of loss is obtained by routing on outside layers. Traces on the surface of the board have some of their *E* field in air. Air is essentially lossless, so long traces on the surface, microstrip, have somewhat lower loss than traces on inner layers, stripline.

On the other hand, routing on the outside layers can yield significantly higher crosstalk than routing on inner layers.

Recommendations

> ■ Evaluate routing long high-speed differential traces on outside layers.
>
> ■ Limit routing of individual traces to layers that share a reference plane.

So when planning the stackup, it is desirable to plan what layers will be used for what signals and to optimize accordingly. For example, if you choose an eight-layer stackup, reserve the outer surfaces for long high-speed signal nets and adjust the dielectric thickness for slightly wider traces wherever possible. If possible, use low-loss material on layers that will be used for long high-speed nets. If economics force the use of FR4, keep in mind that this material comes in a range of quality that varies at least two to one in loss tangent.

There is a final note on the subject of materials used for the board stackup. Some designs have no need for long nets. On such boards, low-loss material, even if economically practical, is not necessarily the best choice. The reason for this counterintuitive situation is that short trace eye-closure tends to be dominated by reflections rather than loss. There is sometimes a "sweet spot" of maximum eye opening. This spot is a function of line length: at longer lengths, frequency-dependent loss tends to close the eye; at shorter lengths, reflections tend to close the eye. If, in a particular design, most of the high-speed nets are dominated by reflections rather than by loss, shifting to a higher-loss material might actually increase the design margins.

Situations like this make it impossible to make a single recommendation that is optimal for all situations. If you really, really want a simple recommendation, it would be to go with a good grade of material and learn to live with its consequences.

Coupling

Numerous flavors of differential pair geometries are available. Some of these can be combined into what might be thought of as hybrids. Three of these flavors can be readily implemented on planar media, or circuit boards. Two work well and one is not recommended. Figure 8.9 shows the three that are going to be discussed. They are, from top to bottom, *coplanar*, *edge-coupled*, and *broadside-coupled*.

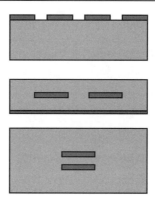

Figure 8.9   Three Differential Geometries

Broadside

Broadside-coupled differential transmission lines are those in which the two sides of the pair reside on adjacent routing layers in the board and are physically one trace above the other. This geometry allows close coupling and has the advantage that corners can be turned without introducing common-mode conversions. It has two disadvantages: an easy one and a hard one. The word "easy" here is meant as relative to each other, not to the whole world of circuit design.

The easy disadvantage is that the two traces lie at different depths in the board, so care is needed in launching signals into this type of pair. You must ensure that the electrical length from other elements to and from the pair sides is equal. This is not particularly difficult, but it does need to be done.

The hard disadvantage is due to stackup registration. When the board is laid out in a computer, all the traces are exactly where you wanted them and everything is perfect. When this perfect layout is turned into a real board, errors are introduced. One of those errors is that various layers are not all exactly lined up with each other. This is called registration error. The registration error between layers separated by core material is typically about one or two thousandths of an inch. Registration error for traces separated by prepreg can be a couple times greater than this. For thin traces, instances that were intended to be on top of each other can end up almost beside each other. For this reason, broadside coupling is not recommended.

Recommendation | Avoid broadside geometries.

Edge-Coupled

Traces that are side-by-side on the same routing layer and referenced to ground or power planes are called edge-coupled traces. These have a problem in that, when a differential pair turns a corner, the trace on the outside of the bend must travel a greater distance than the trace on the inside of the corner. This introduces common-mode conversions in the pair. This can be corrected by adding a wiggle to the inside trace to equalize the electrical lengths of the two sides of the pair. On multilayer circuit boards, this is the most common geometry used for differential pairs. In the absence of overriding reasons, it is the recommended geometry for circuit-board applications.

Recommendation | In general, use edge-coupled pairs.

Co-Planar

The geometry called co-planar waveguide is closely related to the edge-coupled form. In this geometry, ground planes are routed beside the signal line on the same layer. This geometry allows the capacitance of the trace to be increased to help meet impedance targets. The advantage of this is that it allows useful trace impedances to be achieved on single layer boards. It is also often used on test boards to maintain constant impedance while trace widths change.

When a board is constructed for the main purpose of testing some feature, something like a connector, you will want to minimize losses in the traces going to that connector. You do this by using trace widths that are perhaps 20 or 30 thousandths of an inch wide. Then the board stackup is adjusted to get the impedance right. The problem is that the connector spacings may not accept this wide a trace. The solution is that, as you arrive at the connector, you narrow the trace to meet the connector requirements, but you bring in a coplanar ground to maintain the right impedance.

Variations and hybrids, part-way between what here is called edge-coupled and co-planar, are common and useful in many instances. They commonly are found in measurement structures where the two sides of a differential pair need to be separated to make room for probing or for installation of SMA connectors—things like that. Adding a nearby ground can maintain the impedance of traces where coupling between them is reduced.

Recommendation | Use coplanar methods where differential pairs need to be separated to accommodate measurement.

Corners

There are two types of corners. In a single trace, a corner can change the inductance and capacitance slightly and cause a small amount of reflections. The emphasis here is "single trace." On typical circuit boards used in computer and similar applications, this is of little concern. The variations found in normal traces used in such applications is often much greater than those induced by such a corner, so its impact at moderate microwave frequencies is lost in the noise, or the impedance variations normally found on FR4. The other type of corner, the type that is of considerable concern here, is a bend in an edge-coupled differential pair, in Figure 8.10. This one is not to be ignored.

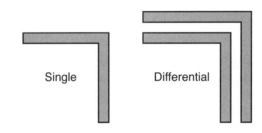

Single   Differential

Figure 8.10   Corners and Bends

In an optimal differential pair, every frequency component on either side of the pair is exactly 180 degrees out of phase with the same component on the other side of the pair. Thus the average, the AC common-mode component, is zero. If edge-coupled traces turn a corner, the trace on the outside of the bend is longer than the trace on the inside edge. This results in a phase shift that is proportional to frequency. Because of the phase shift, the two sides are no longer in precisely opposite phase, so cancellation is no longer perfect—AC common-mode signal is formed. This common-mode signal crosstalks and radiates much worse than does differential signal. The recommendation then is to correct this length mismatch by adding a wiggle to the corner-inside trace. Optimally, it should be added at a distance that is short compared to the minimum wavelength of concern. In a system sending 2.5 gigabits per second NRZ (non return to zero) data, the maximum frequency of concern, established by the rise-time of the signal edges, is likely to be about 3 gigahertz. On FR4, that is going to have a wavelength of about 2 inches so "short compared to wavelength" is probably about 0.2 inch.

If the trace pair jogs back to the same direction in this distance range, it probably isn't worth the effort to try to equalize the lengths individually. Just let the second jog correct for the first. If a bend is not straightened in this distance, add the wiggle to the inside trace, within a quarter inch or so of the bend. Of course, the distance is to be scaled according to the rise-time of the data.

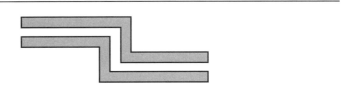

Figure 8.11   A Short Jog

Recommendations

∎ Ignore jogs that restore trace direction in a distance less than about a tenth of a wavelength for the highest frequencies of concern.

∎ Add a wiggle on the corner-inside trace to equalize the lengths at bends that do not meet the previous condition.

A final note on this subject is that, if you are really concerned about the excess capacitance added by having a square corner in a single trace, you can reduce the capacitance by mitering the corner. Another way of reducing the impact of a corner in a single trace is to use an angle that is less than a full 90-degree bend. This strategy can be beneficial, particularly for jogs.

Vias

Vias are one of the more complex aspects of routing signals on multi-layer planar media. In the worst case, a via can add as much loss as an inch or more of trace. In the best case, a via can have an order-of-magnitude less loss than that. So, the first big recommendation is to minimize the number of vias used in any high-speed trace.

Recommendation

Minimize the number of vias used in high-speed traces.

There are two major concerns and a whole bunch of minor concerns in considering a via. First, a via carrying signal that traverses the space between two or more copper planes launches a sizable amount of energy into the planar waveguide formed by those planes. This geometry is illustrated by Figure 8.12.

Figure 8.12   Via Traversing a Planar Waveguide

The second is that through-hole vias that transport signal between close layers on thick boards, as in Figure 8.13, can have stubs that become resonant at high frequencies. That is, if the length of the stub formed by the unused end of the through-hole via approaches a quarter wavelength, it will cause signal-integrity problems. At 10 gigahertz, a quarter wavelength in FR4 is about 0.15 inch.

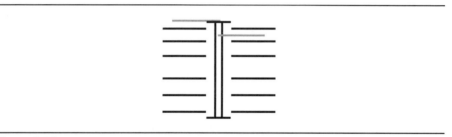

Figure 8.13   Via with Long Stub

The solution to the first concern is always to use well-balanced differential signals when traversing structures that form planar waveguides. As long as the spacing between the vias is small compared to wavelength, only the common-mode component couples into the waveguide. Once again, this was an almost-true statement. It is close enough for practical use in board layout.

Recommendation | Pass through planar waveguides only with closely spaced well-balanced differential pairs.

This recommendation will significantly reduce the loss attributable to the via. You can do better. If the planes are shorted together with "stitch vias" near the point where the signal passes, additional reduction of loss is achieved. Stitch vias are vias that don't carry signal, they merely short the planes together. A single stitch via near the point where the differential pair vias are located significantly reduces loss. A second stitch via helps even more. In this case, "near" is less than about a tenth wavelength at the highest frequency with significant harmonic content. This frequency is sometimes considered to be about three quarters of the bit rate.

Recommendation | When possible, short planes together near the point where signals pass through planar waveguides.

Via Stub

The second major concern with vias is the resonant stub. With frequencies below about 10 gigahertz, or thin boards, this is not likely to be a serious concern. In instances where this is a concern, the typical responses are things such as the use of buried vias or back-drilling the hole to remove the stub. The question is sometimes asked: when will it be necessary to abandon through-hole vias and shift to buried vias? One answer is: when the resonant stubs formed by the via ends become problematic. When board thickness nears a quarter wavelength for the frequencies in use, that time is likely at hand.

These two concerns are not the end of the via story. Experience shows that, if unguided, the layout engineer typically uses vias that are far too capacitive. Heroic measures are not needed, but a via that is useful for microwave frequencies is likely to be a bit different than the typical via for lower frequencies. For board thicknesses in the range of 0.062 inch, it probably is not optimal to use a drill size larger than about 0.014 inch diameter. Many layout tools add a pad on each inside layer. For microwave applications, remove all unnecessary pads. It is not a good idea to make antipads as small as possible. For the above drill, make that antipad about 0.03 or 0.04 inch in diameter. Do these things and, although the via might not be absolutely optimal, it will likely be fairly good.

Recommendations
- Drill holes for high-frequency vias should be about 0.014 inch or less.
- Unused and unneeded inner-layer pads should be removed from vias.
- Antipads should be larger than the minimum mechanically practical size.

Sometimes through-hole-mount connectors must be used for high-frequency signals. Often the vias required for these are much larger than those recommended for high frequencies. In such a case, high-frequency performance can often be improved by removing reference-plane material in the vicinity of these vias to reduce capacitance. And of course, wherever possible, it is always best to optimize via designs by modeling them on a field solver.

Discrete Components

Occasionally, you need to use discrete resistors and capacitors in microwave-frequency traces. Stating the obvious, leaded components are not going to work here. When working at microwave frequencies, you must work with surface mount resistors and capacitors.

NOT a Microwave Component

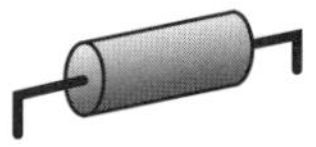

Figure 8.14   Not a Microwave Component

Up to about 1.5 gigahertz, 0603 size components can be used but are not recommended. For frequencies up to about 5 gigahertz, size 0402 are useful. In transmitting NRZ signals at low microwave frequencies, it is not necessary to use so-called microwave capacitors and resistors. Usually inexpensive commodity components are adequate. The loss through such a capacitor, used for DC blocking in a signal line, in the 0603 example above is fairly low. In the same application and frequency, the 0402 capacitor will show about one fifth the loss. So the deal is not so much that larger-bodied capacitors won't work, rather it is that loss seems to grow faster than body size does.

Recommendations

- For signal frequencies up to about 1.5 gigahertz, passive component sizes should be 0603 or smaller.

- For signal frequencies up to about 5 gigahertz, passive component sizes should be 0402 or smaller.

Note that the dominant frequency is half the data-bit rate.

The next question with discrete components is where in the trace to put them? One answer might be to pick a place and run simulations. Perhaps a better response is where *not* to put them. It is not a good idea to place a component where it precisely divides a trace segment length in half. This is most serious in low-trace-loss situations. It also applies to all passive devices, including connectors.

A way of expressing this in a more general form is that it is not a good idea to place any device at a position in a trace such that the trace length on one side divided by the trace length on the other side equals a small integer. The issue is that dividing a trace in such a way can enhance reflections. In this context, the phrase "small integer" can be interpreted as any integer smaller than about 4.

Recommendation | Observe the small integer rule.

Reference Planes and Plane Splits

Both stripline and microstrip trace geometries make use of reference planes. In the ideal world, these reference planes would all be ground planes. In the real world, sometimes they need to be power planes. It is difficult to move a signal to and from referencing a power plane. Part of the reason is that, to minimize loss and mode conversions, the trace images in the reference planes need to maintain continuity as well. Actually, there are difficulties in moving a signal from any reference plane to any other. However, if the planes are not at the same DC potential, you cannot simply short them together to provide a path for image currents. So the problems are just worse if one of these is a power plane. Whenever possible, chose a routing layer, and keep the high-speed differential pair on that layer for its entire length.

Recommendation | Choose a layer and route the entire length of the signal on that layer.

That recommendation is similar to political slogans that sound good but are not very practical. Often you have no option but to change routing layers occasionally. There are several issues with this. The first is that different layers are rarely at precisely the same impedance, so changing layers introduces impedance discontinuities. A monetary cost is associated with specifying controlled impedance on circuit boards. If your design cannot handle this cost, be aware that impedance variations between the target value and the actual value sometimes exceed 20 percent. Achievable impedance tolerances for the differential impedance are usually worse than for single-ended impedance. The change from one layer to another can result in a shift of over 40 percent in impedance. This shift, as detailed in previous chapters, causes notable reflections. Those reflections remove energy at one section of the signal and may add it back at some other section, thus causing jitter. Whereas in long links, loss tends to dominate the signal integrity problems, in short links the jitter caused by reflections tends to be dominant.

That difference should be reiterated; it is important. In long links, the energy reflected by impedance discontinuities often gets absorbed in the loss of the link and so is simply lost energy, increasing overall loss. In short links, the energy reflected is not all absorbed and so ends up simply being redistributed. That redistribution of energy adds to the timing jitter seen at the receiver. Just like long links can fail due to excessive loss, short links can fail due to excessive jitter. Of course there are graduations in between the two extremes.

Recommendation	Minimize the number of reference plane changes a net makes.

Another issue is more subtle but occasionally produces a perplexing result that severely impacts the functionality of the net. This one is important because, while it is uncommon, when it does bite, it occasionally bites so hard that the board becomes unusable. The issue is coupling to plane resonances.

It works like this. Whenever a signal passes through two planes, it radiates energy into the gap between those two planes. Whether intended or not, the region between two reference planes forms a planar waveguide. Signals, once introduced into this waveguide, travel even better than they do on traces—their conducting paths are wider. Since such waveguides are seldom intentionally terminated, reflections can occur at their edges and standing waves can form. If a second via happens to reside at a node of this standing wave, crosstalk can be enhanced. On the other hand, if the planar waveguide has a high Q, a resonance can form and couple into your signal via, or your signal.

Technically, the thing being described is a parallel plane resonator. If the plane has very few holes in it, very little energy will leak out. If it has a lot of holes, as from various vias, a lot of energy will leak out. If it is physically large, the primary resonant frequency will be low. If it is physically small, the resonant frequency will be large. Finally, if it is physically small, there will be less loss between reflections, and resonances will be more likely. So, the worst case is likely to be a small plane that has very few holes in it.

What can be done about it? Obviously, don't run high-speed vias through small planes that have very few holes in them. More importantly, when a differential signal traverses through this planar waveguide, it is primarily the common-mode component that couples into the planar waveguide. Always make sure the differential traces are well matched where they pass through vias. This means, among other things, always place vias symmetrically, never staggered on the differential pair.

Recommendations

| ■ Don't run high-speed signals through small planes that have few holes. |
| ■ Always place vias symmetrically on differential pairs, never staggered. |
| ■ Take the above rule and make it an absolute requirement. |

Slot Lines

For those of us who grew up with signals going down wires, it is somewhat perplexing to be told that signals can also be transmitted through the region between two reference planes. Well step aside, perplexity; it is time for astonishment. Not only can signal be transported in the region between two reference planes, signal can be transported, and quite nicely, in the gap between two planes on the same layer. The antenna guys love this stuff. It is called a slot-line and if you inject signal into it, it will transport that signal just as well as a wire will. What we in the PC industry have called plane splits, the microwave and antenna guys have been calling slot lines. If you can, avoid crossing a plane split. If it can't be avoided, be sure you cross it in a direction perpendicular to the slot.

Recommendation

| Avoid crossing plane splits. |

Also, if you have to cross a plane split, it is, and always has been, a good idea to bridge the gap with a small capacitor near the signal crossing. For single-ended signals this was a necessity. For differential signals it is simply a good idea.

Plane Resonances

Plane resonances were mentioned above. There is absolutely nothing simple about plane resonances. There will be a lowest frequency, and then above that there are typically an infinite progression of higher resonances of progressively lower amplitude; loss increases with frequency. Tools which can analyze a plane and can actually calculate the loss through each hole and energy transported through each via that pierces that plane are exceedingly slow. If you wait a few years before reading this book, perhaps things will get better.

Package Breakouts

Package breakouts, the region near the package where there is usually not enough room to do anything more than barely get all the traces away, let alone add rules about corners and separation and so on, are problematic. Often, particularly on large BGA packages, it is not even possible to keep the desired trace widths and separations. There are some recommendations that really should be followed. First, keep the two lines of the differential pair together. Never break out one trace of a pair on one layer and the other on another. Don't break out one along one path and the other through some other path. It is usually less important to maintain trace widths and separations in this region than follow these two rules. If, as often happens, it is necessary to compromise trace widths or separations, restore them as near the package as possible.

Recommendation | Always keep the two differential traces together.

Connectors

Connectors have problems that are often similar to those of package breakouts. Where it is possible, use a surface-mount connector. This eliminates one of the biggest problems of connectors—highly capacitive vias. Keep in mind that connectors are often centers of crosstalk. Crosstalk is enhanced by common-mode conversions. So always keep line-lengths between the two sides of the pair) equal, both to and through the connector. Select connectors carefully. Impedance matching is fundamental. Occasionally you will encounter connectors where the asymmetry between the two traces of the pair is visible. Given a choice between a symmetrically built connector and an asymmetrically built connector, it is a safe bet that the asymmetric one will have significantly worse crosstalk.

Card-edge connectors can be very good or very bad. A major problem is that the contacts on the plug-in card often have to be physically very large, or capacitive. Never make them longer nor wider than they have to be. Secondly, it can be very beneficial to remove all reference planes below the contacts to minimize capacitance. Another problem is that if the contact slides a long way up a pad, the material below the contact point is, at low frequencies, simply additional capacitance; at high frequencies, it is a resonant stub. So the ideal card-edge connector will have very little travel, or wipe, on the pad. You need some wipe, but not a lot.

Recommendations

- Use surface-mount connectors rather than through-hole.
- Cut away reference planes below card-edge connector pads.

Test Points

Sometimes production lines for manufacturing boards use test procedures that involve bringing test points from every trace to the bottom of the board for automated testing of connectivity. When implemented in the traditional way of a via and a short stub to a surface contact pad, these can be very bad for microwave frequencies. The issue is resonant stubs. An open-circuited stub will resonate at the frequency where the stub length is one quarter wavelength.

A typical traditional test point consists of a via, perhaps .062 inch long, leading to a short trace, perhaps .075 inch long, and ending in a pad about .05 inch long. As a stub, that is a total of 0.187 inch. It will resonate at the frequency whose wavelength is four times that, 0.748 inch. Signal travels through FR4 at about 6 inches per nanosecond. So the resonant frequency will be about 8 gigahertz. If a link is to operate at a low microwave frequency, perhaps 2.5 giga-transfers per second, this is not likely to be catastrophic by itself, but will impact signal integrity measurably. At higher transfer rates, this could well be intolerable.

Recommendation

Avoid stubs in test points.

Impedance Tolerances

One of the biggest problems in the entire field of signal integrity at microwave frequencies is impedance tolerances. It isn't too difficult to find a board-house that will produce boards with ±10% trace impedance tolerances. If you can afford to relax to 15 percent, just about any board house in the world will do for single-ended tolerances. For tolerances better than these, you'll pay a premium; the premium increases as the tolerance gets tighter. This is all well known. If you design boards, you probably already know that.

The problem is that these tolerances are specified for single-ended signals. The tolerances for differential impedance are often worse. In fact, the tolerances for inner layers are not the same as for outer layers. In some cases, tolerance can exceed 20 percent. When it does exceed 20 percent, the impedance shift in transitioning from one layer to another can be over 40 percent. That is another reason to minimize layer changes with high-speed signals.

But that isn't the end of the story. Virtually any simulator will get the impedance right for stripline. Microstrip is another matter. With microstrip, some simulators ignore the presence of the solder-mask layer. With single-ended signals that may not be too big a deal. Adding the solder-mask layer will reduce the impedance by one or two ohms and that isn't too bad. With closely coupled differential pairs, ignoring the solder mask can cause significantly greater error. Using a simulator that cannot account for the solder mask is too bad. No matter what simulator you use for signal integrity analysis, the tool you use to calculate trace impedance should be capable of dealing with the solder mask.

Recommendation | Check your simulator for solder mask capability.

Weave Effects

It is important to maintain the symmetry between the two sides of the differential pair. Conditions that break the symmetry convert differential energy to common mode, and common mode energy to differential noise. It is close enough to true to state as a fact that differential energy does not radiate, common mode does. Common mode energy produces crosstalk at far greater levels than differential energy. Common mode energy couples to board resonances, and so on down the list. All that can be summarized in one statement: common mode is bad, differential is good. Such a summary appeals especially to those of us who want to see a clear distinction between good and bad and who don't particularly like shades of gray.

A ruler can be used to measure the physical length of each side of a differential pair to show that they are the same length, so the differential is maintained; common mode conversion is minimized. That statement is an interesting theory that makes all sorts of sense except that it doesn't work. The problem is that what counts is electrical length, not physical length. By electrical length, I mean the distance the signal travels in some unit of time. The distance traveled depends on the velocity of the signal. The velocity of the signal depends on the dielectric constant. The dielectric constant of FR4 is not a constant; it varies with position.

FR4 dielectric consists of fiberglass fabric impregnated with epoxy. The dielectric constant of a place that has a glass strand under it will not be the same as in a place that has mostly epoxy under it. Those with experience in routing clock signals are fully aware that it is not unusual to route two traces of precisely equal length for 10 or 12 inches across the board and then find signal skews of over 100 picoseconds at the far end. The fiberglass weave causes that. To make it worse, we typically route traces parallel to the edges of the board. The weave typically is parallel to the edge of the board. One signal will spend most of its time over a glass strand, the next might spend most of its time over epoxy.

On the board, some traces spend most of their time over glass fibers, others spend most of their time between glass bundles; timing skew can accumulate at rates as high as 10 picoseconds per inch. That is, traces that are identical in mechanical length can be quite different in electrical length. For differential pairs, electrical length is what counts.

So there is a problem, but can anything be done about it without incurring excessive material costs? Fortunately the answer is yes. Don't run high-speed-differential traces parallel to the fiberglass weave. That is, parallel to the board edges, except where there is a lot of timing margin or where the edge-parallel section is small. This doesn't mean that the traces must be 45 degrees. As little as 5 degrees off is enough to virtually eliminate the effect.

Recommendation
Minimize edge parallelism in high-speed differential pairs.

Special Cases: Measurement Boards

Boards used for reference measurements of passive devices and connectors are a special case. Particularly, boards used in measuring the S parameters of objects need great care. S parameters are measured by use of a network analyzer. The dynamic range of this tool can exceed 100 decibels. That is an impressive range, and to realize it, data distortions caused by the test structures and layout must be minimized. If the test board distorts the voltage measurement by one percent, this corresponds to reducing the useful measurement dynamic range to 40 decibels. The majority of the quality in measured data can be established by the quality of the test board itself.

Every time a measurement is made, it has to be preceded by a calibration of the machine, the network analyzer. Part of this calibration is characterizing the interconnect up to the point where the device under test actually begins. Thus, part of the calibration is establishing the characteristics of the test board so the impact of the test board can be subtracted from the measurement. You need to build an auxiliary trace or set of traces on the test board that allow the measurement of the board characteristics up to the device under test. For the most precise measurements, such test traces must be exactly equal to the traces that connect to the device under test. The major task of the board layout engineer is to achieve that exactness.

A simplistic solution is simply to copy and paste the traces that lead to the device and call the job done. This is part of the solution but by itself is not nearly enough. Traces on typical multi-layer boards are in the range of about 0.004 to about 0.008 inch wide. Both of these are small compared to typical weave spacings in the fiberglass fabrics used on inexpensive multilayer boards. There is a substantial probability that one trace might lay primarily over a glass bundle while another trace might lie over a region of more epoxy content. As has already been explained, these position-dependent differences cause differences in both the velocity of signals, impacting the electrical lengths of the lines, and in the characteristic impedances of the lines. Such differences limit the accuracy of the calibration and therefore the accuracy of the data acquired.

What to do about it is fairly simple. The weave of the glass fabric typically parallels the edges of the board. The impact of the dielectric variations can be averaged by simply skewing the direction of the traces. As little as 5 degrees offset in trace direction referenced to the edge of the test board—the direction of the weave—can improve the stability of velocity and impedance by over an order of magnitude.

Recommendation | On test boards, never run traces parallel to board edges.

The other big issue is not as easy to explain. It is the issue that showed up back in Chapter 4 where the peeling algorithm was discussed. As frequency-dependent loss in the interconnect increases, the accuracy of high-frequency measurements in downstream components quickly deteriorates. A simple way of stating the conclusion: in boards used for measuring and characterizing devices, skinny traces are really bad. The recommendation is to minimize the number of layers on a test board so that dielectric thickness can be maximized with the result of enabling the use of wider traces to the device under test. At times it even makes sense to use simple two-layer boards—reference plane on one side, trace on the other. These recommendations are equally valid when testing with the network analyzer or the time-domain reflectometer.

Recommendation | On test boards, use the widest traces that are practical.

It may or may not be obvious to say so, but also always use high-quality connections between the test equipment and the board under test. Though by far the most expensive, microwave test probes are not always the best solution. The quality of performance with these interconnect devices can be heavily dependent on the board layout. A well designed SMA connector can often outperform a mediocre design with an expensive microwave probe. In some instances, it will outperform a good design with that probe. Usually, the most important issue with an SMA connector is getting the impedance matching right on the circuit board.

SMA connectors are inexpensive and easy to use, but, for good performance, their layout on the board needs to be simulated with a 3D field solver. If you need only one- or two-gigahertz bandwidth, one good footprint will be adequate for most boards. If you need bandwidth near or above 10 gigahertz, the footprint should be tweaked by the signal integrity engineer for the specific number of layers on the board. And yes, it is possible to extend the useful bandwidth of at least one of the commercially available through-hole SMA connectors to beyond 15 gigahertz.

Recommendation | For connections to the test equipment, use footprints that have been analyzed with a 3D field solver.

With a bit of experience, you will find these rules not too difficult to implement and you will find they go a long way toward making your board designs a success.

Chapter **9**

Test Equipment

Only a few types of test equipment apply to the high-speed differential systems of interest here. These include oscilloscopes, network analyzers, time domain reflectometers, and the peripheral devices that are used with these. This chapter introduces the most important of these, adds a bit of detail about what each does, and offers precautions you should be aware of. Some practices will make a person unwelcome in most microwave labs. Other practices are standard and should always be followed. This chapter points them out.

Oscilloscope

The oscilloscope is a tool that is familiar to almost every engineer. Yet, in microwave applications, some aspects are likely not familiar. An objective of this chapter is to describe and explain some of these unfamiliar aspects. First off, there are two types of oscilloscope: analog and digital. For events that occur in nanoseconds of time, analog oscilloscopes are seldom used. There are two types of digital oscilloscope: real-time and sampling.

Real Time

The typical real time digital oscilloscope is a device that samples data at a very high clock rate. It may use a very fast analog-to-digital converter to measure voltages at a series of consecutive, closely-spaced time slots.

These measurements can be done in a number of ways. Some employ multiple flash converters to sample data at alternating time samples. One converter samples the first time slot, the next converter takes the next time slot, and so on. This enables n converters to achieve a data conversion rate that is n times that of a single converter. An alternate method might be to sample the data into an analog FIFO, first-in-first-out pipeline. The FIFO could be a charge-coupled device similar to those found in some cameras. Analog samples are clocked in at a high rate and then clocked back out at a lower rate that can be accommodated by the analog-to-digital converter.

How it is done is not as important as what that means for use. First of all, the data is taken in such a way that consecutive time increments of the display correspond to consecutive time increments of a single wave. The key here is the phrase "single wave." This is an important distinction, because some very good oscilloscopes do not do this. The real-time oscilloscope is capable of capturing an individual pulse at rates limited only by the maximum bandwidth of the scope.

If you need to capture an individual wave, this type of scope is required. The maximum bandwidth of this scope is typically much lower that that of a sampling scope. Also, recognize that "real time" does not mean that this scope captures all events that go by. Typically the duty cycle of this scope is quite low. That is, the scope is only looking at passing data a small percentage of the time. Some types of rare events are very hard to observe unless care is taken to increase the likelihood that the trigger circuitry is actually looking at data when the event occurs.

In examining high-speed differential circuitry, triggering is usually provided separately from the data. Because the data clock is usually embedded in the data, triggering on the data would remove most of the timing information. At the same time, each of the various high-speed serial data transmission standards uses a slightly different clock recovery mechanism, which sometimes makes it impractical for the scope manufacturer to build the clock recovery, trigger, and circuit into the scope hardware. This, by the way, is true for both real-time and sampling scopes. What is apparently done as an alternative is to acquire a buffer full of data and then mathematically extract the timing information. Major oscilloscope manufacturers will thus have built-in clock recovery for established transmission standards. The only thing the user needs to be aware of is that, in measuring any particular type of interconnect, such as SATA or PCI-E, the clock recovery has to be set to match that interconnect type, or the information displayed will be wrong.

Sampling Scopes

Sampling scopes typically achieve bandwidths that are much greater than those of real time scopes. Fifty gigahertz has been available for years. Again, there are various ways that a sampling scope could be designed. One popular and very effective way is to start with a very wideband sample-and-hold circuit. This circuit samples the waveform at a very low rate, usually well under one megahertz. It samples a wave at the trigger time. This sample goes through the analog-to-digital conversion and is stored. Then it samples the waveform at the first time increment after another trigger, and so on till there is a sample for each time increment after the clock.

The situation is that thousands of waveforms go by between each data sample. This situation works well for repetitive wave forms but not for isolated events. The eye diagrams needed for high-speed serial applications work reasonably well with this type of scope, but care must be exercised in acquiring data.

Suppose, for instance that it is desirable to sample each waveform in 10 places to get an acceptable representation of its shape. Suppose also that the stimulus sequence, the data pattern used to generate the eye diagram, is 20 characters long. If the data is 8b/10b encoded, as is often the case, the entire sequence will be 200 unit intervals long, and 2,000 samples are needed to adequately fill the buffer. If scope takes 50,000 samples a second, data must be acquired for 1/25 of a second. But there is no reason to expect the samples to be evenly spread over the waveform. To be safe, it would be a good idea to over sample by at least a factor of 10. It now takes 0.25 second to generate the eye. Some standards specify that compliance is to be based on as many as 1,000 bits. That would bring the acquisition time up to 12.5 seconds.

Now to add interest, some systems allow dithering of the clock. These systems have the capability of tracking the variations in the clock. The clock variations are typically at frequencies of about 30 kilohertz. If the clock recovery system used is rock stable, the clock dithering will make the data look like it has a very large amount of jitter, even though the receiver doesn't see it that way. To really see what the receiver takes as jitter in the eye, the clock recovery circuitry for the scope must be identical to that of the receiver.

As a practical alternative, some systems allow you to turn off dithering for test purposes. If you have this capability, use it for tests. An even better alternative is for the receiver chip to actually output the recovered clock signal so it can be used to trigger the scope.

Yet another method is useful for making a sampled data scope. A flash converter with wide input bandwidth can sample at a moderate rate and store the data in a big buffer. Big means several times larger than the number of samples to be used for a waveform. Now the data in the buffer can be mathematically analyzed to determine the fundamental frequency of the data and can be used to break up the buffer data into a series of waveforms. These waveforms can then be overlaid to yield the effect of a faster sampling rate. This type of scope can have a bandwidth for single events that is one value, and a bandwidth for repetitive events that is several times greater.

In all these cases, clock recovery for triggering encounters the same issues. It is worthwhile to think about clock recovery and triggering. Noise in these circuits, as in any other circuit, is always present. That noise adds some level of jitter in the effective trigger timing. Even at low microwave speeds, jitter margins are often counted down to the last few picoseconds. The scope user needs to be aware of the characteristics of their clock recovery and trigger circuitry. The jitter it adds is going to be something more than zero.

Care

The older, so-called boat anchor oscilloscopes were sometimes good for hundreds of volts input. Internal clamp diodes could absorb any transient that didn't cause dielectric breakdown in the probe itself. This is often not so with multi-gigahertz bandwidth probes. Sometimes these can withstand only a few volts. Those clamp diodes add a lot of capacitance, and that capacitance reduces available bandwidth. This is true for almost all microwave-frequency test equipment. There may be no protection from even minor transients. Any time the equipment is to be connected to live circuitry, first verify that the DC offset of that circuitry can be handled by the equipment. Any time that a cable is to be attached to a port on the test equipment, always first put a terminator on the cable. Many cables can support electrostatic buildups of over 1,000 volts on their inner conductors. Most microwave equipment cannot withstand 100 volts. Some cannot withstand even 10. Applying that terminator discharges the cable and improves the expected life of the equipment. Finally, it is a good idea to make it a habit to keep either terminators or caps on all unused ports of all your microwave equipment. The equipment usually comes with these already in place. For the same reason, if a cable is attached to a port of the equipment, never leave it open on the bench. If it is going to be set down, put a terminator or cap on it.

This habit not only protects against accidentally damaging equipment by electrostatic discharge, it also maintains cables and ports in good condition by simply keeping out dirt.

By the way, the number one rule, the most important, the one you do as a matter of habit: When working around any piece of microwave test equipment, always wear the grounded wrist strap.

Time Domain Reflectometer

The time domain reflectometer (TDR) is a tool familiar to most signal integrity engineers. It consists of a step generator and an oscilloscope. The tool sends a low amplitude voltage step into the device under test and then displays the reflected signal. The output impedance of this tool is a well-characterized resistance; by observing the reflected voltage, you can measure the impedance of the device under test. This allows for very easy measurement of transmission line impedances, crosstalk, connector characteristics, and so on.

The obvious limitation of this device is that reflections from discontinuities further down the line are impacted by the reflections and losses of nearer features. Thus, the accuracy of the displayed image typically decays very quickly with distance through the device under test. Even in a lossless situation, to get any accuracy for downstream characteristics, it is necessary to employ peeling.

A second obvious characteristic is that the tool cannot predict characteristics for rise times faster than its actual output. The loss of typical circuit boards is too large to be ignored, and it causes the rise time of the pulse to quickly degrade. Similarly, crosstalk magnitudes will not be accurate unless the device rise time is set to match the rise time of the aggressor driver. To achieve good rise times, various methods are used. One method is to solder low-loss, or semi-rigid, coaxial pig-tails directly to the pins of the device under test. Another method is to mount the device on circuit board that is as similar as possible to the way it will normally be used, but approach it with traces that are much wider than would be practical on production boards. Of course, the dielectric is made proportionally thicker to get the impedance right.

The maximum resolution of typical TDR machines is in the range of about one percent. It is often said that the useful range of TDR measurements is about 30 decibels. In stating it this way, it becomes easier to compare with the performance of network analyzers, which will be described shortly. To a limited extent, the data that would be acquired by a network analyzer can be derived from that of the TDR. One simply calculates the derivative of the measured wave—yielding the impulse response—and applies a Fourier transform to the result. Useful bandwidths that can be achieved by this method are substantially lower than can be achieved with a network analyzer.

A second mode of measurement that can be made with most TDR machines is the time domain through (TDT) measurement. This measurement is used for such things as making crosstalk measurements. You might use this tool to make such a measurement in several ways. Which method is best depends on what you want the data to do for you.

Suppose you need to compare two connectors to determine which exhibits the least crosstalk. In this case, the procedure might be as simple as mounting each connector on similar test boards and comparing the TDT measurements. It may be as simple as that, requiring attention to only a few details. Obviously, you will want to make the test fair by being sure that the signal edge-rate at the input to each connector is the same. The fact that the edge-rate out of the TDT is the same for two measurements does not necessarily make it the same at the actual edge of the device under measurement. Measure the signal at the edge of the device, and adjust the edge-rate for equality.

Things get a bit trickier if the two connectors don't have the same footprint. You might, for example, try to compare a connector with a single inline arrangement to a connector with a multiport hexagonal array footprint. In the first case, there are two nearest neighbors to measure; in the other case, six. Another difficult case is when signal arrangements place different signal types near your victim signal in different connectors. One percent of a TTL signal is not the same as one percent of a low-voltage high-speed signal. When you encounter problems such as these, you will have to work out a strategy for how you can make the measurements and how you can fairly compare the results.

One possibility is to use some of the material you learned in reading this book and pop back and forth between time and frequency domains. Take your TDT measurement at the fastest edge-rate you can achieve. Calculate the derivative of the data set, yielding an impulse response. Convolve the impulse response with a single pulse of whatever width and amplitude is appropriate for the aggressor signal on the particular port designated as crosstalk aggressor. Note that this step may be more easily done in the frequency domain. You now have the pulse response for this particular aggressor signal through this particular crosstalk link.

More can be accomplished. With the pulse response, you could sum the positive parts of the tail and sum the negative parts of the tail to calculate the worst-case crosstalk that any signal sequence on this aggressor can yield. Such calculations may be complicated, but with the software tools that are available today, scripts can be written to do most of the work for you. Personally, my preference is to make the measurements in the frequency domain and do most of the calculations there.

Network Analyzer

The network analyzer (NA) is an awesome device. It is not surprising to see data that maintains accuracy while spanning a dynamic range greater than 100 decibels. This is equivalent to better than 0.01 percent resolution. Traditionally, oscilloscopes have been in the range of 1 percent. This resolution and this accuracy of the NA are typically available at frequencies up through tens of gigahertz.

The network analyzer is an oscillator and receiver that can be tuned. It outputs a frequency of known voltage and measures that frequency—amplitude and phase—in its receiver. Typical devices have two ports and can measure both voltage reflected and voltage transmitted in both directions. Usually, the engineer specifies a range of frequencies to be covered and the number of samples to be acquired in that range.

To achieve this accuracy, the machine must be calibrated before it is used. In calibration, the machine measures the voltage and phase that its own receiver observes at each frequency in the set, at its own ports. There is no need for the oscillator to output exactly the right voltage at each frequency because the calibration allows it to measure and compensate for deviations. All that is needed is that the machine be repeatable. Of course, the calibration covers more than just this. The tool must be able to accurately measure the signal flowing in and out at each port. It must be able to measure both the amplitude and phase. In all, 12 error terms in the machine are minimized by the calibration routines.

The calibration is specific to the frequency set that the user specifies. If the range or number of points is changed, the calibration has to be repeated. Similarly, since accuracy depends on the repeatability of the machine, it is not a good idea to expect a calibration to remain useful for weeks at a time. The period over which a calibration is reliable depends on things like how much temperature variation the machine is subject to, how much vibration, how badly the line voltage fluctuates, and such environmental variables. There is no fixed answer to how long a calibration is good for; it depends on the environment.

Calibration is typically achieved with the use of a set of precision standards. These are very accurate and very expensive. The set can easily cost many thousands of dollars. They are to be handled with great care.

Typically, the engineer who makes measurements performs the calibration procedure. In instances where the same machine is used by different people for different types of measurements, you may find it necessary to run a calibration every time you come to the machine. On the other hand, if you are the only user and make only a single type of measurement, you may only have to run the calibration once a week. Any time you do things like move the machine or change cables or probes, you must, and my lab expert tells me to emphasize the word must, redo the calibration.

Care

The most obvious rule is that no parts of the calibration kit are ever to be used for any other purpose. That is certainly important enough to say again. Never is any part of the calibration kit to be used for any purpose other than calibration of the network analyzer. When a terminator or a coupler is needed, you may be tempted to use the coupler right there in the calibration kit. Don't do it. When a needed coupler is lost and it takes a week to get in a replacement, slip your schedule by a week and wait rather than using the coupler in the calibration kit. Yes, it is that important.

If a part of the calibration kit is damaged, a month or more may pass before it becomes evident. However long it takes, all work done between the time the damage took place and the time it was recognized is wasted. And when it cannot be absolutely determined when the damage took place, you may have to redo many tests that were actually good. Then, when it is finally established that the calibration kit has been damaged and a replacement part must be ordered, that will take time, too—time that the machine is idle and projects wait.

Terminators and couplers for daily use are much cheaper than those in the calibration kit. Stock enough of various flavors so you won't be tempted to use the ones in the calibration kit. A terminator can be obtained for the price of a milkshake. A good calibration kit can cost as much as a good car.

When using the calibration kit, read, understand, and follow the manufacturer's rules for handling the parts. Align cable ends so that connectors screw on easily by hand. Never use torque to compensate for a poorly aligned cable or connector. Always finish tightening connectors to the specified torque by using a torque wrench. Never tighten the connector with another wrench until it feels tight. Particularly with small parts such as female terminators, it is tempting, it feels natural, to screw the part on by simply rotating the body of the connector into the threads. Doing so damages both the center pin and the flat mating surfaces. Always hold the body of both mating sides while turning only the threaded flange ring. This part provides only force, not electrical contact. As it wears, electrical performance of the part does not degrade. Always hand-tighten the ring before using the wrench on it. Your hand will feel when threads are correctly aligned and moving freely; the wrench may not.

Subtle but catastrophic damage can be done by interconnecting 3.5-millimeter and SMA connectors. They often screw together quite nicely. They fit with no need to force anything. The problem is that the 3.5-millimeter female connector is destroyed by the SMA male connector. The SMA center pin is enough larger than that of the 3.5-millimeter connector that, when they are mated, the contacts on the 3.5- millimeter are permanently sprung. Using hindsight, it is clear that making them look the same and giving them the same threads was a bad idea, but that is water under the bridge. Now the need is to take care not to mix the two connectors.

Finally, any time any wideband test equipment is used, always use a wrist strap grounded to the chassis of the equipment. This practice has two benefits: it makes the wearer look chic and knowledgeable and it significantly reduces the acoustic decibel level from the lab manager. It is a safe bet that microwave test equipment will have no ESD protection.

Application

It was pointed out that the network analyzer can provide extreme resolution, accuracy, and bandwidth compared to TDR and oscilloscope measurements. To achieve these benefits, similarly great care is required in setting up and conducting the measurements. It is usually the skill of the measurer, not the capability of the equipment, that establishes the ultimate accuracy of measurements made with a network analyzer. This does not refer to steadiness of hand or sharpness of eye; it is about skill. It is understanding how to implement a really good calibration of the equipment. It is understanding how to design a test that enables accuracy and repeatability.

Remember when oscilloscope measurements were made by hand-probing a board. A ground lead was attached at some convenient place and the probe tip was held against the test point. Consider a measurement of 6-gigahertz frequency on FR4 board material. Moving the probe tip with respect to the ground by a mere .05 inch, likely the limit achievable by hand, makes a difference of 18 degrees in the phase of the measurement. Clearly, hand-held probes are no longer practical. And yes, the ground placement is as important as the tip placement.

Microwave probes that have very good bandwidths are available. To be used on circuit boards, they need pads specifically designed for them. These probes are usually characterized in terms of their signal and ground arrangement and spacing. They also usually are calibrated through use of a calibration tile that is specifically designed for the specific probe style. Optimal use of these tiles is an art in itself. In one example, a calibration tile was found to yield poor calibration at frequencies above about 5 or 6 gigahertz. It turned out that calibration results improved markedly when a lossy substrate was place under the calibration tile. This sort of thing may be done instinctively by the expert and so may never make it to the descriptions of how to use the device.

Probes are delicate and sometimes tricky to use. Always using a vibration dampening table below any probe station is recommended. One of the costs of doing business with microwave probes is that the first experience most people have with the probe is breaking it. It makes little difference if the user is a lowly lab technician or a PhD, expect the first, maybe the first few, probes to be broken. These probes usually cost in the range of $500 to $1,500 dollars.

How do they get broken? Usually by doing something that seemed perfectly reasonable at the time. Often probes are made of ceramic material in thin sheets. Obviously bumping them with or into anything hard can fracture the tip. But consider this situation: You are to make a measurement on a circuit board that has a pad arrangement with a ground separated by 0.005 inch from a trace that is also 0.005-inch wide. You select a probe with 5 mil tips separated by a 5-mil gap. This is a good choice because there will be little alteration in the fields as the signal transitions from the probe to the signal line. When you get to the board and lower the probe to the surface one side of the probe makes contact before the other for some reason. Perhaps there is a bit of solder on one side. Perhaps the tip is rotated slightly out of level. Whatever the reason, it is easy to turn the vernier height adjustment another quarter turn and get good solid contact on both sides. And then the probe tip goes plink.

So what happened? In pushing the tip down, perhaps you applied a half pound of force on the tip. Let's work with that number. If the tip making contact was 5 mils square, the force you applied to the tip that made first contact was 20,000 pounds per square inch.

When a probe is set on a surface, you cannot rely on feel or force. You must rely on electrical measurement. Turn the machine on while the probe is being moved to the surface. You will see in the signals when contact is made. Measure—perhaps with a multimeter—whether contact has been made with both sides of the probe. If contact has not been made, lift the probe off the surface, tweak the level adjustment, and set it down again until both sides contact at the same time without force.

The network analyzer can make extremely precise measurements, but that comes at the cost of very great care needed in making the measurements, in calibration, and in caring for your equipment.

The recommendation here is to use connectors, such as SMA connectors, wherever possible. These cost a dollar or two and can achieve useful bandwidths as high as 15 gigahertz. The trick is that to achieve these bandwidths, the footprint for mounting the connector on the board has to be very carefully designed—modeled on a full-wave field solver. Also, a calibration strategy has to be carefully devised.

What a Network Analyzer Does

It may not be clear yet just what the network analyzer does. This tool measures the frequency response—amplitude and phase—of a device. It typically measures the frequency response in two directions—forward and backward—through the device. It also measures the frequency response of the reflected wave at both the input and output ports of the device. These measurements are stored in a format called *S* parameters with a table of the frequencies at which the measurements were made. You specify the frequency range and number of points at which measurements are to be made.

Network analyzers usually terminate both ports with 50-ohm termination while measurements are being made, so the data taken describes how the device performs in a 50-ohm environment. Even though many devices are used in environments of other impedances, this is not a problem. As has been described in Chapter 3, it is fairly easy to translate these to any other desired impedances. Similarly, if the device that is measured is a linear, time-invariant device, as most non-magnetic passive devices are, then it is easy to translate the frequency-domain information to time-domain, as has also been detailed in Chapter 3.

Spectrum Analyzer

Most signal integrity engineers will already be familiar with the spectrum analyzer. It is the premier tool used in measuring and tracking electromagnetic emissions. There are numerous books written on this subject, and it will not be expanded here.

Less familiar is the auxiliary tool called the tracking generator. Many signal integrity engineers have never seen or even heard of this useful tool. The tracking generator is a tunable oscillator that couples to the spectrum analyzer and outputs a sine wave that precisely matches the frequency that at any instant is being measured by the spectrum analyzer. This output is used to drive circuitry and devices that are being tested.

As an example, consider a circuit board that is to be tested for resonances. Perhaps a device is known to operate acceptably in numerous applications but on one particular board seems to yield excessive emissions at some particular frequency. Is it a resonance in the board that is producing this result? The tracking generator provides a stimulus for exciting the board at the desired range of frequencies while the spectrum analyzer is making its usual emissions test. Similarly, the tracking generator is useful for testing an antenna, perhaps a slot or patch antenna, or for testing the effectiveness of a chassis at containing emissions.

Though the spectrum analyzer with tracking generator is doing nearly the same thing as the network analyzer does, in instances where the signal is measured in an emissions chamber, the tracking generator is a good choice.

Probes and Probing

Test probes can be used for both network analyzer, TDR, and oscilloscope measurements. These probes consist of devices that are designed to be positioned by a mechanical device and that connect to the measurement tool through a small cable connector—SMA or similar. The probe itself is often implemented as transmission lines on a ceramic substrate that tapers to a small dimension while maintaining a constant impedance. This can be accomplished through geometries such as co-planar waveguide. Tips are typically gold-plated for good contact.

This type of probe has the characteristic that it is brittle. That is, it responds poorly to bumping into things. It also responds poorly to being pushed against things. Consider a measurement that is to be made on a circuit board. For this example, the ground and signal contact points are 0.01 inch apart, but one is 0.001 inch higher than the other for some reason. That means that to push the probe contacts hard enough to make contact, the tip must twist 5.7 degrees. Consider what will happen if you clamp one edge of a sheet of glass and twist the other 5.7 degrees. Don't actually do this, it is likely to be hazardous. Just consider what would happen. Unless it is a very thin sheet of glass, it is going to shatter. So would the probe tip.

Here I am going to repeat what was said only a few paragraphs back in this chapter. Yes, it is that important. Perhaps you are using this as a cookbook and have just flipped to this paragraph heading. You need to know this. When a probe tip is set on a board, it must be tested with a meter to verify low resistance at both signal and ground contacts. If good contact is not made by setting the probe down, lift the probe, rotate it to lower the contact that makes poor contact, set it down and measure again. Repeat this until good contact can be made without pushing the contact against the board. When good contact is made at both power and ground, cables can be connected between the probe and the tester, and testing can begin. Finally, the fact that the probe tips were adjusted to make good contact at a particular test point does not necessarily mean that the level adjustment is right for the next test point.

Some microwave test probes are more flexible than the ceramic ones. When using these, it still is necessary to level the tips using the above procedure. The tips still are delicate and damage can be less obvious. A tip can be bent out of shape but not shattered as with a ceramic tip.

The probes themselves are only one part of a measurement system or strategy. The footprint on the board where the probe makes contact is also part of the measurement. That footprint must be designed specifically for this use if it is to maximize the accuracy of the measurement. Two items need consideration: the impedance of the net must be preserved constant right out to the point where the probe attaches and the ground must provide a low inductance return path. Achieving adequately low ground inductance is sometimes particularly difficult. Another important consideration is that, for the very best measurements, it is not enough that the characteristic impedances match at the point where the probe contacts the device pad. You also want the field shapes to match as closely as possible. As frequency increases, matching the shapes becomes more important.

Consider this situation: A particular probe makes electrical contact over a region that is 0.003 inch wide. That same probe is used to measure a trace that is 0.003 inch wide and a different trace that is 0.02 inch wide. If the impedance, length, and surrounding dielectric are the same for the two traces, will they both read the same electrical length? Probably not. The impact of that width difference is that the current takes some distance to distribute itself into the final long-run configuration on the wide trace. Over that distance where the current distribution is in transition, the characteristics of the trace are not the same as they are through the distance where the current distribution is constant. This effect, by the way, exists not only in measurements, it can also exist in field simulators.

Situations such as this are the reason that on-board calibration structures are needed to get good measurements. Structures, or traces that are identical to the traces connecting to the device, are added to measure the impact of launching the signal. Measurements of those calibration traces can be mathematically manipulated to remove the impact of the launch from the measurement of the device under test. Your success is dependent on the accuracy with which the on-board calibration structures match the traces to the device under test. On-board calibration structures are needed not only for probe measurements, they are needed for any type of board connection.

A useful test is to make five to 10 copies of the same calibration trace and then measure each to see how much difference there is. The distribution of this measurement can help show how well the matching and measurements are, and so how accurate the measurement calibration process can be. Alternatively, refinements of technique that result in better matching of this set of measurements are also likely to yield better overall accuracy.

Auxiliary Equipment

If you are going to use microwave probes to make your electrical measurements, you will need a few pieces of auxiliary equipment. You must have a good stereoscopic microscope. It was pointed out above that very small mechanical distances correspond to significant electrical distances for high frequencies. To obtain the accuracy that the network analyzer is capable of, you will need to be able to position those probe tips with an accuracy of thousandths of an inch. That mandates use of a microscope.

Television cameras that attach the oscilloscope to your computer have gotten very inexpensive. These make it easy to document your procedures with captured images. It is also often easier to view your work directly on the large screen of your computer than through the eyepiece of the microscope. So, even if you decide to not use your computer monitor, be sure that the microscope you get has the facilities for attaching such a camera. Eventually you are going to realize that you need the camera.

Give some thought to lighting, too. Sometimes the lighting system that comes with the microscope produces more glare than is useful. Before you buy, check the lighting system on a real circuit board and find out if it works for you. If it is producing glare, dimming the light merely produces a dimmer glare. It doesn't solve the problem.

A really big issue is vibration. Our environments are often full of low-frequency vibration that we don't really notice. Those big industrial air conditioners on the roof can shake violently, at low frequencies. Cars and trucks on a nearby road are a source of shaking. It may even be just some guy walking down a hall. It isn't always obvious that these things are impacting your measurements. Things may look just fine, but you may find that your measurements are much cleaner after you try a vibration isolation table and see the electrical noise level drop noticeably. Another way you may discover you need a vibration isolation table is when you move your test equipment to another lab and find out that now the noise levels in your measurements are a lot different.

Vibration isolation tables are not particularly expensive. Check them out. Put one on the list of items you need in your lab. You need one.

Cables

Cables are usually not thought of as test equipment nor as part of the test equipment. At microwave frequencies, that thought needs to change. In our lab we have cables that run well over $1,000 per meter. These cables connect to the network analyzer and are part of what makes it capable of its dynamic range and accuracy. They require careful handling to maintain that accuracy.

There are also cables that cost only a few hundred dollars per meter. These are used in less demanding places such as day-to-day connections to the 50-gigahertz oscilloscope. Then the cables that only cost seven or eight dollars a foot are often left laying around on the bench top. Finally, some cable runs only about a dollar a foot. It is not recommended for any sort of measurements.

The easiest way to permanently damage a cable is to bend it in too tight a radius. The more expensive the cable, the more care is needed in avoiding any sharp bends in that cable. The second and third easiest ways to damage a cable are to set something on it, and damaging a connector at the end of the cable. Feel free to use the method that works for you, but please, stay out of my lab. Meanwhile, check with your cable vendor to find out what are safe bend radii for your expensive cables.

Basic Measurements

In the early days of electronics, fundamental quantities that everyone needed to know how to measure included voltage, current, impedance, and time. Now the list changes substantially. We have explained how voltage, current, and impedance vary with position along a transmission line and are highly dependent on how that line was terminated. We have also explained that traditional techniques of oscilloscope triggering on data edges are no longer useful.

Current issues of critical importance are things like worst-case eye opening, impulse and pulse responses, S parameters, and so on. It is no longer useful to make a measurement of a system while ignoring the details of the data being transported as the measurement is made. Basic measurements are simply not as basic as they once were. Seldom can the actual parameter of interest be directly measured. Rather, data is acquired, and parameters of interest are extracted from the measurements. Because of this, it is often true that there is no immediate feedback when a measurement is going bad. Subsequent evaluation of the data is what shows if there was an error. It is probably a bad idea to do something like spend a week in the lab gathering measurements then tear down the test setups and go back to your desk to check the data.

The type of system that is of interest here is the point-to-point interconnect. This system includes drivers, receivers, and the board features that connect them together. The things that need to be measured in such a system are characteristics of the transmitted signal, characteristics of the received signal, and characteristics of the set of features that connect these together. To be useful, these characteristics need to be measured in the environment that is most stressful; that is, in the situation that is most likely to show a design failure. To the traditional extremes of voltage and temperature, now there needs to be added data pattern. One of the most serious issues in measuring whether a link functions reliably is being sure that the test is made while data that is most likely to cause a failure is being transmitted. Initially, one tends to ask how they could know what data pattern might be worse than any other; but, it can be done. The important thing to understand is that the data pattern that stresses one feature may well be benign for other features.

Consider, for example, measurement of jitter and measurement of EMI. Transmission of a simple clock pattern, 101010..., is often the worst case for EMI, but is simultaneously the very best case for jitter. Conversely, transmitting a highly random bit stream makes EMI look good but makes jitter look bad. Clearly, it is not possible to discuss measurement without also talking about the bit streams used to make those measurements.

Transmitter

Among parameters that are typically measured at a transmitter are the worst-case transmit jitter, the minimum and maximum output voltages, unit interval, return loss, clock-to-output jitter transfer, output sensitivity to power supply noise, AC and DC common mode output, slew-rates, and leakage when powered down. Not every system requires every one of these measurements while some may require more.

Jitter

There are various types of jitter, and numerous papers on the subject are available on the web. Some of the individual papers are lengthy, and this book will not repeat everything that has been explained there. Our objective is to introduce you to some of the key concepts while not bogging down in the fine points.

Jitter is the variation of the timing, the position of signal edges, with respect to some reference timing. Initially consider the reference to be a fixed, rock-stable clock. The data edges measured at the pins of the package are likely to deviate somewhat from precisely matching this clock. Those deviations are called jitter. One of the important things to understand about jitter is that it makes a big difference who is asking. If an engineer wants to know what sort of jitter it has in order to determine how the receive eye is influenced by the channel, the answer is that there are two types. If the question is asked by the systems engineer who wants to establish the reliability of the link, the answer is that there are two types. But they are not the same two.

Jitter that is due to clock wandering, that spreads out over several data bits, is quite different in effect from jitter that takes place within a single unit interval. Stated differently, jitter that is distributed over several unit intervals impacts the system differently than jitter of the same numerical magnitude that occurs on a bit-to-bit timeframe. Jitter that is distributed can have impact on receiver clock recovery but will have little impact on channel characteristics—it will add to the jitter observed at the receiver but much less to the voltage opening. Jitter that takes place in a single unit interval will have significant impact on receiver eye voltage opening because narrowing or widening of an individual pulse strongly impacts the low-frequency harmonic content. So the answer that the board engineer tends to look for is the magnitude and harmonic envelope of the jitter.

This type of information can be difficult to obtain with a sampling scope. The better solution is to use a real-time scope with a large data buffer. There the data can be easily examined to find variations in edge-to-edge variations. There are dedicated software packages and even dedicated hardware designed to do nothing but measure the characteristics of jitter.

Jitter is caused by numerous mechanisms. Usually there is jitter in the system clock that the transmit device uses as its reference. The system clock is usually much lower in frequency than the serial data being transmitted, and the actual data clock is generated by a phase-locked-loop, or PLL. This circuit can be sensitive to supply variations and noise in the chip, yielding another sort of timing variation. The data to be transmitted is clocked in circuitry that is sensitive to crosstalk and power supply noise. So jitter happens and it needs to be quantified.

The trigger circuitry of your oscilloscope adds jitter, too. Fortunately, this jitter can be largely eliminated by not overusing the oscilloscope's trigger circuitry. Many oscilloscopes now have large internal buffers, which you want. They allow you to use the trigger circuitry to start data acquisition one time. After that, acquisition continues until the buffer is full. When the buffer has filled, you can examine the data and mathematically determine where subsequent trigger points should have been. That procedure reduces trigger jitter to whatever mathematical accuracy you choose. You are still relying on the stability of the oscilloscope's internal clock, but this usually has far lower jitter than does the trigger circuitry.

It was stated above that the system engineer who is interested in overall link reliability will have a different definition for two types of jitter. The amount of cycle-to-cycle jitter does not tell that engineer how many errors per bit to expect in the working system. That engineer will want to know how much of the jitter is random and how much is deterministic—what is the standard deviation? The error rate can be predicted only when this information is known. Among the values required by various standards are numbers like one error in 10^{12} or even 10^{15} bits. These are big numbers. At a data rate of 2.5 gigabits per second, 10^{15} comes out to one every 111 hours. Of course, if it doesn't fail in a single instance of 111 hours, that proves nothing. It might have just been luck. Measure it for 10 or 100 times this long and then perhaps people will accept that this error rate is likely achieved.

Obviously, this kind of testing is not done. The tests are run but not like this. What is done is careful analysis of jitter profiles. Processes— jitter, noise, rainfall—come in two flavors. They are deterministic or random. A deterministic process is bounded. If so much force is applied, so much velocity results. If the rate of change of current through an inductor is so much, the voltage must be such-and-such. These are deterministic processes. Much of jitter is deterministic. If a bounded parameter drives it, the result will never exceed some specifiable value. Other processes are random. They can have some typical value but, however unlikely, any other value is also possible. This characteristic is sufficient to identify a process as random. It is also worthwhile to note that a process can have random elements and still be deterministic. A good example of this is crosstalk. The amplitude of the aggressor signal is known, and the coupling to the victim net is known. The data patterns are not necessarily known and could even be random. But, the resulting crosstalk is bounded and so is deterministic.

So, what is done in measuring jitter is to carefully measure a bunch of data for jitter values. The values are binned as in a histogram and a curve-fit is done to the profile. This profile is considered to represent the combined deterministic and random components. The curve fitted to the edge is considered to yield the random component from which the standard deviation can be extracted. All of this can be done by software, and the user doesn't have to be particularly aware of the minutia of how the mathematics works. The user does, however, need to be aware that there are different approaches to defining and measuring jitter. When the job calls for measuring the jitter, it must also specify which aspects are to be measured.

Then conditions that maximize transmit jitter must be identified. These conditions are likely to include the level of system clock jitter, data patterns, and noise on the power and ground. Of these, the most difficult to specify is the data pattern. Data patterns that are particularly stressful for the interconnect can be benign for the driver. PLLs in the transmit circuitry often can be a source of transmit jitter, so patterns that tend to interact with the PLL are likely to be effective. However, it is likely that only the silicon-circuit designers really have enough information to make such an identification. One thing is usually true: transmitting a "1010101... pattern stresses nothing but EMI.

The package designer and the board designer have a somewhat different problem, and in many ways it is an easier problem. They have the possibility of directly calculating what data pattern will yield worst-case loss and jitter in the passive interconnect circuitry. The worst-case bit stream can be derived from the pulse response of the interconnect. This is because, as long as the interconnect is passive and has no magnetic components—is linear—and something like TEM mode is presumed, superposition works. That is, the response to any particular sequence of bits can be generated by adding up the contributions of time-shifted copies of that pulse response. The time shift for each individual copy is set equal to the unit interval multiplied by the bit position in the bit sequence. In this way, the channel response to any arbitrary bit sequence can be generated directly from the pulse response.

Similarly, a worst-case bit stream can be derived from the pulse response. Examine the pulse response of the interconnect. Typically, it begins at some level that corresponds to the logical false or zero level. Then it goes to logical true, or one value for one unit interval. And then it returns to false, or zero. During and after this cycle, various ringing and modification of the wave shape takes place. Now divide the graph of this waveform into unit intervals. For discussion here, label the interval that contains the logical true value zero, the next interval one, and so on. The waveform in interval zero will be the starting point for building the worst-case wave. Begin writing a bit sequence by writing down a 1 to represent this bit. Examine the voltage in the next time interval. If it is mostly negative, consider what this means. Had the bit preceding this pulse been a 1, then its remainder would now be adding this negative value to the current pulse. So in the bit sequence that is being written, add a 1 to the left. If, however, the voltage in this time interval is mostly positive, write a 0 to the left. Continue this procedure until the response dynamics have died away. The bit-sequence created in this way corresponds to the sequence that will produce the worst-case 1 at this point in this system.

It is possible to generate the worst-case input sequence for this circuit, independent of unit interval, by using the same procedure but setting the unit interval to an arbitrarily small value. The point of this is that there is no need to simulate a lot of random data in a linear circuit. Worst-case response can be generated from the response to a single pulse. Of course, the designer needs to take into account that the result so generated may be worse than any that can be achieved with the unit interval that the system is actually using.

Signal Amplitude

Place a probe at the package pin, and measure the voltage. That sounds easy enough, but it certainly isn't that simple. There are a whole list of things that make the measurement of the transmit output signal difficult to perform. These include termination issues, data enabling, wave-shaping, and inaccessibility.

The typical high-speed-serial transmitter will have internal termination to some specified impedance level. This will be stated as such things as 50 ohms single ended, or 100 ohms differential. If you measure at a low frequency, perhaps DC, these numbers are what you would expect to find. But what of microwave frequencies? Consider a transmit driver whose combined output capacitance is one picofarad. That is, the combination of the driver transistors, the capacitance of the termination resistors, and of the pad all add up to one picofarad. At a few gigahertz that is effectively in parallel with the termination resistor. At 3 gigahertz, for example, the impedance of this capacitance is nearly down to 50 ohms itself. Similarly, the package can introduce significant impedance and losses that modify the output voltage. This impacts the measurement.

The package will act as one element in a voltage divider. The other element is the impedance of the circuitry being driven. Since that circuitry, the board on which the transmitter is mounted, will have various characteristics, the voltage measured out of the transmitter will be dependent on the board characteristics. Because of this, most standards specify the transmitter output voltage and jitter as measured into a standard resistive load, rather than measured on the user's circuit board.

The output voltage should be measured while the transmit circuitry is being subjected not only to the standard corners of supply voltage and temperature, but also while subjected to worst-case noise on the supplies and worst-case jitter on the system clock. Finally, because the measured parameters will strongly depend on the data pattern being transmitted, standards often specify a particular pattern that is to be transmitted while this measurement is made.

Setting up a system to transmit a particular data pattern can be difficult. Often such measurements must be made while the device is not yet connected into a fully functional system. The solution that is becoming fairly standard is the built-in self test, or BIST. This typically enables numerous types of measurement to be made on devices that are mounted in not yet fully-functional systems. In designing high speed circuitry, be very skeptical of any active device that does not have BIST capability.

Many high-speed transmitters use various types of pre-emphasis to enhance the reach of circuitry. Usually the details will be specified in the standard that defines the particular class of link. In such a standard, not only the minimum transmit eye opening will be specified, but also the minimum for the pre-emphasized part. Thus, there are effectively two eye masks that must be applied to the measurement.

In Chapter 8, the eye mask was defined and illustrated. An eye mask is a geometric shape that is used in graphical displays of serial data. The eye mask designates the region of the graph that must be free of any data traces. Common shapes of eye masks include rectangular, hexagonal, and diamond. Their area defines the minimum eye opening that a particular standard requires.

The final problem in measuring transmitter output levels is that in some types of packages and some types of systems, it can be very difficult to actually access the specified measurement point. Ball grid array packages often fall into this category. In such a case, the engineer needs to translate the measured values that can be obtained at a nearby point, into what they must look like at the point of specification. That is, the specification might require some particular value at the ball of the package. The nearest accessible point may be on the opposite side of the board. The engineer needs to have a good model of the circuitry, from the data taken at the point that is actually available, between the ball and the available measurement point in order to project what is happening at the ball.

Return Loss

It was pointed out in Chapter 4 that the package is effectively one element in a voltage divider. The other element is the circuit board on which the part is mounted. Not enough information is available only in specification of the voltage at the package pin. Required information includes also the return loss of the package. In many specifications, this information is designated in the form of some minimum value, often in decibels. This number can be difficult to measure because circuitry sometimes needs to be active before the actual terminations and capacitors are effectively at their operating values. Because of this, the value claimed sometimes must be based on simulations rather than actual measurements.

Traces

Several important parameters are associated with traces. These include impedance, loss, crosstalk, and others. Two major methods are used to measure these parameters: time domain reflectometry and network analysis. Time domain reflectometry is often easier to perform. The network analyzer yields greater accuracy.

The first parameter to measure is usually the impedance of the trace or pair of traces. Single-ended impedance can be measured with any TDR machine. The procedure consists of calibrating the TDR machine, attaching the TDR probe to the end of the trace, and recording the reading. All measurements begin by calibrating the machine that will make the measurement. The accuracy of the measurement cannot be known unless the machine is calibrated. Occasionally, with a TDR machine, this might be as simple as measuring a 50-ohm terminator to verify that a previous calibration is still valid, but usually it should be the full set of adjustments as specified in the equipment manual.

When the machine is calibrated, attach it to the trace that is to be measured. At microwave frequencies, the measurement ground return is as important as the intended signal path, so take care to ensure that a good valid return path is present. The easiest measurement is made when the trace is terminated into an SMA connector. If this is practical for a given application, it is recommended. Often it is not possible due to layout requirements of the board. A second choice is to use a microwave probe. These probes are typically very fragile, so use care. The microwave probe will require a nearby high quality ground pad. The third possibility, and least recommended, is use of a soldered-on coaxial stub that is itself provided with an SMA connector. Each of these can be the right answer, depending on the situation.

When the machine is attached to an end of the trace, the measurement can be taken. Note that the TDR machine will show not only the trace, but also the circuitry and connectors that attach to it. Identify the point at which the trace itself begins in order to record the impedance of the trace rather than that of the connector. One way of identifying the point in the display where the trace contact is made is to take a metal object such as a screwdriver and contact the trace at the interface with the connector. Observing the display while this is done will clearly show where the connector ends and the trace begins.

Note that impedance variations in the interconnect circuitry between the measurement machine and the trace, and loss in this circuitry, can distort the value measured. See Chapter 4 for a description of the peeling algorithm, which describes this distortion. Some TDR machines have the capability to do peeling themselves; in any case, the recommendation is to minimize loss and impedance variations in the circuitry that connects to your board.

Conclusion

The goal here has been to reduce the chance of your walking into a lab and making a major blunder. Among the major blunders available are: burning out the input of a network analyzer or a wideband oscilloscope, and damaging an element of a calibration kit. Don't. When you bust a probe for the first time, and please delay this as long as you can, the proper phrase is, "I'm sorry, I'm new here." When you bust a probe for the second time, the proper phrase is, "Excuse me while I go and reread all the manuals and application notes." Don't be embarrassed when that first probe is broken, but keep in mind that uses up your allotment. Do be embarrassed if you break a second probe.

I hope you have enjoyed reading this book and find its contents useful. There is a lot more information available and I hope that having read this book encourages you to study more. Virtually all of the subjects and ideas presented in this book have volumes written detailing each. I am not the inventor of any of them. I am the inventor of most of the mistakes you may find here. I did not put in footnotes and references on a page-by-page basis so you would not be distracted from the development of various concepts. Instead, an appendix with references has been added. This appendix presents short reviews of several books and papers that you may find useful in expanding your understanding of much of the material that has been presented here. You undoubtedly know that often you have to read a dozen books or papers on a particular subject before you encounter the one that covers the entire subject clearly and completely. I have tried to list that type of book or paper in the appendix. I am grateful to the authors of those works. They are the giants on whose shoulders we stand.

Appendix **A**

Signal Integrity

While I presume most of you are thoroughly experienced in signal integrity work, there is a possibility that you aren't. In that case, I will say a few words about signal integrity and what the concept means.

Inside your computer, little bits of data are continuously being transported from device to device where they are processed, stored, or maybe evaluated. The signal integrity engineer studies and designs the mechanisms through which those bits of data pass from place to place. The data is carried over wires that are called transmission lines, and their travel is described by an equation called the telegrapher's equation, which describes losses and reflections. Look out a window. You see what is on the other side of the glass. But look closer; you see a reflection of yourself, too. Why is that reflection there? What causes the reflection? The cause is the difference in index of refraction between the glass and the air. In a very similar manner, when an electrical signal is sent down a transmission line, any change in impedance causes a partial reflection to take place.

For the past couple of decades, digital circuitry—computer transmitters and receivers—have been largely implemented in CMOS silicon circuits. One of the dominant characteristics of CMOS receivers has been very high input impedance. This high input impedance dissipates very little energy and so has been one of the very desirable characteristics that made CMOS the technology of choice. The other desirable feature of CMOS silicon was the low impedance of the drivers. They would provide a near short-circuit to the power supply when outputting a one and a near short-circuit to ground when outputting a zero. This again results in very low power dissipation. It was this low dissipation that allowed us to put first thousands and then millions of transistors in individual integrated circuits.

But when digital signals on moderate impedance transmission lines encounter the very high impedance of the CMOS receiver or the very low impedance of the CMOS driver, serious reflections take place. It is not possible to make the impedance of the transmission line high enough to match the input impedance of a normal CMOS receiver. If that were possible, the reflection at that end would be eliminated. But that strategy is not physically possible. So if nothing is done, the signal bounces back and forth between the transmitter and the receiver, slowly decaying to a steady-state condition. Meanwhile, the sum of all reflections on the line can easily be so bad that it is not possible for some time to tell whether the data is supposed to be read as a one or a zero. Lossy diodes called clamp diodes can reduce, but not eliminate, this problem.

What of the transmitter? If the transmitter impedance were set to equal the impedance of the transmission line, there would be no reflection at the transmitter, and all the reflections from the receiver would simply be absorbed at the transmitter. That idea has a better chance of becoming practical. Unfortunately, the precision that can be achieved in generating a target resistance in silicon, while remaining economical, is not very good at all.

Economics is a very important issue in the field of personal computers. The reason you can buy a computer with tens of millions of transistors in it for a few hundred dollars is that at every stage of the design, engineers are carefully evaluating and balancing functionality versus cost. We stay in business by giving you the highest reliability, the best functionality, at the lowest cost. We are not misers, but cost is a very important design parameter.

Back when computers and their data buses ran at only a few megahertz, it was no big deal if it took signals five or 10 nanoseconds to settle enough to be read. When the PCI bus came online, that same 10 nanoseconds represented a third of the total timing budget. Now it was a big deal. The timing budget works something like this: The transmitter outputs a data bit. There is some uncertainty as to precisely when that bit comes out because of manufacturing tolerances. Consider the timing. There is a master clock that dictates when events take place. That clock transmits a rising edge about once every 30 nanoseconds. At some point in time, that clock strobes a bit of data out of a data port, a transmitter. But there is some uncertainty, perhaps one or two nanoseconds, over precisely when the bit departs the chip. After it exits the chip, it travels at a finite rate, about 6 inches per nanosecond, down the transmission line. That transmission line could be over 18 inches long—another 3 nanoseconds. The receiver has two parameters, setup and hold time, that define the timing requirements it needs. The setup time is how long the data is required to be stable at the input before it can be reliably read. The reading takes place at the rising edge of the clock. Let's presume that good engineering practices caused the data to settle adequately by 5 nanoseconds after it arrived, and that the required setup time is another 5 nanoseconds. The same master clock that told the transmitter when to output the bit is also routed to this chip to tell it when to strobe the bit in. There is some uncertainty as to exactly when that clock arrives, because it too encounters reflections and manufacturing variations. We will call this 1-nanosecond uncertainty. Overall, we have used up over half of the original 30-nanosecond budget.

Subsequently, PCI buses doubled in speed. Front-side buses moved to speeds, or data rates, 10 times this. Guaranteeing that the data reliably arrives and settles so that it can be consistently and flawlessly read is the work of the signal integrity engineer. To do this, the signal integrity engineer builds models and runs simulations, makes calculations and weighs the economics of choices.

A bus consists of numerous data lines all starting in one place and going to the same other places. A challenging characteristic of a bus is that it is usually a multi-drop line. The same wire is shared between numerous—more than two—ports. Often, all of these ports, not just the ones at the ends, need to be able to transmit data onto the bus. When one is finished transmitting, it must release the bus and go to high impedance. That is, it turns on and outputs its data bit and afterward turns off so the next transmitter can use the bus. Take a few more nanoseconds off the timing budget we looked at above.

When it was invented, the bus architecture was an excellent solution to an engineering and economics problem. The problem was this: silicon devices cost a lot more than the wires that connected them together. The best trade between the cost of ports and functionality was the bus. The bus enabled a single port to talk to numerous devices; a single receiver to listen, in turn, to numerous devices. Clocks were slow and the few nanoseconds it took a bus to settle were inconsequential.

But driving that bus involves some perplexing problems. The impedance of a typical trace in a bus is about 50 to 70 ohms. When a transmitter is designed with this output impedance and placed at the end of this line, everything works great. But what if this transmitter needs to be in the middle of the line? At places other than the ends, the transmitter sees 50 to 70 ohms to the left and 50 to 70 to the right. It sees 25 to 35 ohms. Now what? Does it make sense to have two values of output impedance for every output? If the drivers at the ends of the line are now tri-stated, they are no longer providing the reflectionless terminations there. How is that solved?

These are the types of problems that the signal integrity engineer encounters and solves daily. The way they are solved is with models and simulations. The most commonly used tool is the program called SPICE. SPICE calculates how various electronic circuits respond, in voltage and current, over time. You create a text file that describes, in SPICE syntax, the components and connectivity of your circuit. This file describes the signal that is to be applied to this circuit. SPICE reads your file and calculates how the circuit responds. Most versions of SPICE include the capability to display the voltages or currents on nodes you specify, much as you would see them on an oscilloscope.

But it is a bit more complicated than that. Buses consist of numerous wires of various lengths within each trace. In your SPICE file, your included variables allow you to vary the line lengths, impedances, receiver capacitance, and driver resistances—all the parameters that can vary in your design. Then you run hundreds of simulations to map the range and combinations of parameters that result in acceptable voltage and timing margins. This step is often implemented through Monte Carlo simulation methods. If no solution is found, you alter the topology and start over. If a solution is found, you document the values and ranges required for the circuit to be successful and pass this information to the various engineers who design and lay out the board itself. Often at this stage, they respond by showing you that the lengths you require cannot be physically achieved within the constraints imposed by the devices required on the board. Again, you go back and start over.

Eventually you get to a solution that looks like it both works and can actually be laid out on the circuit board. Typically, when the board is laid out, you find that though most of your requirements were met, some traces do not correspond to your requirements. Now you take the actual parameters of those traces and simulate them to see if they yield acceptable margins or must be modified in the layout.

It doesn't end there. As the board layout is being completed, various things can go wrong. It would be a very bad idea for a signal trace to pass under the power transistor of a switching power supply. Even if there is a reference plane between the two, this is a bad idea. Another problem that is much more common comes when two routing layers are adjacent with no intervening reference plane. In theory, this layout works well as long as the signals on one layer are horizontal and those on the adjacent layer are vertical. In practice, this method usually results in signals on one layer that are oriented mostly vertical, and on the other layer are mostly horizontal. Thus, there will occasionally be segments of traces parallel and overlaying each other. This situation causes serious crosstalk. You have to set a limit on this condition and watch that the limit, perhaps a half inch, is not exceeded. The layout software might show that the segments on the two layers, though parallel, don't exactly overlay each other. Reality is that when the board is built, there is significant registration variability between layers. You need to be familiar enough with the fabrication process to recognize when the ideals in the layout program will not correspond to the realities in the fabricated board.

That kind of analysis is what signal integrity engineers do. It is exacting work, and requires skill and understanding to be done well. When signals exceeded about 50 megabits per second, signal integrity analysis became vital for reliability. Now a gigabit per second is no longer considered fast, and some engineers are designing at ten gigabits per second on circuit boards. This is one of those fields where there continues to be tremendous progress from year to year. It is a little hectic, but lots of fun.

Appendix **B**

Matlab 101

Matlab is an extremely powerful tool for the types of work we do, and yet many of us are not familiar with this tool. This is an introduction to the most fundamental operations in Matlab. If Matlab is not available to you, a fallback is Octave; however, scripts may have to be tweaked to get them to run on Octave. If you, like many, have been trying to do math in spreadsheets, you will find Matlab very refreshing.

Navigation

When you first start Matlab, it expects to be working in some standard directory. If you accept that and try to do all your work there, that directory soon gets so full of junk that it becomes unmanageable. You have alternatives.

In some ways Matlab acts like a DOS window. You can use several of the standard navigation commands such as `cd` and `dir`. Apparently it does not go to the operating system for execution of these commands, because it also responds to the Unix commands `ls` and `pwd`. If you attempt to use the extensions in either language, such as `dir /p` or `ls -a`, it will not recognize those extensions.

To start out, you open the directory in Windows in which you intend to work. I presume you have your system set up so that the address of the directory is displayed at the top of the directory window. Highlight that address and type `<ctl> c` to copy it. Go to your Matlab window and type `cd`, followed by a space. Now when you type `<ctl> v`, Matlab will pop into your directory.

Well, maybe it will. If there was a space inside the address, such as C:\Program Files, Matlab will balk. No problem, just place quotes around the address and it will work correctly. Well, maybe it will. The quotes you need for this to work are the single quotes not the double quotes. When you specify any string in Matlab using quotes, they need to be single quotes. Look at your keyboard. There is a key next to `<enter>` that has double quotes as the shifted character and single quotes as the lower case character. That lower case character is the one you need.

Now you can work in whichever directory you chose.

Variables

You don't have to declare variables in Matlab, but you do have to be aware that Matlab presumes that all your variables are matrices. Even if you make a statement as simple as `a=1`, it will treat this as a one-by-one matrix. Try it, then check by typing `size(a)`. It will tell you `a` is one-by-one. If you did that, you will have seen some perplexing behavior. You typed `a=1`. It responded:

```
a =

    1
```

You typed `size(a)`. It responded:

```
ans =

    1    1
```

After each of these operations, it likes to display the result of what it just did. Eventually this gets old, and you want it to just do the stuff and leave your screen alone. For each command, you tell it not to print the result on the screen by placing a semicolon after the command.

Try this:

```
b=20;
```

I am presuming you are pressing <enter> after each of these commands. Now it is doing what you wanted it to do. It accepts your command and doesn't immediately print out the result.

The next thing to try is:

```
b(1)=10; b(2)=11; b(3)=12;

size(b)

b
```

An individual element of a vector is specified by using parentheses. When you said b(1)=10, it created a one-by-one matrix for you. When you said b(2)=11, it created a one-by-two matrix for you, kept the values already specified, and plugged in the new value. Each time you added a new value, it went through the entire process of creating a new matrix for you. What would happen if you said b(6)=3? The question mark is not part of what you type into Matlab; and don't append a semicolon at this time. We want to see the result.

It created yet another new matrix, kept the values previously specified, plugged in the new value, and placed zero in all the remaining slots. One last experiment: type b(4)=4 and look what happens. What you see on the screen is pretty much what you expect to see on the screen. But what you don't see is interesting, too. What it didn't do is create a new matrix. It just plugged in the value. In a small matrix like this, the difference is too small to be noticeable. In a large matrix getting the size right first and then plugging in the values makes a big difference.

Ranges

Type b(2:4) and observe the result. It responded with the values of b(2) through b(4). Now try this. Type a=7:12 and see what happens. A vector was created with six elements and the numbers 7 through 12 were plugged in.

Suppose you wanted to create pulse that consisted of 4 out of 100 samples and that was located at some offset from the beginning of the data. Try this:

```
c(100)=0;

c(17:20)=1;

plot(c)
```

Type this:

```
clear

a(1,1:3)=1:3; a(2,1:3)=4:6; a(3,1:3)=7:9;

a

b
```

Undefined? It said b was undefined? *Clear* gave us a new start. Meanwhile, there now is this matrix that is three by three; you can check its size and verify that. Often we read in a huge array of data from our SPICE run but only want one or two columns from that data. You select a particular column by this:

```
a(:,2)
```

That line or command selected the second column. You could save that selection by saying b=a(:,2). On the other hand, if you wanted the third row, you would type a(3,:).

Operations

The standard operations work just like you expect them to—as long as your expectations are right. Add, subtract, multiply, and divide all work as expected. Type $5/17$ and you will see 0.2941, as expected. But try this:

```
a= [ 1, 1/3e9]
```

It displays that second element as zero. Is it really zero? It shouldn't be and we can check it, or you can simply tell the program to display more digits so you can see what is going on.

```
format long e

a
```

Now you have a screen full of numbers and can see that the right value really did get into that second position.

Something else went on there, too. You enter values for an array by placing square brackets. Row elements are separated by commas; columns are separated by semicolons. Usually you would be working with large arrays that you load from data files, but if you have to load something by hand, that's how.

Transpose

When you load your array or vector from a data file, it sometimes comes out wrong. Well, at least different from what you need. What needs to be a column might be a row. This is very easy to deal with. Try these three lines:

```
a
```

```
a'
```

```
a=a'
```

That single quote character transposes a vector or a matrix, and is just as easy if your matrix has 1,000 entries.

Matrix Operations

Now you come to one of the mind-bending parts of Matlab. If you are accustomed to working with matrices, this will seem obvious; if you are accustomed to doing math in spreadsheets, this might be a revelation. Start with a clean slate, but first take a look at what variables you have defined in your explorations.

```
who
```

Yes, type who. The machine responds by displaying the names of all the variables currently defined. For fun, try what and why. Now do this:

```
clear
a=[1,2]
b=[3,4]'
a*b
b*a
```

As stated, the machine does matrix math. So, a*b does not equal b*a. If the two results displayed don't make sense to you, you need to go back and study how matrix multiplication works.

Try out the various fundamental math operators and see how they work with these matrices. This is all well and good, but sometimes you want to treat your data as data rather than as a vector or a matrix. What then?

Element by Element

Sometimes what you want is c(1)=a(1)*b(1), c(2)=a(2)*b(2), and so on. This is not matrix multiplication. It is element-by-element multiplication. Yes, all the standard looping commands are there, and you could do this with a FOR loop, but it would be slow. You do element-by-element operations by prefixing the operator with a period. First, note that we had transposed b above. It needs to be put back or the machine will complain.

```
b=b'
c=a.*b
c=a./b
```

That is all there is to that. It is easier to code this way than with a loop, and it is faster in execution.

Scripts

Half the fun of Matlab is scripting. Once you have worked out a procedure for some operation you want to do, you don't have to type it all in each time you need that procedure again. You can just put it in a script.

A script is a text file that is saved with the extension .m. If the script is in the current directory or on the Matlab path, all you need to do is type the name of the script and it will perform the list of commands as if you were typing them to the screen. As useful as this is, there is a downside to it.

This type of script uses the same workspace that the screen terminal does. If you happen to use some variables inside the script that have the same names as some you have been using, overwriting will take place. Similarly, you might need a lot of temporary variables in completing your script, and when it is done they are all sitting there in your workspace too.

Now you could delete the unneeded variables by using the `clear` statement stating the names of the variables that need to be eliminated, but that is not cool. One way to write the script is to use the command `edit` in Matlab.

Functions

Functions are very similar to scripts, but they have some additional restrictions and benefits. First, from the outside, functions and scripts look the same. They are both text files with the .m extension. One really big difference is that functions have their own working space. Variables in a function will not overwrite variables in your working space. When the function returns, all those temporary internal variables are gone; only the return value remains.

Of course that last statement is only approximately true. But why sweat the fine points in a 101 course? Actually, Matlab has the standard capabilities of most modern languages. You can define global variables. You can define persistent variables, and so on. There are elements and capabilities of functions that I will not describe here. This tutorial is just to get you started. Later you can look up more gory details at your leisure. What is described here enables you to do useful tasks and is very easy to comprehend.

A function starts with the word `function`. It is followed by an optional dummy variable naming the return variable, and an equals sign. Then comes the name of the function, which should be the same as the name of the file except for the extension. The function name is followed by open and closed parentheses. In the parentheses are the optional list of input variables. All that goes on the first line.

On the second line, and this is a requirement, is a comment. There has to be at least one comment line, although there can be more. Comments have a percent symbol in the left column. We haven't talked about the `help` command yet, but there is one. When help is invoked for this function, this one-or-more lines of comment are displayed. This is where you describe what the function does, what its inputs are, and what its output is. `Help` will display every comment it finds, starting at the second line, until any line that is not a comment is found. Other comments can exist and will not be displayed.

The body of your function can be as many lines of code as you need to accomplish your task. When you are finished, plug the return value into the variable named on the first line and simply stop. The return value can be, and often is, an entire matrix.

Looping

Normal programming languages have various flow-control elements and so does this tool. You have *if, for, while, switch,* and more. Rather than write out the details of each, I refer you to the Matlab `help` command. It needs to be pointed out that while these are very similar to the commands you may be familiar with from C or BASIC, they are a bit different, too. Unlike C, the condition statement need not be surrounded by parentheses. The big difference—at least for me—is that each of these must be terminated with an `end` statement.

Note also that the use of any looping statement needs to be suspect. Yes, they work, and work right; that is not the issue. If you can find a matrix manipulation that can substitute for a loop, the procedure will often run hundreds of times faster. That is not an exaggeration—it can be literally hundreds of times faster.

You can check the speed of various implementations by the use of `tic` and `toc`. Tic starts a timer, `toc` prints out how long ago it started.

Files and I/O

There are some good file-manipulation routines available to you; this is good because your data usually is in files. When you have a file with 50,000 data points in it, you don't want to have to enter them by hand. And of course, you don't have to. Typically your data will come as the output of something like a SPICE program, probably in a list file, and will likely contain a lot of other junk besides just your data. None of this is a problem.

The simplest case is when you have a text file that has nothing in it but columns of numbers. This one is so simple that is almost embarrassing. Suppose you have a file named data.csv and you want to load its data to a variable. Try this:

```
d=load('data.csv');

plot(d);
```

I just threw in that plot command for the fun of it. If there are a few thousand data points all in a row, it is easier to plot them than to print them all out to verify they are loaded. Of course, if the file were a matrix, you would specify a particular row or column to plot.

As an aside, the plot function is extremely powerful and well-designed, but I am not going to go into any details about it. It is easy to look up and use the information provided by the help function. This is available in both Matlab and Octave, but in my opinion, this is one place in which Matlab clearly excels.

The SPICE list file has a lot of junk before you get to the data, and a lot of junk after. You can deal with it. Matlab can read text just as well as data. Start by opening the file. The syntax is very similar to what you have seen in other programming languages.

```
fin = fopen('filename.ext');
```

Now you need to read down through the file until you find the data. In HSPICE, the beginning of data is demarked in an easy-to-identify manner. There is a line with the single symbol, x, on it. Read until you find this line.

```
while ~strncmp(line,'x',1);line=fgetl(fid);end
```

As I told you, all the standard flow control and looping features are here, and I closed the while statement with end, as required. The looping condition ~strncmp() is not inside parentheses, nor should it be. The string comparison function is strncmp(). The tilde that precedes it is the negation that Matlab uses. So what this says is: "While it is not true that the first character in the variable line is 'x'", read the next line in the file.

That gets us past the junk but there is a bit more. Now there is a list of the node names identifying the data columns. But first, there is a line that needs to be skipped.

```
line=fgetl(fid);              % Skip the blank line

nodes=fgetl(fid);             % Read the node list

nodes1=fgetl(fid);

disp( 'Nodes found: '); disp( nodes);disp(nodes1);
```

Having read the list of node names, you may want to print them out on the screen so the disp command can be used. This is the easiest way you can print. Actually, there is a formatted print command that is very similar to the syntax used by C. You can use this to write to files, too.

There is a text command that allows you to extract tokens, one by one, from the text line. The standard conversion functions allow you to pull numbers out of text strings. Overall, it is not difficult to work with files in Matlab.

Help

The reason I expect to get away without giving you all the details of file handling and plotting and flow control is that there is an excellent help system. If you know the name of a command, there is no problem. If you don't know the name of a command, it gets a little more difficult, but not much. Here is how it works.

As stated above, every function has a built-in help section. When you write a function, all you have to do is type `help` and name your function, and that help section will be printed on the screen.

Suppose you want to find out if there is a FOR command and how to use it. You type `help for` and the screen fills with information about the command. It will give you the syntax, examples of use, and a list of related commands you might also want to study. It is a good idea to look this over and use similar formats for the help sections you put in your own functions.

On the other hand, particularly when you are starting, you might not know the precise command you want to know about. You might, for example, want to concatenate two strings but have no idea what the command is. Then you just type `help` by itself. The result is a list of the categories that are available. Looking at this list, you see there is a category of string functions named `strfun`. So you type `help strfun` and get another list. This list is all the string functions. It more than fills the page, so scroll up to see what is there. In this list, you see that the command you are looking for is probably `strcat`. You can confirm this by typing `help strcat`.

There is an alternative method. Just type `helpwin` to see an alternate presentation of the help. This is more convenient when you are just beginning, and possibly less convenient when you already know what function you are looking for. Learn both methods; you will use both.

It is that easy, in most cases. Sometimes you are sure there must be a function that relates to what you need, but you can't find it in these lists. It may be there, but for some reason it is not popping out at you. There is a solution, but it is a bit slower.

Suppose you are looking for a function that relates to the IFFT, but you don't know its name. What you type is `lookfor ifft`. This sets a search in motion that is going through the help section of every function it has. Any time it finds the word you specified, it will report the function that word was found in. Unfortunately, it appears that this procedure only looks in its own functions. It does not search the functions you wrote and placed in the current directory.

For looking up keywords and their syntax, the built-in help system seems very good. It is worth your while to spend some time exploring and studying what is there.

As with most subjects, there is a lot more than has been said here, but this should be enough to get you started. And of course, there are manuals. I'm talking big, fat, manuals. I'm talking the type of manuals we used to set on our desks to intimidate other engineers. They'd see all those big, technical-looking manuals on the desk and say to themselves, "Wow, what an engineer that must be!"

Of course, now they all come in PDF files. You can get one of those little USB drives and put the entire set of manuals, thousands of pages, into it. The drives often come with a lanyard, so you can hang it around your neck. When other engineers see that hanging around your neck they are impressed, although in a somewhat different way than back in the days when technical manuals were big and fat.

Anyway, the manuals are well worth reading.

Appendix C

Further Reading

Throughout this book, you have not been subjected to footnotes, references, and various distractions. You may have wondered where to find more information, get alternate explanations, and find out about some of the unnamed sources. This appendix is the answer, as it is partly a list of references and partly a set of reviews. To some extent, it is ordered. That is, more important books and papers tend to come earlier. The list is not exhaustive, and the venerable old tome your alma mater used may not be included.

Electromagnetic Fields and Interactions

This book by Richard Becker truly classifies as a venerable old tome. If it was not used at your alma mater, it should have been. It is the correct starting place for anyone who wants to actually understand field theory. When Maxwell published his equations, very few people, even engineers, understood what he was talking about. So, in 1894, August Foppl wrote a detailed explanation. Over the years, that explanation was expanded and refined by various authors. It was the standard work on the subject. In 1930, with its eighth edition, Richard Becker took over the job of keeping the work current. At Becker's death, the book was in its sixteenth edition. This book, *Electromagnetic Fields and Interactions*, is the 1964 edition of that work. It could well be the best book ever written to explain Maxwell's equations.

The book starts with fundamental mathematical definitions—vectors, components of vectors—things at that level. It proceeds through how and why the mathematics works. Then it goes into fields, the curl, and divergence. It continues into electric fields and magnetic fields—the discoveries that Maxwell used in forming his equations. By the time you actually begin encountering Maxwell's equations, you have been led through enough background material that further explanation is almost unnecessary; you know what they mean and why they mean it.

This is one of those science and math books whose copyright ran out long ago and now can be obtained in paperback for about $15. It is not only informative, it is a pleasure to read.

Microwave Transistor Amplifiers, Analysis and Design

A first impression might be that you don't intend to design microwave transistor amplifiers so why buy this book by Guillermo Gonzales? If you aren't going to buy it, at least check it out of the library. Its first couple dozen pages have the best, most precise, explanation of S parameters I have ever encountered. It is extremely terse. Much of it seems to be almost a list of simple mathematical expressions. But a wealth of information is packed into those expressions. Some of the pages can be reread every week, and every week new meaning and insight is found.

As irrelevant to signal integrity work as the title sounds, this book should be familiar to everyone who does signal integrity work at microwave frequencies. Again, it is a pleasure to read.

The Transmission-Line Modeling Method TLM

Don't let the name fool you. This book by Christos Christopoulos is about a particular type of field solver. It does a very good job of describing and explaining the theory that makes this field solver work. But that is not the only reason this book is recommended. Along the way, it provides some of the clearest developments of fundamental transmission line mathematics you will ever encounter. If you aren't going to buy it, at least check it out of the library and read the first 25 or so pages.

Among the things you will find are:

■ How to derive the equation that relates characteristic impedance to inductance and capacitance.

■ How to derive the equation that relates velocity to inductance and capacitance.

■ How to derive the tangent equation that relates impedance at a point in a line to distance from the termination.

Or, you may want to understand how a second type of full-wave field solver really works at its core. This book will tell you that too.

Numerical Methods for Scientists and Engineers

Now here is a fat book that every engineer, in this field or not, should have on the shelf. This is your reference by the engineer of engineers, R. W. Hamming. It is over 700 pages of mathematical wisdom and insight, and in paperback, available for a pittance. In 700 pages, there is room to cover a lot of ground, and it does. It covers subjects as diverse as roundoff, series, matrix inversions, and random numbers. It covers interpolation and derivatives, differential equations and eigenvalues, the fast Fourier transform, and quantization. This book contains more than just numerical procedures, it also includes insights and wisdom. It is an enjoyable book to read. At about $15, how can you afford not to have it?

Analysis of Multiconductor Transmission Lines

Clayton R. Paul wrote this, and reading it is a real slog. This book is one I cannot recommend as reading for fun. It is over 500 pages of heavy mathematics. Rather than attacking fields from the perspective of curl equations, it seems to really like integral equations. Yet, it has some important information that was only touched in my book here. An example is the development that shows under what circumstances, and how, you could derive the L and G matrices from the C matrix. This information is valuable because, as you will see in this book, that derivation will be valid for stripline.

Paul's book has good information on loss, both copper loss and dielectric loss. It develops on the skin effect to derive surface impedance. Subjects that I have only devoted a sentence or two to, he devotes pages to. Though I will not recommend this as a fun reading, I will recommend it as important reading.

Transmission Line Design Handbook

Here is a book by Brian C. Wadell that is interesting. It is very different than any of the books mentioned above. What it does is develop models for an extremely wide range of geometric structures. It covers things like a coaxial line. It covers a circular conductor in a circular shell. It covers the case where the dielectric only partially fills the outer shell. It covers the case where the center conductor is offset. It covers the case where the outer shell is square. It covers the case where the center conductor is square, or both are rectangular. Then it proceeds on to other variations.

It covers stripline structures, coplanar strips, with and without ground, covered coplanar, with and without ground. It covers steps in width and stubs. It covers various types of gaps. It covers corners and various strange growths on corners. Spirals of various flavors are certainly here. But what does it do with all this? Well, for the most part, it provides equations that are to be used to generate L-C models of the geometric object.

The book gives equations that are curve fits to enable you to generate your SPICE models. It is an interesting book and may be worthy of having in your collection.

Principles of Microwave Circuits

This is a 1948 book by C.G. Montgomery and others. If you are going to design waveguides, definitely read this book. Have I told you of the joy of hitting yourself in the head with a hammer? The joy is that it really feels good when you finally decide to quit. I am told that this book is the source for much of the book by Ramo Whinnery and Van Duzer, which is almost as much fun to read as this one is.

Microstrip Lines and Slotlines

Here I will get serious again. This book by K. C. Gupta and others is not easy to read, but you really should try anyway. In the personal computer industry we grew up with signals transported from place to place on wires. Initially we were soldering wires between point *a* and point b. Then we shifted over to wire-wrap, and then circuit board. But always our signals were carried through strips of copper.

Meanwhile, the microwave industry, the radar people, and the satellite people were sending their information through hollow pipes. They did that because the nothing inside a hollow pipe has less loss than copper does, and they could do it because they were operating at really high frequencies. But wait! Now we are beginning to operate at the same frequencies that they used to send down hollow pipes.

Is it possible that we, too, could send signals along paths other than those defined by wires? Gupta's book says that we can send information down a path that consists of the gap between two planar conductors. The structure is called a slotline. In fact, it looks a lot like structures you will find on many printed circuit boards. These are structures signal integrity engineers call plane splits. If you inject signal into the gap of a plane split, will it transport just like a slotline? If it looks like a duck, and quacks like a duck, is it a duck?

Foundations for Microwave Engineering

Now here is a book that is a book. This tome by Robert E. Collin is the sort of thing that you used to have nightmares about back in college. This book is so big that it deserves a prominent place in your bookshelf. It is guaranteed to intimidate any engineer that comes into your office.

Actually, this is an excellent reference that you probably should check out. Some of its subject matter is a little off-target for signal integrity, but look it over anyway. You might learn about how to make microwave filters on planar media, and things like that.

Finite Elements for Electrical Engineers

This book by Peter Silvester and Ronald Ferrari is something you would read if you wanted to write your own finite elements field solver. It is nearly 500 pages of information and code examples. There are a lot of books on finite elements, but most are written for mechanical engineers. Those books are going to show you how to set up a system to calculate how much a beam is going to bend. The good thing about this particular book is that it is written specifically for electrical engineers. That is, it doesn't talk about the bending of steel girders at all.

The examples are written in Fortran, rather than C or Matlab.

Numerical Solution of Initial Boundary Value Problems Involving Maxwell's Equations in Isotropic Media

With a name like that, this has got to be an IEEE paper, not a book. This work is what I believe to be a seminal paper. It was written back in 1966 by Kane S. Yee and details the core of the methodology that we now call the finite difference time domain (FDTD) method of solving fields. The paper is only about six pages long, so there is no reason not to read it. It is a seminal work, the original idea, the terse and beautiful development of the mathematics and concepts that became the FDTD field solver.

Ok, perhaps you have no intention of ever writing a field solver. Read it anyway. It is a great example of clear thinking and clear communication. It is an example of what a technical paper should be.

Starting with Maxwell's equations, it shows the equivalent finite difference equations. It proceeds to boundary conditions and to stability criteria. It gives an example in two dimensions with a discussion of numerical computations, with graphs of computed values. It closes with a comparison of the solution calculated by this method, and with the best alternative solutions known at the time.

Time-Domain Methods for Microwave Structures, Analysis and Design

This book is a collection of the major IEEE papers related to the FDTD field of study. It is some 500 pages of such papers. I don't think there is anything there that you could not find by searching your IEEE papers. But it does bring them all together and save you the time of figuring out enough keywords to search and find them yourself. If you have an interest in the FDTD method, this is a book worth reading.

Arbitrary Pulse Shape Synthesis via Non-uniform Transmission Lines

This IEEE paper by Scott C. Burkhart and Russell B. Wilcox is the best description I have found for the mathematics needed for the peeling algorithm. It is only five pages long, but a lot of information is packed in those five pages.

Microwave Engineering

This is a general book on microwave engineering, written by David M. Pozar. It is highly recommended.

Glossary

ABCD A matrix that defines the voltage and current out of one port of a device, in terms of voltage and current into another, single, port.

adaptive equalization In a serial receiver, the process of adjusting circuit parameters in a manner that reduces the impact of intersymbol interference or of crosstalk.

balun A contraction of the phrase balanced-to-unbalanced converter. A balun is a three-ported device that can convert single-ended signals to differential, and differential signals to single ended.

boundary conditions Values assigned at the edges of a field or the limits of an equation that allow you to solve for actual values rather than just relative relationships.

broadside In the context of differential transmission lines, this is a coupling where the two lines are on adjacent layers and stacked one above the other.

c As a lower-case letter, c is often used as the speed of light in free space, $3*10^8$ meters per second.

cgs Centimeter, gram, second.

chaining A process in which the combined effect of two matrix operations can be found by the simple process of finding the product of the two matrices.

characteristic impedance The relation between current and voltage for the forward-traveling wave in a device. It can also be viewed as the impedance that will terminate a transmission line in a manner that produces no reflections. It is usually designated by the symbol *Zo*.

circuit solver A program such as SPICE that solves for currents, voltage, and time in a circuit by treating the circuit as nodes separated by discrete devices: resistors, capacitors, etc.

common mode The part of the signal on several conductors that consists of the average of the signal on all the conductors. Typically, there will be a DC common mode and an AC common mode.

common-mode rejection The ability of a receiver to ignore common-mode signals.

complex conjugate A number that is the mirror image of a complex number. The complex conjugate consists of a real part equal to that of the original number, and an imaginary part that is equal in magnitude but opposite in sign to the imaginary part of the original number. [That sounds pretty darned complex to me!]

complex number A number that has two parts, called the real and the imaginary parts.

complex propagation constant A part of the exponent in solutions of the wave equation. This exponent is complex whenever the system includes losses.

constitutive equations A set of definitions that relate Maxwell's equations to a specific measurement system such as MKSA or cgs.

coplanar waveguide A type of transmission line, either single or differential, where the reference plane is on the same layer as the signal line. It is a form of edge-coupling.

copper loss The phenomenon in copper that converts electrical energy into heat.

core Epoxy-fiberglass material used in the manufacture of circuit boards. Core is fully cured epoxy, usually coated with a copper film on both sides. See also *prepreg*.

CPU Central Processing Unit.

Cramer's rule A method of solving some types of matrix systems by simple column interchanges and division by the determinant.

crosstalk The current or voltage in a circuit, resulting from unintended coupling of current or voltage from some other circuit.

curl A mathematical operator; the value obtained by applying that operator. Taking the curl of a field is the operation of calculating the cross product of the three-dimensional spatial derivative and a field. It is calculating the tendency of a field to circulate around a point.

decibel Literally, one tenth of a Bell. The decibel system is a logarithmic system of designating ratios. In terms of voltages, the decibel quantity is 20 times the log, base 10, of the ratio of the voltages.

deconvolve Undo the operation of convolution.

del A mathematical operator whose symbol is an upside-down capital Greek Delta. It consists of the full set of spatial partial derivatives. That is, the rate of change of the quantity in each direction.

De-skew Removal of the effects of skew through either mechanical means or electrical means. At microwave frequencies, de-skewing is usually accomplished by electrical means.

determinant A number that can be derived from a square matrix.

dielectric loss The phenomenon that converts electric energy in a dielectric to heat.

differential Data, driver, mode, receiver, signaling, voltage.

> **differential data** Data that is transmitted in a differential format. It has two data streams; the voltages of one stream are the complement of the voltages of the other stream.

> **differential driver** A driver circuit that is designed to transmit differential data. Such a driver has two signal outputs and usually is designed to be very symmetrical.

> **differential mode** That aspect of a field or signal characterized as the difference in voltage between two points. The voltage between two points can be fully described by two orthogonal quantities: the differential part, describing the difference between the two, and the common part, describing the average of the two.

> **differential receiver** A circuit with two inputs, designed to maximize sensitivity to the voltage difference between the inputs and minimize sensitivity to the average voltage on the inputs.

differential signaling Transmitting data in a differential format.

differential voltage The voltage difference between two points.

directional coupler A three-port device used to introduce a unidirectional signal into a bidirectional transmission line or to extract a portion of signal from such a line.

displacement current A term invented to account for current that derives from changing fields rather than from charge movement. It accounts for current through capacitors and for radio waves.

divergence A three-dimensional value that can be derived from a field. It relates to the rate of flow of a field quantity away from some point in the field. See *curl*.

DUT Device under test.

edge rate The time it takes for a signal voltage to change from one value to another.

edge coupled A term applied to differential transmission lines on planar media. It designates a geometry where the two conductors are on the same plane and adjacent to each other.

effective dielectric constant The dielectric constant of a hypothetical uniform dielectric surrounding a conductor and producing the same capacitance as the real, non-uniform dielectric.

embedded clock A term associated with serial data that indicates that constraints have been placed on data-edge placement to facilitate extraction of a clock at the receiver. A common form of this is a requirement of a maximum allowable number of data bits between edge transitions.

EMI Electromagnetic interference, the undesired emission of radio-frequency energy.

ESD, human body model ESD is electrostatic discharge. The human body model is a standardized circuit that is intended to yield an energy profile equivalent to a charged person touching something with their finger.

even mode impedance The characteristic impedance seen in a circuit when that circuit and adjacent circuits are all driven by the same voltage.

extrapolation A mathematical procedure to find a number that is outside a given data set, but that might be an extension of the data set.

eye The oscilloscope pattern that results from accumulating the images of many data bits while triggering the scope with a clock set to the data bit rate. The eye diagram is often used to indicate the quality of a data link. Two parameters are typically specified as requirements of acceptable eye pattern. One is the vertical opening, the minimum voltage range clear of any data traces. The other is the horizontal opening, the minimum time duration that is clear of any data traces.

FDTD Finite difference time domain, a type of field solver. This type of field solver is obtained by discretizing Maxwell's curl equations.

feature This word is used to denote any change from a straight, uniform transmission line. A feature could be a component, a change in width, a change in trace coupling to other objects, or even a bend.

FFT Fast Fourier Transform. This is a modified version of the Fourier transform that is, where it can be applied, much more numerically efficient than the original Fourier transform.

field A mathematical quantity that has a value at every position in space. Fields of interest in this book are the electric field and the magnetic field. A key aspect of the concept of a field is that it has a value that is associated with position.

flux A term that once meant flow, as in a liquid, but now is just a relic of the terminology that grew up around field theory.

Fourier transform A mathematical procedure that is used to decompose a voltage waveform into a series of sinusoidals.

FR4 Circuit board material composed of fiberglass and epoxy. Related terms are *core* and *prepreg*.

full wave A term used to describe field solvers that account for the time it takes fields to travel through space. See *quasi-static*.

fully terminated Terminated by the complex impedance that results in no reflections.

Gamma A Greek letter used in various ways in microwave literature. The capital gamma is used to designate the steady-state reflection coefficient—as opposed to lower-case rho, the transient refection coefficient. Lower case gamma is used to designate the complex transmission coefficient in a lossy transmission line.

Gibbs phenomenon A sinusoidal data pattern superimposed on a data set and associated with sudden transitions in magnitude.

gigabits 1,000,000,000 bits.

Green's function A mathematical formula that produces the impulse response of a system at a point in space.

higher order modes Transitory modes of signal propagation that take place around geometrical transitions. Higher order modes are usually much lossier than the primary modes of signal transmission and sometimes account for substantial losses near geometrical transitions.

ideal transmission line A hypothetical lossless, uniform transmission line, whether single ended or differential.

IFFT Inverse fast Fourier transform.

imaginary One of the two parts of a complex number. The other part is called the real part.

Impedance The number that describes the relationship between current and voltage in a device or at a point in a circuit.

impulse response A mathematical ideal, the response of a circuit to a pulse of unit area and infinitely short duration.

insertion loss The number that describes the voltage or current out of a port in terms of the voltage or current into another port. Insertion loss is often described in decibels.

Interpolation A mathematical procedure to find a number that lies somewhere between two known data points. See *extrapolation*.

inter-symbol interference The degradation of serial data caused by an accumulation of artifacts from previous data bits.

jitter Timing variation. Jitter is deviation in the position in time of the edges of a signal or a clock with respect to some ideal time reference.

limpts A SPICE keyword used to specify the maximum number of output data points allowable.

linear sweep In reference to SPICE, data points evenly spaced in frequency.

lossless An ideal that shows neither copper nor dielectric loss. In practical application, it can be used whenever energy converted to heat is very small compared to energy inserted to a device.

loss tangent A number that expresses the rate at which a dielectric converts electrical energy to heat.

low-loss material A dielectric material that has a loss tangent that is small compared to some arbitrary standard.

Maxwell's Equations A set of four equations that describes electric and magnetic fields.

microstrip A transmission line on an outer layer of a board, which uses an adjacent plane below it as the reference plane. See also *stripline*, and *planar waveguide*.

microwave probe A device designed to connect a test equipment to a circuit. Usually, microwave probes are characterized by great bandwidth, low loss, and fragility.

MKSA Meter, kilogram, second, ampere.

mode conversion The phenomenon in which energy that enters in one mode, such as differential, and exits in another, such as common mode.

Multi-pole algorithm An algorithm that speeds up calculations by selectively grouping objects whose distinctiveness has little impact on the accuracy of a calculation.

Neper The unit of measurement of the loss factor in the complex propagation constant. It is often described in terms of Nepers per meter.

non-uniform In reference to transmission lines, not constant in either characteristic impedance or signal velocity.

normal A direction that is perpendicular to all vectors that can be formed tangent to a surface.

odd mode impedance The characteristic impedance seen in transmission line when that line is part of a differential pair and the pair is being driven by a purely differential signal.

offset stripline A variation of stripline transmission line where the line is not spaced midway between the two reference planes.

Omega A Greek letter that, in capitalized form, designates frequency in radians per second; that is, the frequency in hertz, multiplied by two pi.

patch antenna An antenna that consists of a metal region on the surface of a planar medium, or a circuit board.

PC Personal Computer.

PCI Personal Computer Interface bus. A standardized interface for peripherals in personal computers.

peeling A method of deriving a circuit model from time-domain reflection measurements of the device.

per unit length Refers to the practice of normalizing capacitances and inductances to the unit of measurement of length. This practice is essentially universal in field solvers.

pi network A two-port network connected in the following manner: a component from the input node to ground and another from the input node to the output node; a final component from the output node to ground.

planar waveguide The region between two conducting planes on a circuit board. This region can become a transmission line for microwave signals.

prepreg Partially cured epoxy-fiberglass material used in the manufacture of circuit boards. Unlike core, prepreg is not encased between two layers of copper. See *core*.

propagation constant A part of the exponent in the solution of the wave equation. This part describes the rate at which waves travel. In the case of a lossy medium, this has two parts: a real and an imaginary part. The real part describes an amplitude decay due to loss. The imaginary part describes a wave propagation.

quasi static As though it were static. This term is used to describe field solvers that make the presumption that all dimensions are small compared to wavelengths.

real One part of a complex number. Note that there is nothing more real about the real part of a complex number than there is about the imaginary part. They could have just as well been called part a and part b.

reference plane A conducting plane in a circuit board. For a particular transmission line, it is the plane, or planes, where most of the *E*-field lines terminate.

reflection coefficient A number that expresses the relationship between incident and reflected energy.

resonant modes Various patterns that produce various resonances in the same physical structure. Unlike classical discreet circuits, or distributed circuits, objects that are large compared to wavelength often develop resonances that are caused by signals bouncing between two or more reflecting boundaries. In such a situation, there is not one resonant frequency, but rather, if the circuit is lossless, an infinite series of resonant frequencies. This series is referred to as the resonant modes of the object. Usually, the greatest interest is in what is the lowest frequency in this series.

return loss The number that describes the relationship between the reflected wave at a port and the forward wave into the same port. It is often described in decibels.

rise time The time a circuit requires to change from one voltage level to another.

scattering parameters Matrix elements that describe a device in the frequency domain. The scattering parameters describe the device in terms of reflected and transmitted sinusoidal, steady state, and energy.

skew Difference in length between various transmission lines. Also, difference in signal delay between various transmission lines.

skin depth A number that relates to skin effect. The skin depth is the thickness of conductor that would yield the same surface current density if the current were evenly distributed throughout the conductor. It is used to calculate the effective resistance of the conductor at the specified frequency. The skin depth is inversely proportional to the square root of the frequency and the magnetic constant.

skin effect The phenomenon where current at high frequencies tends to flow only near the surface of a conductor.

single-ended impedance The characteristic impedance seen by a transmission line, either in isolation or when all adjacent lines are held at a constant voltage.

slot antenna A type of microwave antenna that consists of a hole cut in a conductor.

slot line A transmission line that consists not of a metal conductor but rather of the gap between two planes.

Smith chart A circular graph used to display various complex quantities such as impedances.

SPICE A venerable old computer program that is used to solve for currents and voltages in circuits. The acronym stands for simulation program with integrated circuit emphasis. At this time it is used for the analysis of all kinds of circuits, not just integrated circuits.

step response The time-domain response of a circuit to a unit step in applied voltage. The derivative of the step response is the impulse response. The Fourier transform of the impulse response is the frequency response of the circuit.

Stokes's Theorem Not to be confused with Stokes's law that has to do with how marbles travel through liquid. Stokes's Theorem shows how a surface integral can be reduced to a line integral around an edge of an opening in that surface.

stripline A transmission line in a planar medium, or circuit board, that is sandwiched symmetric ally between two reference planes. See also *microstrip* and *offset stripline*.

T line An ideal transmission line model found in SPICE solvers.

T matrix A rearrangement of an *S* matrix to a form that allows chaining.

tan-delta An alias for loss tangent, a number that quantifies the rate of energy loss in a dielectric.

TDR Time domain reflectometer.

telegrapher's equation A single-dimensional version of the wave equation. The telegrapher's equation describes the signal amplitudes in a wire, in terms of forward and reflected voltage or current.

time domain A descriptor for data that is characterized as a function of time, rather than of frequency.

training The process of transmitting pre-determined data patterns across a link to facilitate the receive circuitry in adjusting its parameters to achieve optimal data integrity.

transfer function A mathematical formula that relates an output to an input.

vibration isolation table A device, or table, that is designed to dampen mechanical vibrations. It is used to isolate objects set on the tabletop from mechanical vibrations below the table.

wave equation An interpretation of Maxwell's equations. The wave equation describes the time-derivative of electric and magnetic fields in terms of the derivatives of position in space. It can be derived from Maxwell's curl equations by taking the curl of those equations. It can be used to derive the telegrapher's equation by reducing it to a single dimension and substituting a phasor for the electric field.

Zo Characteristic impedance.

Index

Continuing Education is Essential

It's a challenge we all face – keeping pace with constant change in information technology. Whether our formal training was recent or long ago, we must all find time to keep ourselves educated and up to date in spite of the daily time pressures of our profession.

Intel produces technical books to help the industry learn about the latest technologies. The focus of these publications spans the basic motivation and origin for a technology through its practical application.

Right books, right time, from the experts

These technical books are planned to synchronize with roadmaps for technology and platforms, in order to give the industry a head-start. They provide new insights, in an engineer-to-engineer voice, from named experts. Sharing proven insights and design methods is intended to make it more practical for you to embrace the latest technology with greater design freedom and reduced risks.

I encourage you to take full advantage of Intel Press books as a way to dive deeper into the latest technologies, as you plan and develop your next generation products. They are an essential tool for every practicing engineer or programmer. I hope you will make them a part of your continuing education tool box.

Sincerely,

Justin Rattner
Senior Fellow and Chief Technology Officer
Intel Corporation

Turn the page to learn about titles
from Intel Press for system developers

Beyond BIOS
Implementing the Unified Extensible Firmware Interface with Intel's Framework

By Vincent Zimmer, Michael Rothman and Robert Hale

ISBN: 0-9743649-0-8

Beyond BIOS: Implementing the Unified Extensible Firmware Interface with Intel's Framework describes a set of robust architectural interfaces, implemented in C, that has been designed to enable the BIOS industry and Intel customers to accelerate the evolution of innovative, differentiated, computer platform designs. The Framework is Intel's recommended implementation of the Extensible Firmware Interface (EFI) specification for computer platforms based on the Intel® Architecture.

The EFI specification is an industry standard that defines a new model for the interface between operating systems and computing platform firmware and provides a standard environment for booting an operating system and running pre-boot applications.

Intended for BIOS developers, firmware designers, and software professionals, this book covers one of the most important new developments in computing platform evolution.

Beyond BIOS: Implementing the Unified Extensible Firmware Interface with Intel's Framework provides the reader with solid examples of how to implement the EFI specification from booting a system based upon this technology to the constituent elements of building a platform with the Framework. Included is the rationale for design decisions, code fragments that implement the concepts, and samples from many different platforms. Each operating environment imposes different requirements on the system software. Operating system developers have learned that the successful support of a complex operating environment is the result of adaptation of existing basic software concepts to a new landscape. The reader of this book will learn how to use just such a strategy in turn to build pre-boot firmware and understand the new world of standards-based operating system booting.

Beyond BIOS

Implementing the Unified Extensible Firmware Interface with Intel's Framework

Vincent Zimmer, Michael Rothman, and Robert Hale

Intel PRESS   Books by Engineers, for Engineers   (intel)

66 *This book is for you if you'd like to understand the UEFI/PI architecture and the Framework implementation; that is, to understand how to move beyond BIOS ...For any student in this field, this book provides an important bridge between normative specifications and the informative details of the development.* 99

Dong Wei, Vice President and Chief Executive, the Unified EFI Forum
HP Distinguished Technologist

Introduction to PCI Express†
A Hardware and Software Developer's Guide

By Adam Wilen, Justin Schade, and Ron Thornburg
ISBN 0-9702846-9-1

Written by key Intel insiders, this introduction to the new I/O technology explains how PCI Express† is designed to increase computer performance. The authors were instrumental in implementing Intel's first generation of PCI Express chipsets and they work directly with customers who want to take advantage of PCI Express. The book explains in technical detail how designers can use PCI Express technology to overcome the practical performance limits of existing multi-drop, parallel bus technology. The authors draw from years of leading-edge experience to explain how to apply these new capabilities to a broad range of computing and communications platforms.

> ❝ *This book helps software and hardware developers get a jumpstart on their development cycle that can decrease their time to market.* ❞
> *Ajay Kwatra, Engineer Strategist, Dell Computer Corp.*

PCI Express Electrical Interconnect Design
Practical Solutions for Board-level Integration and Validation

By Dave Coleman, Scott Gardiner, Mohammad Kolbehdari, and Stephen Peters
ISBN 0-9743649-9-1

Learn how to translate PCI Express electrical specifications into a reliable and robust interface implementation. PCI Express† Electrical Interconnect Design is a how-to guide for system design engineers, board and layout designers, signal integrity engineers, designers of high-speed communication devices, test engineers and technicians, and validation engineers. Intel experts relate their insights and experience, thoroughly explaining each step from design through validation. Developers can directly apply this knowledge to improve both quality and time-to-market for desktop, server, workstation, mobile, and communication platform designs.

Your guide to simulation, layout, and measurement

● Serial ATA Storage Architecture and Applications

Designing High-Performance, Low-Cost I/O Solutions

By Knut Grimsrud and Hubbert Smith
ISBN 0-9717861-8-6

Serial ATA, a new hard disk interconnect standard for PCs, laptops, and more, is quickly becoming a serious contender with Parallel ATA and SCSI. Computer engineers and architects worldwide must answer important questions for their companies: "Why make the change to Serial ATA? What problems does Serial ATA solve for me? How do I transition from parallel ATA to Serial ATA and from SCSI to Serial ATA?" The authors of this essential book, both Intel Serial ATA specialists, have the combined expertise to help you answer these questions. Systems engineers, product architects, and product line managers who want to affect the right decisions for their products undoubtably will benefit from the straight talk offered by these authors. The book delivers reliable information with sufficient technical depth on issues such as Phy signaling and interface status, protocol encoding, programming model, flow control, performance, compatibility with legacy systems, enclosure management, signal routing, hot-plug, presence detection, activity indication, power management, and cable/connector standards.

> 66 *This book provides explanations and insights into the underlying technology to help ease design and implementation.* 99
>
> Rhonda Gass, Vice President,
> Storage Systems Development,
> Dell Computer Corporation

● Building the Power-Efficient PC

A Developer's Guide to ACPI Power Management

By Jerzy Kolinski, Ram Chary, Andrew Henroid, and Barry Press
ISBN 0-9702846-8-3

An expert author team shows developers and integrators how to address the increasing demand for energy conservation by building power-managed personal computers. From key engineers responsible for developing ACPI Power Management at Intel,® gain the practical knowledge and design techniques needed to implement this critical technology. The companion CD includes sample code, complete power management documentation, Intel power management tools, and links to references.

Learn how to build power-efficient PCs from the experts

Special Deals, Special Prices!

To ensure you have all the latest books
and enjoy aggressively priced discounts,
please go to this Web site:

www.intel.com/intelpress/bookbundles.htm

Bundles of our books are available,
selected especially to address the needs
of the Developer. The bundles place
place important complementary
topics at your fingertips, and the
price for a bundle is substantially less
than buying all the books individually.

About Intel Press

Intel Press is the authoritative source of timely, technical books
to help software and hardware developers speed up their development
process. We collaborate only with leading industry experts to deliver
reliable, first-to-market information about the latest
technologies, processes, and strategies.

Our products are planned with the help of many people in the developer
community and we encourage you to consider becoming a customer advisor.
If you would like to help us and gain additional advance insight to the latest
technologies, we encourage you to consider the Intel Press Customer
Advisor Program. You can register here:

www.intel.com/intelpress/register.htm

For information about bulk orders or corporate sales, please send e-mail to
bulkbooksales@intel.com

Other Developer Resources from Intel

At these Web sites you can also find valuable technical information
and resources for developers:

developer.intel.com	general information for developers
www.intel.com/software	content, tools, training, and the Intel® Early Access Program for software developers
www.intel.com/software/products	programming tools to help you develop high-performance applications
www.intel.com/netcomms	solutions and resources for networking and communications
www.intel.com/technology/itj	Intel Technology Journal
www.intel.com/idf	worldwide technical conference, the Intel Developer Forum